EXPERIENCE AND EDUCATION – TOWARDS AN ALTERNATIVE NATIONAL CURRICULUM

Experience and Education – Towards an Alternative National Curriculum

EDITED BY

Gwyn Edwards and A. V. Kelly

P·C·P

Paul Chapman
Publishing Ltd

Paul Chapman Publishing Ltd
144 Liverpool Road
London
N1 1LA

British Library Cataloguing in Publication Data

Experience and education : towards an alternative National Curriculum
1. Education – England – Curricula 2. Education – Wales – Curricula
I. Edwards, Gwyn, 1947- II. Kelly, A. V. (Albert Victor), 1931-
375'.00942

ISBN 1 85396 272 4

Typeset by Anneset
Printed and bound in Great Britain.

A B C D E F G H 4321 098

Contents

Notes on the Contributors

Dave Boorman is currently Lecturer in Primary Physical Education at Goldsmiths' College, University of London. He has previously taught in primary and secondary schools in South East London, and was for two years an ILEA Youth Officer in Southwark. He has recently completed an M.Phil. thesis which provides a critical analysis of Primary Physical Education.

Lynne Broadbent is currently Deputy Director of the BFSS National Religious Education Centre at Brunel University. She formerly lectured at Goldsmiths' College, University of London, and was Head of the South London Multi-Faith Religious Education Centre. She has considerable experience in in-service training for teachers and has published both articles and resource materials in the field of Religious Education.

Daniel Davies is currently Lecturer in Primary Science Education at Goldsmiths' College, University of London. He has previously taught in primary schools in the London Boroughs of Lambeth and Southwark and in the Inner London Education Authority. He has also worked as Design Education Officer for The Design Council. He holds a B.Sc. in Physics from University College, London, a PGCE in Primary Education from the University of London Institute of Education and an MA in Design Education and Curriculum Studies from Goldsmiths' College. He is currently engaged in research for a Ph.D., and has published in the area of science and technology education at the primary level.

Gwyn Edwards is a Lecturer in Geographical Education and Curriculum Studies at Goldsmiths' College, University of London. Previously, he spent twelve years teaching humanities subjects in schools in Leicestershire and Kent. His publications include *Change and the Curriculum* (1992) (with G. M. Blenkin and A. V. Kelly) and *Dimensions of Action Research: People, Practice and Power* (1993) (with G. Plummer [eds.]).

Paul Ernest is a graduate of the universities of Sussex and London, and has taught in London, Cambridge and Jamaica. Currently a Reader in Mathematics Education at the University of Exeter, he chairs the Mathematics Subject Area in the School of Education and leads the Masters Degree in Mathematics Education. He is founding chair of the International Philosophy of Mathematics Education Network and editor of the electronically published *Philosophy of Mathematics Education Journal* (location: http://www.ex.ac.uk/~PErnest/). He is general editor of the Falmer Press *Studies in Mathematics Education* series. His publications include *The Philosophy of Mathematics Education* (Falmer 1991) and *Social Constructivism as a Philosophy of Mathematics* (SUNY 1997).

Vic Kelly is Emeritus Professor of Curriculum Studies at Goldsmiths' College, University of London. His publications include *The Curriculum: Theory and Practice* (third edition 1989), *Knowledge and Curriculum Planning* (1986), *The National Curriculum: A Critical Review* (updated edition 1994) and *Democracy and Education: Principles and Practices* (1995).

Alex Moore is a Lecturer in Educational Studies at Goldsmiths' College, University of London. Previously, he spent eighteen years as a teacher of English at a number of secondary comprehensive schools in London. He has published numerous articles and book-chapters on a range of educational issues, including, centrally, explorations of cultural bias in schools curricula and pedagogy.

Malcolm Ross is Reader in Education at the School of Education, University of Exeter. He teaches a range of postgraduate courses in the arts and is currently directing a national study of the arts in secondary education, funded by the Calouste Gulbenkian and Paul Hamlyn Foundations and due to report in 1997. His publications include *The Creative Arts* (1978), *The Aesthetic Impulse* (1984), *The Claims of Feeling* (1989), *Assessing Achievement in the Arts* (1993) and *State of the Arts* (1997).

John Saxton is currently course tutor for the PGCE in Design and Technology (secondary) at Goldsmiths' College, University of London. He also works on the undergraduate and postgraduate programmes (MA) and as part of the Technology Education Research Unit (TERU) team with Richard Kimbell on sponsored research contracts. He was a senior researcher for the APU Design and Technology Project and before this taught for fifteen years in secondary schools. During this time he ran a large Technical Studies department and a Design Faculty and undertook a significant amount of in-service work for HMI and LEAs. His work in schools was featured in the DES video 'Technology Starts Here'. His publications include *Making Things Work* (CUP).

Preface

The National Curriculum established for state-maintained schools in England and Wales by the 1988 Education Reform Act has proved to be as flawed as many people predicted. Some of its more obvious deficiencies were removed on the recommendations of Sir Ron Dearing who was invited by the Secretary of State in 1993 to undertake a review of the current requirements. That invitation, however, did not extend beyond practical concerns, in particular a reduction in the volume of what had to be assimilated, simplification and clarification of the programmes of study and a diminution in the levels of prescription. And so the revision which followed was largely cosmetic, quantitative rather than qualitative in its thrust. Nevertheless, it was decreed that no further changes should be made for a period of five years.

That period is now coming to its close; the interim has seen a change of government; and, although there has been no indication as yet that the change heralds a significant revision of the school curriculum, there is reason to hope that any forthcoming review of the National Curriculum might be more open, more democratic and thus more fundamental. We need a genuinely open debate which will go beyond the superficial and identify the essential components of a national curriculum for a democratic society. In the hope that there is to be such a debate, this book is offered as a contribution to it, and, in particular, as an invitation to consider the merits of an *adjectival* curriculum, one which will *de*scribe rather than *pre*scribe the kinds of educational experience to which all young people have an entitlement in a democratic society.

Introduction

The extensive attempts at curriculum development which were a feature of the 1960s and 1970s, not only in the UK but elsewhere too, were prompted by two main considerations. The first of these was the need to support through the school system the continued economic development of society. The second was to do this while at the same time providing an equality of entitlement for all children to educational provision of a kind that would enhance and enrich their lives as individuals. These two purposes were well expressed as early as 1959 by the Crowther Committee (CACE 1959, para. 83, p. 54) in the phrases education as 'a national investment' and education as 'the right of every boy and girl to be educated'.

By the middle of the 1970s, it was becoming apparent, from both research and experience, from theory and practice, that the attainment of these aims would require the establishment of a curriculum framed in terms of the common principles and processes which should underpin every child's educational provision rather than a simple statement of the content every child should be required to assimilate (Stenhouse 1975, Kelly 1977).

It was also becoming clear that a genuine form of entitlement would require that any statement of these principles and processes would need to include some delineation of the range of experiences every child should have access to. A survey of secondary education in England and Wales, published by Her Majesty's Inspectorate (HMI) in 1979, drew attention to, among many other things, the lack of balance in the curricular experiences of many of the pupils in the schools which the survey covered (DES 1979a). And that feature of the current practice became as strong an argument as any for the establishment of some form of national curriculum – an entitlement curriculum, in which 'entitlement' was to the full range of educational experiences.

The case for this was developed extensively by HMI in a publication, *Curriculum 11–16* (DES 1977a), in which they offered the notion that a common curriculum might be planned by identifying the 'broad areas of experience that are considered to be important for all pupils' (op. cit., Supplement). And they went on to identify eight such areas of experience, which they set out in the form of eight adjectives – aesthetic/creative, ethical, linguistic, mathematical, physical, scientific, social/political and spiritual. The notable omission of 'technological' was later recognized and rectified.

It was also argued at the time (Kelly 1977), and has been reiterated many times subsequently (Kelly 1982, 1989, 1990) that this is the *only* route to the achievement of genuine educational entitlement for every boy and girl.

And, at the level of practice, the notion of a curriculum framed in terms of 'areas of experience' became the basis for what was called the 'entitlement curriculum', which was the subject both of a subsequent HMI publication, *Curriculum 11–16: towards a statement of entitlement* (DES 1984), and of an attempt to translate it into practice in six local authorities.

That experiment seems to have foundered because it failed to recognize the extent of rethinking which was required, and attempted to graft this approach on to an incompatible subject-based structure. It is worthy of note, however, that those responsible for that experiment also saw genuine educational entitlement as attainable only through this kind of provision.

In the event, this kind of experimentation, along with any developments it might have led to, was overtaken by the institution of a National Curriculum for England and Wales, through the 1988 Education Act, which ignored all thinking of this kind and adopted a content approach, listing core and foundation subjects, and, within those subjects, detailing the content to be taught and learned. The notion of planning by means of areas of experience was, for several reasons which are not difficult to identify, and which will emerge very clearly in all of the contributions to this book, firmly rejected and/or ignored.

One of the most vociferous claims made for this National Curriculum, however, has been that it is an 'entitlement curriculum'. Yet, if those earlier claims, based on both theory and practical experimentation, that genuine entitlement can only come from a form of curriculum which is quite differently conceived, have any validity, then such entitlement will not, and cannot, be attained by a National Curriculum of this kind.

It is not surprising, then, that it has already become plain that the National Curriculum has not achieved what it was claimed it would achieve. In particular, there is clear evidence that, as had been predicted, it has not provided that entitlement which was claimed to be a major part of its *raison d'être*.

It is becoming increasingly clear that a major reason for this failure is a lack of clarity over the full meaning of the concept of entitlement. The term 'entitlement' is a moral term; it encapsulates the notion of rights. And, in a democratic context, the rights any individual has are intended to benefit him/her rather than society at large. Thus the right to an 'entitlement curriculum' is a right to a form of education deliberately designed to promote the development of each individual. The education system might, indeed must, at the same time promote the economic health of society, but this cannot be sensibly described as an entitlement, except in so far as society itself may feel entitled to some return on its 'national investment'. The notion of entitlement must be interpreted as the right of each individual to a form of education which will advance his/her development as an individual, which will offer enrichment and, indeed, social and political empowerment.

In a civilized society education is central to the civilizing process; it is the main means by which we seek to enable human animals to develop into human beings. This is something, however, which the current National Curriculum seems not to have done very well, and, for the reasons we touched upon earlier, cannot do very well. For there is evidence of a growing concern in many different quarters over the personal growth and development of children and young people, particularly in the light of the kind of 'law and order' problems we hear of – and sometimes experience – increasingly. And this is accompanied by a growing sense that in the context of a curriculum centrally geared to attainment targets, especially those which appear to be readily measurable, there is neither scope nor allowance for other important, if more elusive, aspects of the educational process.

This inadequacy is felt by many to be especially disturbing when viewed against the backcloth of a society which is characterized by rapid technological change and the moral consequences of such change, which is ethnically diverse, which must recognize value-pluralism and which is consequently subject to cultural, moral and spiritual uncertainty.

These features of twentieth century societies must be acknowledged, not least because they are likely to increase in significance as we move towards the next millenium, and a curriculum must be developed which will both take account of them and prepare the young for life in such societies. This cannot be done, however, by adding to the current National Curriculum bolt-on 'crosscurricular themes, topics or dimensions', as SCAA and the National Curriculum Council (NCC) before it have advocated. For a genuine form of personal education must be more than a bolt-on afterthought of curriculum planning, and in any case there is a fundamental mismatch between what these additional forms of provision are designed to do and the principles upon which the National Curriculum itself is founded, so that this kind of policy must lead to distortion of the curriculum as a whole.

A form of education which will genuinely promote the personal development of all children and young people on all fronts requires a complete reconceptualization of the principles which must underpin the school curriculum, if it is to be appropriate for the twenty-first century. For we must devise a curriculum which will focus on the pupils who are its recipients as well as on the needs of the society they are being prepared to enter, and, further, on the interaction of these two factors in the curriculum equation.

And so, again one is beginning to hear and read about areas of experience as a strategy, perhaps the only strategy, for producing a national curriculum which might ensure entitlement to personal development, quality of provision and, at the same time, appropriate forms of accountability, while not imposing the rigidity which characterizes the existing National Curriculum or erecting the barriers to personal development which it creates. Furthermore, there is increasing evidence that such a form of curriculum is coming to be recognized, even in countries, such as Japan, which have been long committed to a rigid, centrally controlled national curriculum, as a more effective route to economic success as well as to personal development and social stability.

What one hears and reads about areas of experience, however, does not always give one the assurance that those who are resurrecting the phrase understand what a fundamental shift of curriculum philosophy it implies, any more clearly than those who attempted to implement this kind of curriculum in the early 1980s. For it is not a matter of merely rewriting our syllabuses, orders, attainment targets, programmes of study or whatever in a less restrictive and more open form, or of giving teachers increased freedom in relation to choice of subject-content, although both of these would be prerequisites of such a shift. The notion of a curriculum planned in terms of areas of experience requires a complete reconceptualization of curriculum, not merely a rethink about the methods by which it is to be offered. And it requires a similar reconceptualization of every school subject, in order to identify what, if anything, each subject has to offer to the pupil's development and how it must be viewed and approached if its potential is to be effectively tapped.

It is not merely a change of methodology which is required. The notion of education through experience points us towards a new educational philosophy – or, at least, a reassertion, supported by a clearer articulation, of those educational principles which current policies have rejected.

It is this kind of reassertion, combined with appropriate forms of reconceptualization, that this book seeks to make. It is an attempt to develop earlier theorizing and practical experience in order to indicate appropriate directions towards an alternative form of national curriculum, which might achieve the educational ends stated to be desirable while avoiding the worst of the current flaws.

Those changes in the fabric of society to which we have already referred have not only made this more of a priority than it perhaps was in 1977 when the term 'areas of experience' first came into prominence; they have also changed the emphases within this scheme. This change in emphasis we have sought to reflect in our analysis of the areas to be explored.

Hence, we begin from a conviction that such a reconceptualization must be undertaken with full awareness of the prime thrust we are, or should be, seeking. For us the priorities which need urgently to be addressed are those which relate directly to the need to prepare the young for entry into a genuinely democratic society which will offer them the kind of life-enhancement that democracy must seek to offer and, within that, the ability to take charge of their own destinies in the context of an acknowledged and accepted responsibility for the collective destiny of human society. For, to adapt Artistotle's famous dictum, education, like the state, exists for the sake of the good life and not for life only. The concern must be to develop a form of curriculum which will genuinely prepare the young for entry, as full and competent participants, into the democratic society of the future, a curriculum which will offer personal enrichment and empowerment in addition to a preparation for a productive economic role.

For it is also our view that it is only through offering every member of society this fully emancipatory form of education that economic needs can in the long term be most effectively served. We cannot see the polarization of the 'liberal' and the 'vocational', or 'education for society' and 'education for personal development' as anything other than a false dichotomy, which must prove damaging to the quality of both. For there is still much to be said in favour of what the Crowther Report (CACE 1959, para. 91, p. 60) said about 'the quickening of enterprise . . . the stimulation of invention or . . . the general sharpening of those wits by which alone a trading nation in a crowded island can hope to make its living'.

And so, our key adjectives relate largely to the kinds of experience which are likely to help pupils to develop as autonomous, responsible and productive members of the democratic society of the future – even the global society. And, through an exploration of each of these key dimensions of individual development, we shall be seeking to offer pointers towards an alternative national curriculum, a set of educational policies which are quite differently grounded from those currently in place, and which, perhaps most importantly, are intended to help pupils to see the essential interrelatedness of these several aspects of human existence.

This last point alerts us to a further important feature of our alternative national curriculum which should be noted here. For the main significance of employing adjectives rather than nouns to delineate the several dimensions of such a curriculum is that they can be seen as describing different aspects of what is essentially a single entity, the developing experience of the individual, rather than as discrete elements to be kept forever apart. An adjectival curriculum, unlike a substantive curriculum, cannot be so readily viewed as an agglomeration of separate entities; it is what they all add up to which constitutes education in the full sense and which also constitutes the entitlement of every individual in such an education. For the entitlement is, or should be, to a coherent set of experiences, not to a heterogeneous conglomerate whose cohesiveness is left to chance.

In a genuinely democratic society educational provision must go beyond the demands of economic success and social control; it cannot consist merely of forms of vocational preparation and training in obedience; it must, above all things, offer social and political empowerment and opportunities for personal enrichment.

And this means that it must be based on the offering of genuine educational experiences to young people. In order to be genuine, these experiences must be their own and must relate in some direct way to the development of their own thinking, their own attitudes, their own views and values. Such a form of education must offer something of positive and direct value to its recipients beyond the wherewithal to secure a job and earn a living, important as these are.

This is not to say, however, that it will bear no relation to vocational advancement or the economic health of society. For, as we have already suggested, an alternative national curriculum planned in this way will, we believe, offer an enhanced contribution to economic stability.

It will also reflect a proactive approach to those 'law and order' problems which are looming increasingly large in present societies, since it will seek to obviate these by providing a genuine form of entitlement as the democratic right of all pupils, in order to enhance their sense of belonging to, and thus sharing a responsibility for, the society of which they must learn to see themselves as a valued part. Above all, therefore, it will contribute, we also believe, to a major shift towards a more truly democratic society for the twenty-first century.

The book begins with a 'scene-setting' chapter which develops the general curriculum issues – what is implied by the notions of education as development and of education through experience, the lessons to be learnt from earlier experience of curriculum development and the inadequacies of a National Curriculum which appears to have ignored these.

Subsequent chapters are contributed by specialists in the main areas of experience, and seek to illustrate the degree of rethinking which subject specialists need to engage in if they are to contribute in a worthwhile manner to this form of curriculum, and, in particular, if they are to assist young people to develop a cohesive and unfragmented understanding of the world of which they are a part.

We have kept the personal, social, moral and the socio-political to the end, because we hope that, as the focus narrows and concentrates on the development of the individual as a moral agent in a social, political and, indeed, economic setting, exploration of these aspects of educational experience will draw together many of the threads which by that stage will have emerged from earlier discussions. In this way we hope to provide coherence and to underline our central concern with the interrelatedness of all aspects of the experience of being human.

The overall intention is to try to get beyond mere criticism of the National Curriculum and to offer an alternative blueprint for a national curriculum which would offer all pupils, from 5 (or even earlier) to 16 (and beyond), a genuine entitlement to the kind of curriculum which will enhance not only their employment prospects but also their personal lives, while at the same time ensuring the benefits which must follow for society as a whole if those lives are led in a genuinely participative democratic setting.

1

Education as Development Through Experience

Gwyn Edwards and A. V. Kelly

Everyone who has contributed significantly to the educational debate during the last two centuries has begun from a concept of education as personal development. And all have acknowledged the corollary of that, that such development can only be promoted by genuine forms of personal experience. This necessary connection was first adumbrated by Rousseau in his *Emile*, and it has been reiterated by every theorist since, perhaps most tellingly in the work of John Dewey.

More recently, the same point was emphasized from an opposite perspective by A.N.Whitehead (1932). For he roundly criticized those forms of education whose focus is on education as the transmission of knowledge and its assimilation by largely passive recipients. He described the kind of knowledge purveyed by that form of 'education' as 'inert ideas', and he claimed that 'education with inert ideas is not only useless; it is, above all things, harmful' (op. cit., p. 2), since 'knowledge does not keep any better than fish' (op. cit., p.v).

His claim was taken up explicitly in the Hadow Report on Primary Education (Board of Education 1931), and this view of education as development was implicit in all the major government reports on education published in the UK in the earlier years of this century.

> We must recognise the uselessness and the danger of seeking to inculcate what Professor Whitehead calls inert ideas – that is, ideas which at the time when they are imparted have no bearing upon a child's natural activities of body or mind and do nothing to illuminate or guide his [or her] experience. (Board of Education 1931,para.74)

And that is a major part of the basis for the report's now famous assertion that 'the curriculum is to be thought of in terms of activity and experience rather than of knowledge to be acquired and facts to be stored' (para.75).

We also noted in our Introduction that the Crowther Report (1959), in considering the education of young people from 15 to 18, stresses the notion of education as the right of every boy and girl as of equal importance to

1

its function as a national investment. 'There are many persons the justification for whose education must be sought almost entirely in what it does for them as individuals' (op. cit., para 86). The Newsom Report (1963), in its Introduction (p. xiv), tells us that 'each [pupil] is an individual whose spirit needs education as much as his [or her] body needs nourishment. Without adequate education human life is impoverished.' And, more recently, Nelson Mandela in his autobiography has described education as 'the great engine of personal development' (1995, p. 194).

We must finally note the extent to which this notion of what it means to be educated is, or was until very recently, a major part of the meaning of 'education' in common parlance. An 'educated' person has long been seen as someone whose educational experiences have had a recognizable impact on the development of character, and thus on life-style and general behaviour (the opposite kind of person usually being described as 'ignorant').

Such personal development, however, does not just happen, nor must it be left to chance. And so, unless we are to deny altogether this dimension of education, as the instrumental ethos of the current National Curriculum encourages us to do, the school curriculum must be planned in such a way as to seek to ensure that it does happen, that those who are exposed to it do develop as persons through that exposure. A prime focus of any truly educational curriculum must be on the individual development of its recipients.

THE EVOLUTION OF AN ENTITLEMENT CURRICULUM

Against this backcloth, therefore, we cannot be surprised to discover that the changes which were occurring in the actualities of schooling during the 1960s and 1970s, or at least the changes which some people were attempting to bring about, were characterized by this view of education as personal development.

It is customary to date deliberate attempts at curriculum change to the launching by the USSR of the space satellite, Sputnik I, in 1957, although extensive changes were already under way in the primary, and especially the early years, sectors, prompted by those recommendations of the Hadow Report (1931) which we have noted. At secondary level, however, the period before 1957 was characterized as one of 'drift' (Hoyle 1969).

All this was to change at the point where, both in the USA and in the UK, serious concerns began to be felt at the thought that the west might be falling behind in the 'space race'. For that thought prompted, on both sides of the Atlantic, a focusing of attention on the school curriculum and a conviction that it must now not only begin to change but also to do so on the basis of careful forward planning.

Thus there began that period which Lawrence Stenhouse (1980) was later to describe as the curriculum development movement. This was the period which saw the establishment of the Schools Council for the Curriculum and

Examinations, and the consequent generation of a plethora of curriculum projects, as well as other similar initiatives supported by private sponsors such as the Nuffield Foundation.

The origins of this movement would suggest that its prime motivation was to be found in the enhancement of scientific and technological education, that its focus was on the economic, national investment function of educational provision. However, from the outset it recognized that, as we argued in our Introduction, technological development depends crucially on human development, and, further, that it brings with it extensive social and moral change, so that the initiatives which it spawned were characterized to a similar, even perhaps a greater, extent by that concern with education as personal development which we explored above.

And, although, not unnaturally, it began by working within a mainly subject structure, most of its early projects being concerned with specific curriculum subjects, many of its working papers raised issues of a cross-curricular kind, which shifted the focus onto the children themselves rather than merely the content of their curricula. Thus projects were set up whose concern was with gifted children, for example, with travelling children, with disadvantaged children and with children with special needs.

The general tenor of curriculum development at this time, then, was underpinned by a view of education as at least as much concerned with what could be offered to the individual child as with potential advantages to society and its economy. Indeed, there was a general recognition of the interrelationship of these two concerns. And running parallel to this was the desire to ensure equality of entitlement for all pupils.

The same features can be seen in those less formalized and thus often less public developments which were occurring in individual schools and local authorities. Many authorities were experimenting with various systems of secondary comprehensivization – from all-through comprehensives to three-tier systems, involving either middle schools or sixth form colleges – long before Circular 10/65 required them to do so. Within schools, there was much experimentation with both grouping systems and with the curriculum itself. Mixed ability classes began to appear throughout the secondary sector (they had by this time become largely the norm in primary schools) and, with the advent of such groupings, there appeared new 'subjects' on the timetable, a reconceptualization of some traditional subjects and consequent changes in public examinations, especially those made possible by the institution of the Certificate of Secondary Education (CSE).

A major phenomenon of the time, for example, was the arrival of a variety of forms of 'integrated studies', and in many cases these were accompanied by significant changes in teachers' methods, especially a move towards offering pupils greater scope for independent study. Such work was then examined by the submission of extended projects rather than by formal tests of memorization and regurgitation.

And similar developments were occurring within subjects. For this was the time of 'modern mathematics', of Nuffield science, of Geography for the Young School Leaver; this was the time when 'handicraft' was beginning its development into CDT and, later, Design Studies, when classics was becoming classical studies, and various combinations of subjects were coming together as humanities. All of these were developments designed, among other things, to make what they had to offer more accessible to all pupils and no longer the preserve of the more able and more privileged, and to do so in order to support the personal development of pupils through first-hand experience of a genuine kind.

And, in the meantime, informal education was growing in the primary sector, boosted as it had been by the support of the Plowden Report (CACE 1967).

The more one contemplates these developments the more they appear to constitute some kind of natural evolution, a process by which the school curriculum was attempting to free itself from the shackles of tradition and move into the twentieth century, to match those rapid advances in technology with which we are all familiar and, above all, to keep in phase with the massive social changes, most notably the establishment of universal education, which have accompanied those advances.

Indeed, it was at this time that Basil Bernstein (1967) wrote about open schools for an open society. And he writes from a clear assumption that there is identifiable movement towards both. Society is becoming more open, characterized by a form of social integration which emphasizes unity in difference rather than similarity or conformity, and by the achievement rather than the ascription of social roles. And in schools there is to be seen a shift 'from a pedagogy which . . . was concerned with the learning of standard operations . . . to a pedagogy which emphasises the exploration of principles; from schools which emphasise the teacher as a solution-giver to schools which emphasise the teacher as problem poser or creator' (op. cit.), and 'to more personalised forms of control where teachers and taught confront each other as individuals' (op. cit.).

To say this is not of course to suggest that changes as dramatic as this were to be discerned in every school. That is not our point. It is to say, however, that the general climate of educational thinking was one in which the superior importance of the pupil to the content of the curriculum was beginning to be recognized. And it was being increasingly acknowledged that a prime purpose and justification for education was to be found in its contribution to the development of the individual – not in isolation from society, but as a member of a social and cultural collective, the continued health – social, cultural and economic – of which depended centrally on the quality of life of each member.

It was this kind of thinking and this evolutionary process which was reflected in the HMI publication, *Curriculum 11-16* (DES 1977a), to which we referred in our Introduction as the source of the term 'areas of experience', and which, listing these in the form of 'eight adjectives', argued the essentiality of such an approach to education for the attainment of educational entitlement.

It begins by telling us, for example, that 'we have to ensure that the curriculum does everything possible to help pupils to develop as individuals' (op. cit., p. 1). It goes on to express the belief that only through a curriculum framed in terms of its 'eight adjectives' 'can pupils' common curricular rights and the society's needs be met' (op. cit., p. 6). It speaks of 'the responsibility for educating the "autonomous citizen", a person able to think and act for herself or himself, to resist exploitation, to innovate and to be vigilant in the defence of liberty' (op. cit., p. 9).

This document, therefore, gave this concept of education some kind of official status and sanction.

Less than two decades later, in a context of political policies in which most of what this chapter has offered so far may appear outmoded, even naive and of historical interest only, it becomes pertinent to ask why this evolutionary process has ground to a halt (and, indeed, whether the open society disappeared along with the open school). For the National Curriculum evinces none of the characteristics we have been describing, and is in fact an exact opposite. Nor does it reflect the claim of *Curriculum 11-16* that 'there is no intention . . . of advocating a centrally controlled or directed curriculum' (p. 1), a claim which is clearly in phase with the document's recognition of the different needs of pupils 'which depend not only on their ability and maturity but also on the range of their previous experience and the degree of support received from home' (p. 12) and which thus require that 'schools must . . . be capable of adopting methods suitable to different needs' (ibid.).

One explanation for this complete turn-around is undoubtedly to be found in the economic recession which followed the oil crisis of 1974, and which has led to continued reductions in the funding of all social services since that time. For the kind of education we are here describing is far more costly than the limited offering of economically useful knowledge; and the deletion of one of the two major purposes of education which the Crowther Report (CACE 1959) proposed is clearly a major source of financial saving.

For no-one has been under any illusions that a proper form of education, designed to benefit the individual as well as society, is a costly business. The Newsom Report recognized this, but declared, 'We make no apologies for recommendations which will involve an increase in public expenditure on the education of the average pupils' (CACE 1963, p. xiv). The Plowden Report said, 'The cost of the proposals we have made is large. This is in part the cost of bringing a system designed for "other people's children" up to the standard which "a good and wise parent" would accept for his [or her] own children' (CACE 1967, para. 1230). And earlier the Crowther

Report had clearly drawn attention to the fact that 'whatever their nature and whatever their purpose, all these things will cost money' (CACE 1959, para. 88). It had gone on to say, however, that 'it is not beyond the country's means' (ibid.) and to assert, as we saw in our Introduction, that 'we find it difficult to conceive that there could be any other application of money giving a larger or more certain return in the quickening of enterprise, in the stimulation of invention or in the general sharpening of those wits by which alone a trading nation in a crowded island can hope to make its living' (op. cit., para. 91). Again we must note the conviction in these words that this is the only route to economic stability as well as personal development.

One of the reasons why the evolution we have been exploring has come to a halt is that recent governments have not accepted the validity of this last point, and have certainly not been prepared to devote public money to the provision of forms of education which they regard as having no economic 'pay-off'. Traditionally, this form of education had everyone's support when it was being made available only to those children whose parents could afford to pay for it. The advent of mass education, provided by the state for all children, brought with it much reduced notions of what should be on offer, and those notions seldom went beyond the provision of useful forms of training, allied with equally useful forms of social control. The evolution we have been describing was a process by which some were seeking to make these expensive forms of education available to every child, from a conviction that, in a democratic society, entitlement entails this. Recent governments have sought to halt that process and have preferred to allow the quality of state-provided education to deteriorate rather than to increase taxation to maintain its quality as a genuine source of enrichment to all. This is the key to the genesis of the National Curriculum for England and Wales which reflects a rejection of the view of educational provision as concerned to support the development of the individual person.

A second reason for the block on this evolutionary process, however, which is central to the case we are developing here, is that its momentum has always been retarded by a lack of clarity over what it entails, so that, as we saw above, its theory far outstripped its practice and it has been easily overturned. For example, although *Curriculum 11-16* declared that none of the areas it listed 'should be simply equated with a subject or group of subjects' (p. 6), the document then devoted most of its subsequent text to supplementary papers by HMI Subject Committees.

It is absolutely vital, therefore, if we are to propose the resurrection of this form of education as a viable alternative to what is currently on offer as the National Curriculum, that we become much clearer than most people once were about its implications, practical as well as theoretical. For, as we suggested in our Introduction, it requires a complete reconceptualization of both theory and practice.

THE JUSTIFICATION OF AN ENTITLEMENT CURRICULUM

First, however, we need to address the question of why the notion of an entitlement curriculum should be accepted, why a society should seek to provide this kind of empowering curriculum for all its young people. And the main reason why we must address this question is because there are many people who do not accept this as any kind of imperative, and who would thus dismiss our case for an alternative national curriculum framed in such terms as unnecessary or even as ideologically unsound.

From the beginning of state-provided education, there have been major ideological disagreements and conflict concerning the point and purpose of such provision. And a strong case has been made (Gordon and Lawton 1978) for acknowledging that the dominant ideology has always been that of the group which Raymond Williams (1961) described as 'the industrial trainers', those who have seen the justification of a state-maintained education system entirely in terms of its contribution to the national economy and of a parallel concern with social control, a 'gentling of the masses'. The case for the former of these two purposes has weakened considerably as advancing technology has reduced the need for a trained workforce of previous proportions, so that some of those who have taken this view, perhaps foolishly ignoring the social consequences, can find little continuing justification of any kind for state-maintained education. This is one reason why recent policies have revealed a progressive shift away from the idea of education as person-centred or as 'the right of every boy and girl'.

Denis Lawton (1989, p. 7) has identified 'four ideological positions concerning the debate between those who would plan education and those who would leave education to market forces'.

First, there are the 'privatizers' who would leave education entirely to market forces and regard parents' choices for the education of their children as limited only by their ability to pay. The introduction of vouchers for nursery provision (now discontinued) may be seen as a major step towards such a system.

Second, there are the 'mimimalists' or 'segregators' who believe that the state should provide merely a basic schooling for every child and leave it to parents to buy additional extras or to opt out of the state system entirely; under such a policy, children would be separated out by social class or suppposed intellectual ability, even by gender, so that regular testing and the publication of 'league tables' becomes central.

The 'pluralists' want to see the establishment of a sound state-maintained system, but one which is based on a meritocratic view of educational progress, and thus of equality of opportunity; they favour the metaphor of the 'ladder of opportunity'. The re-introduction of selection into our education system, whether accompanied by the resurrection of the grammar school or not, may be seen as a significant current example of this ideological position.

Finally, there are the 'comprehensive planners', who wish to see the state providing a good general education for all, a genuine system of mass education, a 'broad highway' to educational achievement and empowerment.

It will be clear, then, that, if all of these ideologies exist and are currently seeking to influence the planning of the country's education system, we need to make a case out here for aligning ourselves with the last group, the 'comprehensive planners', and advocating a national curriculum which, unlike the currently established version, will genuinely seek to provide appropriate educational opportunities for all pupils.

The first line of justification we would offer for advocating this last stance is purely pragmatic. For it is our view that current problems of social control, those 'law and order' difficulties we referred to earlier, the emergence of an underclass in our society of quite massive proportions, can no longer be dealt with by traditional devices for 'gentling the masses'. Nor are they problems which, once created, can be cured; they can only be prevented. And a major strategy for their prevention has to be found in the creation of an appropriate education system for all, one which will offer a worthwhile set of experiences for everyone rather than subjecting a major proportion of the school population to failure, rejection and the alienation which must inevitably follow from negative experiences of that kind. It requires an education system which will support the personal development of every child and young person, and which will seek to involve and engage them fully in a concern for the society of which they are a part.

Secondly, it is also our view, as we have indicated in our Introduction, that this kind of education is also the best route to economic stability. It is naive to take the view that economic stability depends on narrow forms of vocationally oriented training. It is far more dependent on the development of independence of thought, creativity and imagination, as we have seen the Crowther Report (CACE 1959) claiming.

However, the major theoretical justification that we would offer for advocating this approach to education derives from the proclaimed democratic context in which this debate and the planning of a state system of education are both taking place (Kelly 1995). For, within any society with pretensions to being described as democratic, access to a genuine and complete form of education for everyone must be recognized as a human right, as one of the 'commmon curricular rights' of *Curriculum 11-16* (DES 1977a, p. 6). As John Dewey once said (1916, Ch. 7, Summary) it is part of the essence of democracy that it 'makes provision for participation in its good of all its members on equal terms'. Further, 'a true community . . . , to maintain itself as a community, requires universal education' (Rosenthal 1993, p. 385). And, as Raymond Williams (1961, p. 144) said, 'All members of the society have a natural right to be educated, and that in any good society depends on governments' accepting this principle as a duty'. To this we would add that it is a *sine qua non* of any democratic society. For it is difficult, if not impossible, to offer a definition of democracy in terms of privilege or of a democratic system of education in terms of competition or social divisiveness.

If this is so, then a democratic society requires a public system of education which offers equality of opportunity and entitlement to all, regardless of wealth, social class, gender or ethnicity.

Finally, it must be added that, at the most basic level, it makes little sense to place the responsibility for government, even at the minimal level of electing a body of politicians to rule on one's behalf, in the hands of every citizen and then adopt a policy which will ensure that not every citizen is educated to fulfil that responsibility as thoughtfully and as meaningfully as possible. To do so is to suggest that an ill-informed electorate is one's best route to achieving or maintaining political power and to reveal a cynical disregard and contempt for democracy itself. It raises questions, therefore, not merely concerning how serious the advocates of such policies are about education but also about how serious they are about democracy. For such a policy is certainly not consistent with democratic principles, since 'the primary role of education in a democracy is to provide all its future members with the opportunity to develop those intellectual and moral qualities which meaningful participation in democratic life requires' (Carr 1991, p. 185), to educate the 'autonomous citizen' which *Curriculum 11-16* asserts as a major responsibility of the education system (DES 1977, p. 9).

The case for universal entitlement to education of an appropriate kind, then, derives not only from a common-sense appreciation of the complexities of modern societies but also from both the theory and the practice of democratic government. And it cannot be denied without an accompanying denial of democracy itself – and perhaps of common-sense too.

We must now turn to an examination of some of the underlying principles of this appropriate kind of education which both common-sense and the notion of democracy provide an entitlement to.

EDUCATION FOR EMPOWERMENT

Fundamentally, in a democratic society every citizen has a right to the kind of education which will offer him/her empowerment, in the form of a proper preparation for an active role in the government of that society, whether this involves participating directly in that government or merely evaluating the actions, the decisions and the policies of those who do. It is essential that every citizen be offered a sense of genuine involvement in the collective destiny of the society of which (s)he is a part. And it is a major task of the education system to promote such a sense. This in turn means creating a form of education which will seek to develop all capabilities and not merely those which are regarded by those currently – and temporarily – in power as likely to contribute to the economic health of society. The social, cultural and intellectual health of society has to be seen as being of equal importance.

It has been argued with some cogency, particularly by Elliot Eisner (1982; 1996), that educational provision is currently conceived in terms which are far too narrow and constricting. 'Concern for the quality of education is most often expressed as the desire to return to what is fundamental in schooling, that is, acquiring literacy and achieving competency in the use of numbers. In sloganese, the demand has been to "return to the basics" ' (1982., p. xi).

Eisner's argument is that human experience goes far beyond these two areas of competence -important as they are. In particular, he is concerned to stress 'the identification of the role of the senses in human conceptualization and the description of the forms humans use to make their conceptualizations public' (ibid.). The latter he calls 'forms of representation'; they are 'the devices that humans use to make public conceptions which are privately held' and 'the vehicles through which concepts that are visual, auditory, kinesthetic, olfactory, gustatory, and tactile are given public status' (op. cit., p. 47). And his major theme is that education should seek to provide a facility of operation within *all* of these modes of cognition and communication.

> Thus, insofar as education is concerned with developing the individual's ability to secure diverse forms of meaning through experience, then the ability to encode and decode the content embodied in different forms of representation is also of crucial importance. (op. cit., p. xii)

The case which Eisner makes out for giving our concept of education this kind of breadth, or of defining educational breadth in this way, can perhaps be seen as an extension of the case which we have already noted was made by HMI through their 'eight adjectives' (DES 1977a). And their reasons for making that case were much the same. In particular, there was that conviction we have already noted that all pupils are entitled to a 'broad' and 'balanced' curriculum, to a range of 'areas of experience' covering all the major aspects of human cognition and communication.

That entitlement, then, which we have seen to be an essential aspect of educational provision in a democratic society, is not merely an entitlement to tuition in a range of school subjects, an experience which may or may not prepare one for an active life in such a society; it is an entitlement to a process which will develop all of one's capacities to the fullest possible degree. It thus requires a form of education, and a concept of curriculum, whose emphasis is on individual development rather than on the acquisition of subject knowledge, a curriculum which requires an approach to planning which is adjectival rather than substantive. For adjectives describe, whereas substantives tend to prescribe; and description is permissive and permeable, whereas prescription is rigid and incapable of adaptation to individual circumstance.

EDUCATION AS EXPERIENCE

A key feature of such a form of education is that it must involve genuine experiences on the part of the person being educated. We must plan for such genuine experiences on the part of pupils; we must seek to ensure that what they learn makes a difference to them in some real sense and is not just, as Whitehead (1945) put it, 'plastered on'.

Such experience, however, while it must be personal and authentic and must contribute significantly to the development of the self, must not be viewed as taking place in some kind of social, or even intellectual, vacuum. This is the view of the self and of the development of the self to which we are led if we view the issue solely from a psychological perspective.

However, we do not experience events as autonomous individuals but as situated actors. Hence education through experience is a social rather than an individual process. As Inglis (1993, p. 205) observes,

> Whatever experience is, it is so in virtue of its intersubjective and trans-individual definitions and meanings, constituted by the language and symbols we have for interpreting and therefore giving experience its meaning and value. Experience on this account is not yours or mine; it is ours. It is not private but public.

We might also note here the words of Lawrence Stenhouse (1967, p. 9), that 'though people can think *for* themselves, they cannot think *by* themselves. They think within cultures associated with human societies'. For this point has an important relevance for the issue of the relationship of culture to the curriculum – a further central dimension of education through experience.

In accepting the significance of the role which culture plays in the development of the individual, however, we must avoid the risk of slipping into a deterministic view of the construction of self, since this would deny any concept of education as empowerment or as concerned with the development of individual autonomy, and thus would invalidate the central message of this book. For, to quote from the work of Lawrence Stenhouse again (1967, p. 9), 'culture is often seen . . . as a determinant of thought and behaviour' and 'if we were to accept this position without reservation, we should have to concede that to transmit culture . . . would determine [pupils'] thoughts and outcomes...Education would become . . . a constricting indoctrination.'

An acknowledgement of the socio-historical construction of our consciousness, however, need not lead to that form of over-deterministic view of humankind. For, while never being wholly or truly autonomous, individuals need not necessarily be unwitting replicas of the underlying social order. There is at least the potential for a dialectical interpenetration of self and society. People can transform themselves by acting on the world in ways which transform the socio-historical structures and processes. Pupils must be encouraged and assisted to respond critically and creatively to both

culture and experience. They must be invited, even driven, to reflect upon
the cultural experiences they have or are given. For 'to reflect means to gain
control over culture rather than to be controlled by it' (Stenhouse, op. cit.,
p. 28) and 'the object of education is to make culture more a resource and
less a determinant' (op. cit., p. 20).

We need, then, to adopt a sociological as well as, or perhaps instead of,
a psychological perspective on the process of learning through experience.
For, on the one hand, as Oakeshott (1933,p.14) has pointed out,

> a self, replete with opinion, prejudice, habit, knowledge is implied in every actual
> experience; and to exclude self from any experience whatever is an absolute
> impossibility.

On the other hand, as Dewey (1916, p. 87) claimed, 'each [individual] has
to refer his own action to that of others and to consider the actions of others
to give point and direction to his own'. It is for this reason that this
approach to education is being advocated here, as it was advocated by
Dewey himself, as the only approach which is appropriate in a democratic
social context.

If education is to be viewed as development through experience, then,
both the process of development and the experiences which promote it
must be firmly located within the social context. Hence, again, those who
advocate an approach to education through experience regard the educative process as essentially one of collaboration rather than competition, as
democratic rather than elitist.

And this would seem to reflect the same kind of thinking as that which
we have seen led Eisner to stress the public dimension of the 'modes of
representation', to emphasize that these are not only modes of cognition
but also, and crucially, modes of communication. Experience is a matter not
merely of how the world is conceived but of how it is *expressed*, and education is not a matter only of providing experiences but of promoting the
development of a capability to reflect on, to communicate and to express
those experiences, the acquisition of what, as we saw earlier, Eisner (1982,
p. 47) calls 'forms of representation' – 'the devices that humans use to make
public conceptions which are privately held'.

There is thus a powerful argument here in favour of viewing education
not as the mere learning of 'facts', inert or otherwise, but as a form of
human development through genuine experience within a social and cultural context. There are also strong pointers as to what such an approach
to educational provision entails. These will be explored in all the chapters
which follow.

For it is clear that, while we must acknowledge the subjectivity of learning through experience, we must also recognize the importance of the social
context of such learning, and, in particular, the many ways in which the
socio-historical and cultural context of learning affects the nature of the
experiences themselves. Furthermore, genuine experience is not something

that happens to us, and marks us, but something we construct from and through our situatedness within the world. Hence any form of education which seeks genuinely to empower the individual, especially by developing an awareness of the cultural forces which, in the absence of such awareness, will limit experience and inhibit social and political empowerment, must seek to promote the widest possible development of intellectual, including, above all, critical, capacities.

Two further points must be noted here which will emerge more fully in the chapters which follow. First, what we have learned about the social and cultural context of experience must imply an acceptance of the multicultural nature of that context. It must point us towards a multicultural, even an intercultural curriculum – rather than, as with the National Curriculum in its present form, a monocultural one – a curriculum which is designed to acknowledge, to welcome, even to celebrate the different social and cultural contexts in which pupils' experiences are situated rather than to impose on these some form of spurious and totalitarian hierarchical structure.

Secondly, education through experience, when both are conceived in the ways we have suggested they must be, requires active rather than passive forms of learning. True and genuine experience implies active forms of interaction between the individual, the social and cultural context of learning and the experiences which that context offers. Anything less than that falls short of any concept of education as empowerment, and thus of any concept of education which is defensible in a democratic political context.

The notion of education as development through experience, then, is not new. It is not outmoded, except in the rhetoric of those who have a vested political interest in debunking it. Nor does it represent merely an alternative teaching methodology; it constitutes a serious alternative ideology, social and political as well as educational, which involves a quite different conceptualization of education and curriculum from that enshrined in the traditional ideology of the National Curriculum.

However, before beginning the exploration, to which the rest of this book is devoted, of what might be a more acceptable alternative to the National Curriculum currently in place, we must first consider the question of whether any kind of centrally determined curriculum is appropriate to, or necessary for, the kind of education we are advocating and the democratic context for which we are advocating it.

THE CASE FOR A NATIONAL CURRICULUM – DEMOCRATIC ENTITLEMENT

We might begin by noting that, as John White (1988, p. 120) pointed out at the time when the National Curriculum was being created, 'there is no virtue in a national curriculum as such. Hitler had a national curriculum, and so did Stalin. The basic issue is: what *kind* of national curriculum is Mr Baker giving us?'. There are thus two issues to be addressed – that of the justification of the imposition of any form of national curriculum and that of the nature of whatever national curriculum it is planned to impose.

There are three main kinds of argument for the establishment of a national curriculum, and it is important to be clear that each appeals to a quite different set of values and derives from a quite different concept of education and its purposes. Each line of argument, therefore, leads to a quite different kind of national curriculum.

First, there is the argument which sees education as primarily concerned with the maintenance and transmission of human knowledge and high culture.

The basis of this case is a particular view of human knowledge, and of human values, as objective and in some sense permanent, and a consequent view of education as concerned primarily with the induction of the young into this knowledge and these values. On this view, certain kinds of knowledge and certain forms of human activity are regarded as qualitatively superior to alternative forms, so that it is this knowledge and these activities which education must be centrally concerned with. And so education becomes initiation into these 'intrinsically worthwhile activities' (Peters 1966).

This argument, therefore, leads us to the idea of a compulsory national curriculum which will aim to ensure that all pupils are offered such initiation. The intention of such a curriculum, then, although beginning from a desire to secure the maintenance and the extension of these qualitatively superior forms of human knowledge, is equally to ensure equality of access to what is worthwhile for all pupils. In this connection, it is worth noting that the assertion of the need for a compulsory curriculum to achieve this was a direct response to those attempts to offer differentiated forms of curriculum and to reconceptualize many curriculum subjects which we noted earlier (White 1973). For, on this view, such reconceptualizations run the risk of diluting those pure forms of knowledge which its advocates posit.

A variation on this theme, or another perspective on it, is offered by those who have proposed a common curriculum planned around the notion that education should seek to transmit a society's culture, what Matthew Arnold once described as 'the best that has been thought and said', so that the curriculum should consist of a selection from that culture (Lawton 1975). Again, we must note that this kind of case also has two purposes – to preserve and develop that culture but also to ensure equality of access to it for all pupils.

This line of argument has much to recommend it. For we do not want an education system which will lead to the demise of what is valuable in human knowledge or in cultural achievements. Nor do most of us want a curriculum which will deny access to these to significant groups of pupils.

It falls down, however, because of its assumption of permanence for both human knowledge and culture. For if the intrinsically worthwhile exists only in the eye of the beholder, if what is best in our culture is a matter of opinion, if we are to acknowledge the force of postmodernism and its view of human knowledge as 'transformatory rather than cumulative' (Doll 1989), if we are to recognize, and to accept, the cultural pluralism of present-day societies, then to impose any one version of knowledge or any one culture on the next generation through the school curriculum begins to look more like indoctrination than education, more like totalitarianism than democracy.

The concern for equality of entitlement which this kind of view displays must be acknowledged, and the case made for a common, compulsory, national curriculum in those terms is valuable. What is questionable, however, is the kind of national curriculum their basic stance on knowledge leads them to. For that curriculum is framed in terms of the knowledge-content its advocates regard as intrinsically worthwhile, and tends to evince little regard for the impact of this on the learner. In short, this argument for a compulsory curriculum is founded on a particular view of the purposes of education which is at odds with the developmental view, and thus leads to a form of compulsory curriculum which is equally at odds with that which we are advocating here.

This form of argument for a compulsory curriculum has also offered a source of rhetoric for those who have wished to establish a national curriculum for quite different reasons – considerations of a political and/or economic kind. And this is the second form of argument in support of a nationally determined curriculum which we must consider. This kind of case has little to do with entitlement, although that term is often a major part of its supporting rhetoric. For, as we suggested in our Introduction, entitlement is a moral concept; it is concerned with human rights; and the political case is instrumental and pragmatic, a matter of economic and political expediency.

We saw earlier that, from the beginning of state provided education in the UK, a major influence on its establishment and on its subsequent development has been that of those whom Raymond Williams (1961) called the 'industrial trainers', those whose view of the state system has always been that it is there to provide a trained workforce and to 'gentle the masses' by ensuring some form of social compliance. These are the people, then, whose case for a national curriculum goes no further than a desire to produce fodder for industry and to exercise social control.

It must be noted, however, that such people seldom, if ever, offer their case in this stark form. It is always dressed up in, even concealed by, the rhetoric of other, moral arguments. As Denis Lawton (1988, p. 19) has said of the current National Curriculum for England and Wales, the 'plan for a national curriculum may be accompanied by some of the common curriculum rhetoric, but does not show its ideals'. Thus we hear of 'entitle-ment', of 'spiritual, moral, cultural, mental and physical development', of 'a broad and balanced curriculum' and many more high sounding phrases which appeal to moral considerations in support of what is essentially an amoral case. When we consider the reality beyond the rhetoric, however, all is very different.

A second feature of this argument which we must consider is that, in a society characterized by high levels of unemployment, in which the need for a trained workforce is becoming progressively less pressing, the case of the 'industrial trainers' is rapidly diminishing (although the force of the 'law and order' case remains, and perhaps is becoming even greater). It is not surprising, therefore, to find that there is emerging a number of views of educational provision which would significantly reduce what is seen as the entitlement of every pupil – those ideologies of the political right which, as we saw earlier, Denis Lawton (1989) has identified. For, however these ideologies are dressed up for presentation, at root they are taking the view that there is no case for state provision of anything but a minimal form of education, since the economic needs of society justify nothing more and they do not recognize the force of any kind of moral consideration.

The third argument for the provision by the state of a common national curriculum is an overtly moral argument, and it is this argument which underpins the case for viewing education as personal development. This is the argument we noted earlier when we were examining the concept of entitlement. And, as we noted there, it begins from an acceptance of democ-racy as a moral concept, and of human rights and equality as central prin-ciples of that concept, and deduces from this that a democratic society has a moral duty to provide all of its citizens with the best possible form of education appropriate to their individual needs (Kelly 1995).

This is an argument, then, which is firmly based on what are seen to be the rights of each individual. It will thus in practice lead to a form of common national curriculum which is different in many respects from that which emerges from a concern with intrinsically worthwhile knowledge or from the economic needs of society. For, on this view, the entitlement is not merely to access to certain bodies of knowledge or to training for employ-ment, although neither of these is necessarily excluded; the entitlement is to a form of curriculum which will cater appropriately to the growth and development of every capacity, which will promote the acquisition of those understandings which will facilitate intelligent participation in democratic processes, which will offer genuine social and political empowerment, and which will in general enrich and enhance the life potential of every indi-vidual.

Simply to describe a curriculum as an entitlement curriculum does not make it such, at least in this sense of entitlement. One must always ask what is the entitlement to. And if the entitlement which a particular form of curriculum offers is not to the kinds of benefits we are describing here, then such a curriculum is not adequate for a democratic society.

The kind of curriculum which this view of entitlement requires is that which we attempted to delineate in the earlier sections of this chapter. It requires the kind of reconceptualization of curriculum which we explored there; it demands a curriculum framed in terms not of subjects but of 'forms of representation' and/or areas of experience. And its underlying first principle must be the empowerment of the individual.

Curriculum 11-16, in its 'General Introduction', said, 'There is no intention anywhere in the papers which follow of advocating a centrally controlled or directed curriculum' (DES 1977a, p. 1). The case it made out, however, for ensuring adequate exposure of all pupils to all the areas of experience it outlined, along with the evidence offered by the subsequent secondary survey (DES 1979a) of the paucity of experience being made available to many pupils, would suggest that, if this kind of entitlement is to be fully realized, some central direction, some kind of national curriculum, is necessary.

The notion of entitlement as a democratic and human right, then, offers a moral justification for a national curriculum. The kind of national curriculum it justifies, however, is very different from that which is based on political and economic expediency. It is thus very different from the National Curriculum which has been imposed on the state maintained schools of England and Wales.

TOWARDS AN ALTERNATIVE NATIONAL CURRICULUM

If we have been right to claim that the only *moral* justification for the imposition of a compulsory, common, national curriculum in a democratic society is that which is premised on the development and empowerment of the individual, then the only kind of national curriculum which this can lead to is one which is similarly premised. At the very least, we need a national curriculum which reflects *both* of the aims set out for education in the Crowther Report (CACE 1959), a curriculum which does not ignore the demands of education as a national investment, the economic function, but which at the same time gives equal weight to the social service aspects of educational provision.

And the first thing that we must note is that this latter function cannot be met by the provision of a simple unitary curriculum for all pupils, regardless of their origins, interests, background, culture, language and all those other characteristics which make them the *individuals* they are and must be encouraged to be. Uniformity of provision can never lead to equality of opportunity or entitlement. As Mary Warnock (1977, p. 26) said a long time ago, 'there is a difference between claiming that everyone has an equal right to education and saying that everyone has a right to equal education'. To promote a genuine form of entitlement, a curriculum must not only be common to all, it must also be 'genuinely suitable for all, not suitable only for the middle class or most academic' (op. cit., p. 84).

To provide a uniform curriculum, built on the public school model, for pupils from a wide range of very different backgrounds will never lead to any kind of productive educational achievement on the part of most of them, let alone to anything remotely comparable to political empowerment. All the evidence indicates that it leads to the opposite – to disaffection, alienation and rejection, and, as a consequence, to those 'law and order' problems of which we are becoming increasingly aware. However, as Mary Warnock goes on to say (ibid.), 'it is possible to devise a curriculum which is both common and non-middle class, adaptable for all, and within which no-one is doomed to failure or frustration', and 'a system must be devised so flexible that it can be made to accommodate everyone, whatever his [or her] ability, whatever his [or her] cultural background'.

The devising of such a curriculum, however, as we have sought to show, and as subsequent chapters will also reveal, requires an intellectual sophistication, an administrative flexibility, a trust in the professionalism of teachers and, above all, a commitment to democratic ideals at a level far beyond that shown – or, indeed, not shown – in current policies.

For, as we have seen, it necessitates a complete reconceptualization of curriculum as a concept far more complex than a subject syllabus or collection of subject syllabuses, and as requiring a level of intellectualism and professionalism in its framing which go well beyond a simplistic listing of levels and attainment targets. And it demands a form of assessment which will reveal more sophisticated educational attainments than the retention and regurgitation of subject knowledge, and will genuinely seek to assess what exposure to the processes of education has done for the developing pupil.

This is the real thrust behind an 'areas of experience' approach to educational planning. Its concern must be not merely to provide a breadth and a balance to the educational experience of every pupil, but to ensure that the experiences enjoyed are genuine experiences rather than 'inert ideas'.

Further, if, as we have argued, the fundamental rationale for a national curriculum in a democratic society is the concept of democracy itself, then, as we have also argued, the developmental experiences we provide as the essential constituents of such a curriculum must be firmly rooted in a democratic social context. And this means that education must be recognized as a collaborative rather than a competitive activity.

For education in any real sense, especially within a genuinely democratic society, is not, and cannot be, a competitive matter. No-one ever became an educated person in isolation from his or her cultural environment, as we noted earlier, or in competition with his or her fellows. On the contrary, education is advanced by cooperation, by what Paulo Freire (1976) once called 'dialogue', based on a 'faith that I can only become truly myself when

other people also become themselves' (op. cit., p. 45). 'Education is fur-
thered the more it is shared . . . In direct opposition to market exchanges,
educational exchanges flourish most with the unpaid gifts of others and
develop the more they are *not* mediated by private possession and profit'
(McMurtry 1991, p. 212).

We have accepted that to devise such an alternative form of national curriculum, one which might offer all, or at least most, pupils the kind of social
empowerment and personal enrichment which we are claiming to be the
sine qua non of a democratic curiculum, is far from easy either conceptually
or practically. It should not surprise us, however, to find that to devise a
curriculum which will support the development of human beings is a far
more complex undertaking than the authors of the present simplistic
National Curriculum appear to have been able to recognize.

Nor is complexity to be shied away from, especially when, as in the present context, the stakes are so high. While recognizing, therefore, that the
task is far from easy, and that the damage done already by recent and current policies will be difficult to repair, those who are dissatisfied with those
policies must be prepared to make the effort to find an appropriate alternative.

Unlike the present curriculum, that alternative must be firmly based conceptually and practically viable. It must reflect sound practice underpinned
by clear, honest and coherent theory. Subsequent chapters will explore, from
both of these perspectives, all the major dimensions of the kinds of experiential learning which such an alternative curriculum must embrace if it
is to support the growth of individuals towards empowerment, enrichment
and a sense of social responsibility, and the development of society towards
a more genuinely democratic form.

2

Questioning School Mathematics

Paul Ernest

Recent years have seen a major reorganization of the mathematics curriculum and its assessment in Britain, through the central imposition of a
national curriculum for state schools (excluding Scotland). The associated
curriculum innovations and developments in assessment have been rushed
into implementation with little new reflection on the nature or purpose of
the mathematics curriculum, since the landmark Cockcroft Report (DES
1982). Although there was a broad trend in educational thought leading
towards a whole curriculum, the deeper issues of the nature and purpose
of mathematics in schools in the context of the whole curriculum had
scarcely been posed before the National Curriculum was formulated and
enshrined in law in 1988. Subsequent revisions in 1991 and 1995 have
merely been technical tinkering with a rigid curriculum structure.
The underlying assumption is that mathematics is an inert body of knowledge and skills which needs to be taught to all for purely utilitarian reasons. In this chapter I wish to pose some of the unasked but much needed
questions about the mathematics curriculum. What are the aims of teaching mathematics and what should they be? If school mathematics is thought
of in terms of areas of experience, what contexts, experiences, entitlements
should it be providing for learners? In fundamentally reconsidering
the nature and aims of the mathematics curriculum, what are the key
issues that emerge? In other words, I wish to submit mathematics to the
same fundamental critique that this book is applying to the whole
curriculum.

There are a number of especially pervasive problems facing the reconceptualization of the mathematics curriculum. First of all, mathematics is a
recondite subject. Thus many of the theorists of the whole curriculum, not
being properly acquainted with the subject, have had a limited or distorted
view of it. Phenix (1964) identifies mathematics as part of his realm of meaning entitled `symbolics'. As I agree below, the symbolic nature of mathe-
matics is a vital part of it, although it is one half of a complementary duality
that also incorporates the conceptual and imaginary part. But in the discussion by Phenix, mathematics is dominated by set theory and other
aspects of 'modern math' that over-emphasize mathematical formalism and

formalistic conceptions, and which have little to do with meaningful school mathematics.

Secondly, mathematics is an ideologically saturated subject. Part of the ideology of mathematics is to deny that it is subject to any values, interests or distortions, and that it is purely objective and logical. A corollary of this position is that mathematics is isolated and discrete from science and other areas of knowledge and values. In the areas of science and technology the issues of social and environmental impact are clear, although the successive formulations of the National Curriculum eliminated almost all such concerns. In the area of mathematics, the notion of its social responsibility is virtually unthinkable. How could mathematics, pure, objective, remote and inevitable, be held accountable for its distant and unintended uses? This position leads to paradox, with mathematics seen as utilitarian knowledge, but also completely detached from its uses.

With such considerations as a backdrop, a fresh consideration of mathematics in the curriculum in terms of areas of experience first requires some reconceptualization of the subject. In particular, there are a number of conceptions, misconceptions perhaps, that dominate the character and place of mathematics in the school curriculum, especially in the era of the National Curriculum, which need to be addressed. These are as follows:

- There is unanimity about the nature of mathematics and the aims of the teaching and learning of mathematics
- Mathematics is primarily a utilitarian subject whose function is to provide employment skills and enhance industry
- Mathematics is an abstract subject which in diluted forms is applied in a variety of contexts
- Mathematics is a fixed and inert (if growing at the edges) body of knowledge and set of symbolic and conceptual tools
- The mathematics curriculum should carve out a piece of this body of knowledge and then let students progress up it as far as they can.

Contrary to these assumptions, I think a fundamental re-examination is needed of the following issues:

- the nature of mathematics, and its relation with other areas of knowledge
- the aims of teaching mathematics
- the range of experiences learners of mathematics are entitled to have
- the character and structure of the mathematics curriculum, and its relationship with different groups of students.

In the sections that follow, each of these issues is addressed in turn.

THE NATURE OF MATHEMATICAL KNOWLEDGE AND ITS RELA-
TIONSHIP WITH OTHER AREAS OF KNOWLEDGE

For some time a prevailing absolutist conception of mathematics has dominated both academic and popular thought. In the philosophy of mathematics two traditional assumptions concerning the nature of mathematics are that first, mathematical knowledge is absolutely secure objective knowledge, the cornerstone of all human knowledge and rationality (the assumption of absolutism), and second, that mathematical objects such as numbers, sets, geometric objects all exist in some objective superhuman realm (the assumption of Platonism).[1]

Absolutism in the philosophy of mathematics is primarily an epistemological position concerned with how to best justify mathematical knowledge, but it has consequences for views about the nature of mathematical knowledge. In simplified terms, absolutist perspectives describe mathematical knowledge as an objective, absolute, certain and incorrigible body of knowledge. According to absolutism mathematical knowledge is timeless, although we may discover new theories and truths to add; it is superhuman and ahistorical, for the history of mathematics is irrelevant to the nature and justification of mathematical knowledge; it is pure isolated knowledge, which happens to be useful because of its universal validity; it is value-free and culture-free, for the same reason.

The outcome therefore is a philosophically sanctioned image of mathematics as objective, fixed, pure, abstract and wholly logical, which is the traditional and often negative image of mathematics held by many persons. If this is how many philosophers, mathematicians and teachers describe their subject, small wonder it lends support to a public myth of mathematics as cold, hard and inhuman. Although absolutist philosophies of mathematics can be defended as rational, they are often incorrectly associated with such negative myths and beliefs about mathematics and in the interests of successful schooling and a scientifically literate populace this connection should be severed.

In contrast, Kitcher and Aspray (1988) describe a 'maverick' tradition in the philosophy of mathematics which emphasizes the practice of, and human side of, mathematics. This position has been termed quasi-empiricist and fallibilist, and is associated with constructivist and post-modernist thought in education (Glasersfeld 1995), philosophy (Rorty 1979), and the social sciences (Restivo 1992). A growing number of modern philosophers of mathematics and mathematicians espouse fallibilist views of mathematics (Ernest 1997, Tymoczko 1986).

Most versions of fallibilism view mathematics as the outcome of social processes. Mathematical knowledge is understood to be fallible and eternally open to revision, both in terms of its proofs and its concepts. Despite the rigour and precision of mathematical concepts and proofs, which humans have developed to extraordinary, austere and beautiful lengths, mathematical knowledge never attains a final, ultimate form. Fallibilist views reject the notion that there is a unique, fixed and permanently enduring hierarchical structure comprising mathematical knowledge. Instead fallibilist views see mathematics as made up of many overlapping structures. These, over the course of history, grow, collapse, and then grow anew like icebergs in the Arctic seas or like trees in a forest (Steen 1988). Fallibilism embraces as legitimate philosophical concerns the practices of mathematicians, its history and applications, the place of mathematics in human culture, including issues of values and education – in short, it fully admits the human face and basis of mathematics.

One of the innovations associated with a fallibilist view of mathematics is a reconceptualized view of the nature of mathematics. It is no longer seen as defined by a body of pure and abstract knowledge which exists in a superhuman, objective realm – the World 3 of Popper (1979). Instead, mathematics is associated with sets of social practices, each with its history, persons, institutions and social locations, symbolic forms, purposes and power relations. Thus, academic research mathematics is one such practice (or rather a multiplicity of shifting, interconnected practices). Likewise, each of ethnomathematics (culturally embedded informal mathematics) and school mathematics is a distinct set of such practices. They are intimately bound up together, because the symbolic productions of one practice are recontextualized and reproduced in another (Dowling 1988).

Another important implication of fallibilist views of mathematics is that it is not seen as discrete and wholly separated from other domains of knowledge. Lakatos (1976) terms his version of fallibilism 'Quasi-empiricism' because he argues that there are ineliminable empirical elements to both the development and justification of mathematical knowledge. Thus mathematics has some of the character of science, and vice versa, and mathematics, science and other areas of knowledge overlap and interpenetrate, although it is not claimed that they lose their identities. Similarly, Quine (1960), and others, have long argued for epistemological holism – that all forms of human knowledge form a single connected web and that the division of this unity into subjects and disciplines has contingent and arbitrary aspects.

Mathematical knowledge is thus the result of one of the forms of human knowing, which are all founded on the powers of understanding of the human subject, connecting all realms of knowledge.

> The various forms of knowledge can be seen in low-level developments within the common area of our knowledge of the everyday world. From this there branch out the developed forms which, taking certain elements in our common knowledge as a basis, have grown in distinctive ways. (Hirst in Brown et al. 1981, p. 230)

Traditional absolutist conceptions notwithstanding, this applies as much to mathematics as any other discipline or area of the curriculum.

School mathematics is not the same as academic or research mathematics, but a recontextualized selection from the discipline. Consequently it can be expected to share some of its key features with the parent discipline. What then are the implications of these developments in mathematical philosophy for the curriculum? First, that mathematical knowledge should not be viewed as a finished product, but as an area of culture that is still growing and being refined to suit human purposes. Mathematical concepts are not God-given, but rationally developed to suit human purposes and to fit with the established rules and patterns of mathematics. Mathematical knowledge and results are not right or wrong because of the dictate of authority, but need to be argued for and established by reason. Thus a fallibilist mathematics is not an irrational mathematics, as some of its critics fear. It is rather an area where knowledge depends centrally and irreducibly on rationality and the exercise of human reason and argument.

Second, mathematics is not something that is divorced from other human areas of thought and knowledge, but instead impacts on all areas of human thought (and reciprocally is influenced by many areas of human activity). Thus the relationships between mathematics and other disciplines and subject areas need to be explicitly incorporated in the curriculum. There is a long tradition of mathematical isolation to be overcome, which has undoubtedly been reinforced by the dominant absolutist conceptions of mathematical knowledge as separate. For example, in an HMI survey of 10% of English and Welsh schools, the most widely made recommendation to mathematics departments was that greater co-operation with other subject departments was needed (HMI 1979). This recommendation was made to two thirds of all schools inspected, thus illustrating the common perceptions of isolation and 'apartness' of school mathematics.

Third, if as modern theorists suggest, mathematics is a shifting multiplicity of practices, comprising 'the motley of mathematics' (Wittgenstein 1956), then school mathematics should not be seen as a fixed, unified and monolithic subject. It should be recognized that the selection of mathematical experiences, concepts, processes and contexts for inclusion in a school mathematics curriculum is a matter of context-dependent and contingent decision. The outcomes of such decisions are dependent on a multiplicity of factors including student age, aptitudes, interests, intended future study or work, cultural contexts and needs. In other words, the multiplicity of mathematics as a discipline strongly supports the idea of a multi-centred, multi-natured mathematics curriculum whose variations are determined by differing student needs. Of course this formulation raises the problem of whose perceptions of those needs is to count; but a sensitive, responsive, and to some extent bottom-up curriculum can overcome the inherent problems of imposition.

Already a consideration of recent developments in the philosophy of mathematics and their implications for school mathematics has provided a partial critique of the National Curriculum in mathematics as determined by law during the period 1988–1995. This critique extends beyond mathematics, for it concerns the structure of the curriculum for every one of the 10 subjects that make up the National Curriculum. The criticism is this. The structure of the National Curriculum promulgated by the DES (1988a) and underpinning the whole National Curriculum is that of a fixed, hierarchical structure. Mathematics, like the other subjects, is made up of a few topic strands, each of which is specified at 10 levels (rearranged into 9, after 1995) for all students in normal state schools in England, Wales and Northern Ireland. During their statutory schooling, i.e. from 5 to 16 years of age, these pupils are expected to work their way up these levels in the same fixed framework of mathematical knowledge. A single curriculum framework is intended to serve for all, irrespective of age, aptitude, interest and need. Elsewhere I have analysed and critiqued the National Curriculum in mathematics in terms of its ideological features including integral hierarchical conceptions of school mathematics, learning and mathematical ability (Ernest 1991). My claim is that the implicit views of mathematics schooling and society constitute a socially reproductive position.

An illuminating analogy is that between the National Curriculum structure and a fractional distillation device as used in chemistry or the petrochemical industry. Fractional distillation ensures that different types of products are produced and tapped off at different heights in the distillation tower. Likewise, pupils at age 5 are fed into the National Curriculum structure, and tapped off at different heights from the framework. Low-grade products come out at levels 1-4, medium grade products come out at levels 5-6, high-grade products come out at levels 7 or above. My claim is that both social class and future career prospects of students correlate with these levels. Low gradings corresponding to the semi-skilled, unskilled and unemployed. Medium gradings corresponding to skilled blue and white collar workers. High level gradings correspond to managerial and professional occupations.

These correspondences are of course simplistic and crude, and what will be found is at best a statistical correlation between mathematical achievement and occupation. However, the use of mathematical qualifications as a 'critical filter' for entry into higher education and higher paid occupations has been long noted by researchers in gender and mathematics (Sells 1976; Walkerdine 1988, 1989). Thus my claim is that a unique curriculum structure for mathematics for all students serves social reproduction purposes rather than defensible educational purposes.

Although my complaint with the model of knowledge in the National Curriculum is that it is divisive both in terms of the separation of school subjects and in terms of the social outcomes of the mathematics curriculum, there are also more positive opposing forces built in. One of the innovations of the National Curriculum is to give weight to and pay special attention to cross-curricular dimensions, themes and skills (NCC 1989c, 1990a). These are cross-curricular elements which are supposed to be common to all the subjects of the school curriculum. The curriculum model is made up of ten vertical strands, which are the different subjects of the National Curriculum, woven together into a partial unity by the horizontal strands of the cross-curricular dimensions, themes and skills. These are made up as follows:

- Cross-Curricular Dimensions: (i) Equal Opportunities, (ii) Multicultural, (iii) Special Educational Needs.
- Cross-Curricular Themes: (i) Economic/Industrial Understanding, (ii) Careers, (iii) Health, (iv) Citizenship, (v) The Environment.
- Cross-Curricular Skills: (i) Numeracy, (ii) Literacy, (iii) Oracy, (iv) Information Technology skills, (v) Personal and Social skills.

The inclusion of these elements thus serves to partially overcome the criticism that the underlying epistemology sees school subjects as wholly discrete and isolated.

Unfortunately this inclusion is largely one of rhetoric, rather than implementation or reality. The cross-curricular elements seem to be diminishing in importance in revisions of the National Curriculum and official statements of its aims. Thus most recently attention has been devoted to promoting the basic cross-curricular skills of numeracy, literacy, and to a lesser extent, information technology (often expressed in the form of criticisms of the basic skills attained by school leavers), whilst the remaining cross-curricular skills, dimensions and themes have been neglected.

THE AIMS OF TEACHING MATHEMATICS

The aims of mathematics education are often discussed in isolation from the social and political context. However, aims are expressions of intent, and intentions belong to individuals or groups. Educational aims are thus the expression of the values, interests, and even the ideologies of certain individuals or groups. Furthermore the interests and ideologies of some such groups are in conflict. Elsewhere, building on Raymond Williams' (1961) seminal analysis, I distinguish five interest groups and show that each has distinct aims for mathematics education and different views of the nature of mathematics (Ernest 1991). These groups, their relations to Williams' analysis, and some of their views, are summarized in Figure 2.1.

Thus the different social groups have different political orientations, differing views of the nature of mathematics, and in a special relationship with these, partly consisting of consequence, partly of coherence, different aims for the teaching of mathematics. The aims of the five groups distinguished in Figure 2.1 can be expanded as follows:

Figure 2.1: Five interest groups and their aims for mathematics teaching

INTEREST GROUP	RELATION TO WILLIAMS (1961)	SOCIAL LOCATION	MATHEMATICAL AIMS	VIEW OF MATHEMATICS
1. Industrial Trainers	Reactionary part of Williams' (1961) group of 'industrial trainers'	Radical 'New Right' conservative politicians and petty bourgeois	Back-to-basics numeracy and social training in obedience (authoritarian)	Absolutist set of decontextualized but utilitarian truths and rules
2. Technological Pragmatists	Progressive part of Williams' group of 'industrial trainers'	Meritocratic industry-centred industrialists, managers, etc.	Useful mathematics to appropriate level and certification (industry-centred)	Unquestioned absolutist body of applicable knowledge
3. Old Humanist Mathematicians	Mathematical cultural restorationist version of Williams' group of 'old humanists'	Conservative mathematicians preserving rigour of proof and purity of mathematics	Transmit body of pure mathematical knowledge (maths-centred)	Absolutist body of structured pure knowledge
4. Progressive Educators	Liberal progressive part of Williams' group of 'public educators'	Professionals, liberal educators, welfare state supporters	Creativity self-realization through mathematics (child-centred)	Absolutist body of pure knowledge to be engaged with personally
5. Public Educators	Radical activist part of Williams' group of 'public educators'	Democratic socialists and radical reformers concerned with social justice and inequality	Critical awareness and democratic citizenship via mathematics	Fallible knowledge socially constructed in diverse practices

1. Acquiring basic mathematical skills and numeracy and social training in obedience (authoritarian, basic skills centred)
2. Learning basic skills and to solve practical problems with mathematics (industry and work centred)
3. Understanding and capability in advanced mathematics, with some appreciation of mathematics (pure mathematics centred)
4. Confidence, creativity and self expression through maths (child-centred progressivist)
5. Empowerment of learner as highly numerate critical citizen in society (empowerment and social justice concerns).

In my analysis I suggest that these aims (and the groups to which they are attributed) can be seen at work in the development of the National Curriculum in mathematics through a number of alliances. Aims 1 and 3 are conservative, and both support the National Curriculum model, with the lower elements of knowledge and skill, together with external testing, partly achieving the basic skills centred aim (1), and the higher elements of knowledge and skill directed at the pure mathematics centred aim (3). These aims are directed at goods external to the students and embody views of knowledge and skills as decontextualized.

Aims 2 and 4 both supported the inclusion of a progressive, personal knowledge-application dimension which has survived through all versions of the National Curriculum in mathematics, namely the processes of 'Using and Applying Mathematics'. For aim 2 supporters, this is seen as the embodiment of practical skills in being able to apply mathematics to solve work-related problems. For aim 4 supporters, this is seen as the embodiment of exploratory and creative self-realization through mathematical activity. However, the language of Using and Applying Mathematics in the National Curriculum is clearly utilitarian and more overt references to progressive 'personal qualities' in early draft versions were expunged fairly rapidly. Thus, the notion that the processes and applications of mathematics derive some value because of their relevance to the experience and life situation of the learner *qua learner* is marginal in the National Curriculum. Primarily the purposes of the Using and Applying component is preparation for using knowledge productively in work and industry. However progressive educators have consoled themselves that it legitimates the presence of the processes of mathematics within the National Curriculum.

Aim 5, concerning the development of critical citizenship and empowerment for social change and equality through mathematics, has played no part in the development of the National Curriculum, and is virtually absent from any curriculum development in mathematics education too. Thus although progressives see mathematics within the context of the individual's experience, the notion that the individual is socially located in an unjust world plays no part. Moving towards a critical mathematics education – making mathematics (and all schooling) relevant to critical citizenship for all – is not only neglected by the alliances who formed the National Curriculum: it apparently did not figure in the discussion and planning for the National Curriculum in mathematics.[2]

The outcome of these contests and processes is that the National Curriculum may be said to serve three main purposes. First of all, much of the National Curriculum in mathematics is devoted to communicating numeracy and basic mathematical skills and knowledge across the range of mathematical topics comprising number, algebra, shape and space (geometry and measures), and handling data (incorporating information technology mathematics, probability and statistics).

Second, for advanced or high attaining students the understanding and use of these areas of mathematics at higher levels is included as a goal. Thus, there is an initiation into a set of academic symbolic practices of mathematics *for the few* (e.g. 'A' level studies for 16–18 year olds).

Third, there is a practical, process strand running through the National Curriculum mathematics which is intended to develop the utilitarian skills of using and applying mathematics to 'real world' problems.

Each of these three outcomes is to a greater or lesser extent utilitarian, because they develop general or specialist mathematics skills and capabilities, which are either decontextualized – equipping the learner with useful tools – or are applied to practical problems. The slant of this outcome comes as a surprise to no-one, because the whole thrust of the National Curriculum is recognized to be directed towards scientific and technological competence and capability.

What is more surprising is that there has been very little, if any, fundamental criticism of this thrust of the National Curriculum. Representatives of each of the five interest groups have argued that their aims need to be given more priority. Recently the mathematical community and users of mathematics in higher education have been critical of school mathematics because of the perceived mathematical weaknesses of entrants to university mathematics, science and technology courses. Part of this criticism is that 18 years olds do not have an adequate understanding of mathematical proof, advanced algebra, etc. This criticism mainly concerns the claimed inability of new students to understand or produce the technical proofs which are characteristic of university mathematics. Thus, the criticism is directed at the higher level mathematical capabilities of university entrants.

There may well be some justification behind these criticisms. However, the point I wish to make is that this is not a root-and-branch critique of the National Curriculum in mathematics. Rather it is the criticism by one interest group, albeit a significant one, that the outcomes of the school mathematics curriculum do not serve the needs of a small minority of students in terms of the development of high-level skills.[3] Thus the goals of the National Curriculum in mathematics seem to be either tacitly accepted, or at least acquiesced with, by the mathematics teaching community. The criticism that I wish to direct at this mathematics curriculum, apart from the rejection of the public educator position and its values, is that the aims for school mathematics neglect the culture and intrinsic value of mathematics. Some experience and appreciation of this, I wish to argue, should be a part, however limited, of every child's educational entitlement in mathematics.

THE RANGE OF LEARNING EXPERIENCES

The previous discussion leads to a distinction of direct relevance to the range of learning experiences a learner is entitled to have.

Capability versus Appreciation

In technology education, curriculum theorists distinguish between developing technological capability, on the one hand, and appreciation or awareness, on the other (Jeffery 1988). In brief, technology capability consists of the knowledge and skills that are involved in planning and making artefacts and systems. Technology appreciation and awareness comprise the higher-level skills, knowledge and judgement necessary to evaluate the significance, import and value of technological artefacts and systems within their social, scientific, technological, environmental, economic and moral contexts.

In the development of the National Curriculum, the draft syllabus for Technology included a major appreciation strand, but this was virtually eliminated in the transition to the statutory framework. Likewise the draft syllabus for Science included significant elements of appreciation and awareness, including attainment targets devoted to the development of science within its historical context, the nature of science and scientific inquiry, and the discussion of the social, environmental, and economic contexts of science. These too were virtually eliminated in the final statutory frameworks. Thus the National Curriculum in science and technology ended up as being concerned with capability rather than appreciation. This is in keeping with the perception of the National Curriculum as an intentionally utilitarian curriculum framework which is not concerned to promote reflection, appreciation and critical awareness amongst the masses.

In contrast to the above history, although the end result was the same, the issue of appreciation in the above sense arose at no stage in the development of the National Curriculum in mathematics, except insofar as capability and appreciation might overlap. The three outcomes of the National Curriculum listed above all concern capability. The following question can therefore be meaningfully posed. Is school mathematics all about capability, i.e. 'doing', or could there be an appreciation element that was overlooked in the National Curriculum?

There is a well-known view that 'mathematics is not a spectator sport', i.e. it is about solving problems, performing algorithms and procedures, computing solutions, and so on. Except in the popular domain, or in the fields of social science or humanities which comment on mathematics as opposed to doing mathematics, nobody reads mathematics books: they work through them. Furthermore, the language of both school and research mathematics is full of imperatives, ordering the reader to do something, rather than follow a narrative (Rotman 1993, Ernest 1994). Thus the capability dimension of mathematics, and of school mathematics in particular, is dominant and perhaps universal. Of course, if mathematics is to be given a major role in the curriculum, as it almost invariably is, some large capability element is necessary, for unquestionably it does serve a number of useful functions. Furthermore, a minimal mathematical capability is essential, a *sine qua non*, for the development of mathematical appreciation. But is capability enough on its own? Has any published curriculum addressed anything other, such as appreciation? Would the development of mathematical appreciation be a worthwhile and justifiable goal for school mathematics? If so, what is mathematical appreciation and how could appreciation be addressed?

The first question that needs to be answered is the following. What does or might appreciation of mathematics mean? In my view, a provisional analysis of what the appreciation of mathematics means, understood in a broad sense, involves the following elements of awareness:

- Qualitatively understanding some of the big ideas of mathematics such as infinity, symmetry, structure, recursion, proof, chaos, randomness, etc.
- Being able to understand the main branches and concepts of mathematics and having a sense of their interconnections, interdependencies, and the overall unity of mathematics.
- Understanding that there are multiple views of the nature of mathematics and controversy over the philosophical foundations of its knowledge.
- Being aware of how and the extent to which mathematical thinking permeates everyday life and current affairs.
- Critically understanding the uses of mathematics in society: to identify, interpret, evaluate and critique the mathematics embedded in social and political systems and claims, from advertisements to government and interest-group pronouncements.
- Being aware of the historical development of mathematics, the social contexts of the origins of mathematical concepts, symbolism, theories and problems.
- Having a sense of mathematics as a central element of culture, art and life, present and past, which permeates and underpins science, technology and all aspects of human culture.

In short, the appreciation of mathematics involves understanding and awareness of its nature and value, as well as understanding and being able to critique its social uses.

Perhaps it is worth drawing the analogy between capability and appreciation of mathematics, on the one hand, and the study of language and literature, on the other. Mathematical capability is like being able to use language effectively for oral and written communication, whereas mathematical appreciation resembles the study of literature, in that it concerns the significance of mathematics as an element of culture and history, and the artefacts of mathematics are understood in that context, just as great texts are in literature.

My purpose in contrasting capability and appreciation in mathematics is to draw attention to the neglect of the latter, both in theory and practice. To be a mathematically-literate citizen, able to critique the social uses of mathematics, which is the aim of the public educator position, would go part way towards realizing mathematical appreciation, if it were implemented. However there would be another element still lacking, even if this were achieved. This is to develop an appreciation of mathematics as an element of culture, and of the inner culture and nature of mathematics itself. Despite the love for mathematics felt by most mathematics teachers, educators and mathematicians, the fostering of mathematical appreciation, in this sense, as an aim of mathematical teaching is not promoted. It might therefore be said that mathematics professionals both undervalue their subject and underestimate the ability of their students to appreciate it.

Appreciation is not entirely neglected in mathematics education. As a psychological category it is well known. In a review of the psychological research on the learning of mathematics, Bell et al. (1983) offered a breakdown of the types of outcomes in school mathematics into the categories of facts, skills, conceptual structures, general strategies and the appreciation of mathematics. This last component was described to mean appreciation of the nature of mathematics and attitudes or affective responses to it. This involves a few but far from all of the components of appreciation listed above. This treatment of appreciation also fits with the tradition in educational psychology to classify evaluation, defined as making judgements using internal evidence and external criteria, as coming at the highest level in the taxonomy of educational objectives in the cognitive domain (Bloom 1956). For evaluation involves some of the intellectual skills implicated in appreciation. However, the sense of appreciation given by these treatments is restricted and decontextualized, and does not include the various contexts of mathematics, and the deeper relation between the knower and the subject suggested above.

There are many other factors that can be considered as part of the desirable range of learning experiences in school mathematics, and more are considered in the context of the mathematics curriculum.

THE MATHEMATICS CURRICULUM

Having considered some of the controversies over the nature of mathematics and over the aims of teaching mathematics the following question arises. What thoughts and recommendations are appropriate concerning the character and structure of the mathematics curriculum, and its relationship with different groups of students? Further, in the context of the overall theme of this book, how can, might or should the school mathematics curriculum relate to areas of experience, and in particular, to students' areas of experience? What are the relevant areas of experience for mathematics? A number of issues have been raised that will help to define them.

First of all there is the relation between mathematics and other areas to consider. This suggests that the contexts of mathematics are an important factor.

Second, there are the different teaching outcomes and styles mentioned in connection with the aims of mathematical teaching. This could include, for want of a better place to include it, the distinction between mathematical capability and appreciation, although this has already been discussed at length above.

Third, related to the previous category but not identical with it are the various modes of understanding, communication and assessment experienced by learners. This encompasses the differences between alternative ways of understanding and representing mathematical ideas and helps to define the contexts and areas of experience of learners.

Lastly, there is the conventional distinction between mathematical topics, which is the traditional means of dividing up the school curriculum. The National Curriculum divides this content into the areas of Number, Algebra, Shape, space and measures, Handling data, including probability and statistics, and the mathematical processes of Using and applying mathematics. This division is relatively uncontroversial, and, except to say that all students should be entitled to experience all of these areas of mathematics, as is part of the National Curriculum rationale, I shall not comment on this further.

The listing of these factors which serve to distinguish different areas of experience in mathematics is not claimed to be complete. Furthermore, there may well be overlaps and redundancies, and it is not claimed that the factors can all be combined meaningfully. In the following pages I discuss each of the first three factors, devoting most attention to those factors which have not been discussed above.

The Context of Mathematics

First of all there is the issue of relation between mathematics and other contexts and areas of experience to consider. As I argued above, the notion that mathematics is context-free is increasingly rejected. Mathematics either constitutes a context of its own, or relates to other contexts and areas of experience. Furthermore, students invariably bring with them knowledge, skills, experiences and other intellectual resources into any context which provide both the basis for their understanding and participation, and resources which can be utilized by the teacher in developing the learning context and areas of experience. The range of possible contexts to be considered in schooling include the following.[4]

1. School mathematics as a set of conceptual tools

The first context is that of school mathematics itself. This is a self-subsistent context and set of practices in which mathematics is treated and developed as a set of useful symbolic and conceptual tools. This is the domain in which mathematical capability is developed. It is the invisible 'base' context which it is proposed to revise by the inclusion of the elements listed here. This context provides the legitimate location for mathematical exercises, activities, procedures and problem solving aimed at developing mathematical facility per se.

2. The culture of mathematics

The culture of mathematics includes appreciation of internal aspects of mathematics including qualitative understanding of 'big ideas' such as infinity, symmetry, pattern, as well as the understanding of the overall unity of mathematics and the nature of mathematical knowledge. To experience the culture of mathematics it is necessary to appreciate some of the concepts, results and global understandings that mathematicians have and which they value about their discipline, although clearly this appreciation needs to be restricted to what is feasible for the appropriate stage of schooling. However, one must be careful about prejudging what is appropriate or accessible to schoolchildren. One of the arguments against encouraging the appreciation of ideas like infinity is that it is 'too difficult' for schoolchildren. However, many an interested 8 or 10 year old will happily discuss the infinite size of space, or the never-ending nature of the natural numbers. An argument that has been widely put by mathematics educators is that experiences in developing mathematical process skills, such as in problem solving, mathematical modelling and investigational work, allow students to enter into a corner of the culture of mathematics as experienced by mathematicians.

3. Mathematics in every-day life, work and the social context

All mathematics students bring with them an extensive range of knowledge and experience from the social and cultural milieu in which they live. These include their knowledge of and involvement in local affairs, leisure activities, pastimes, hobbies, clubs, and the media including music, television, films, magazines and newspapers.

There is an extensive range of issues involved, including local, national and global politics, environmental issues, health, fitness, sport, nutrition, drugs, education, policing and law and order, finance, housing, transport, accidents, and so on. These contextual factors provide a rich range of issues, shared to a greater or lesser extent by students, which can be drawn upon as meaningful resources for contextualizing the teaching and learning of mathematics. These contexts can be drawn upon and exploited for the mathematics classroom in two ways.

First of all, there are all the out-of-school terms, concepts, knowledge and experiences which students bring into the classroom with them which can be drawn and built upon in developing understanding of school mathematics. These provide the basis for student understanding and participation in school mathematics in accordance with constructivist learning theory, which shows how learning always builds on previous knowledge.

Secondly, resources drawn from the range of everyday life, work and the social context in general can be utilized to link mathematical learning with the external contexts of its use. Authentic materials, social statistics, and other resources provide a basis for understanding how mathematics is used and applied in the world outside school. In particular, they can be used to teach students to begin to identify, interpret, evaluate and critique the mathematics embedded in social, commercial and political claims, and the uses made of them in advertisements and claims in the mass media to those of political party and government claims. Thus there are two uses indicated here: illustration of the uses and application made of mathematics in society, and the development of critical mathematical literacy and citizenship. In each case independent critical judgement is developed in the student, but in the second case it is applied in a way which can be seen as more controversial and more individually empowering to the student.

At Key Stage 4 (age 14-16 years), in the final years of a student's compulsory schooling, students may well have general ideas about the career, vocation or occupation that they wish to embark on and the possibility of relating the school mathematics to those interests would add a further dimension and interest for the student, as well as providing an appropriate preparation for adult life. As I shall suggest below, the possibility of some degree of optionality or specialization in mathematics, i.e. of curriculum differentiation, is an important issue that needs to be included in a revised entitlement curriculum.

4. Mathematics in other areas of the curriculum

Another context to be considered is the mathematics in other areas of the curriculum. Mathematical concepts and skills are used in science, technology (including both design and technology and information technology), geography and history, in the statutory 5-16 curriculum, as well as a whole host of 'A' level subjects such as psychology and computer studies. As I noted above, there is evidence that the level of co-operation between mathematics and other school subjects is poor, and presumably this means that little attention is devoted to the mathematics used in other areas of the curriculum, or the applications in these other areas which serve to illustrate the uses and applications of mathematics. If it is accepted that the school curriculum is a unity, then it is desirable that links and connections between subjects are made and strengthened. This involves drawing upon other subjects as contexts for mathematics.

5. Mathematics in history and cultures

Mathematics not only has a long history stretching back 5000 years, but it is one of the first disciplines to emerge in history and indeed with writing formed part of the first school curriculum, in Mesopotamia (Høyrup 1980).

Mathematics is widely presented as a decontextualized and ahistorical subject. Many school mathematics texts in the UK and USA, for example, concentrate on developing students' skills and concepts with little or no reference to either the social context or the history of mathematics. In his modest survey Stander (1989) found little evidence of the teaching or use of the history of mathematics in the UK and limited use of it elsewhere world-wide, in school and undergraduate educational contexts. This contrasts with the near universal teaching of mathematics.

However, the history of mathematics has an important role to play in the teaching of mathematics. In his survey, Fauvel (1991, p. 4) reports that the use of the history of mathematics in teaching has the following outcomes:

• helps to increase motivation for learning
• makes mathematics less frightening
• pupils derive comfort from knowing they are not the only ones with problems
• gives mathematics a human face
• changes pupils' perceptions of mathematics.

Thus, the location of classroom mathematics problems and methods in a historical context can help to communicate mathematics as a living, humanly created area of knowledge, subject to the same vicissitudes, false starts, cul-de-sacs and distortions as any other human endeavour, instead of the perfect discipline the absolutist myth promotes.

It is widely remarked in the mathematics education literature that student and teacher attitudes and perceptions of mathematics are important factors in learning (e.g. Ernest, 1991). Indeed, much of the research on girls and mathematics talks of the problems caused by the stereotypical perceptions of mathematics as a male domain (e.g. Walkerdine, 1988). Thus, an important area of impact of the history of mathematics is on student (and teacher) attitudes to and perceptions of mathematics. Furthermore, a number of experimental teaching programs use a historical approach and have positive outcomes (e.g. some Italian experiments described by Bartolini-Bussi, 1991).

An important area of impact of the history of mathematics is in correcting Eurocentric myths about the origins of mathematics. These often claim that mathematics originates in Ancient Greece, which with minor input from India and Arabia was developed in the Renaissance, to become modern European mathematics. This view is now rejected and the current view accepted by scholars is that oral proto-mathematics and ethnomathematics have developed in all human cultures. Thus the words 'tik' meaning finger, digit, one, and 'pal' meaning two have been identified by linguistic theorists in the conjectured proto-language out of which all human languages developed. In the great civilizations of the past – Chinese, Indian, Sumerian, Egyptian, Mayan – written mathematics developed as a discipline connected with accountancy and central administration. In the millennia that followed elements of this knowledge were transformed and elaborated by the Greek, Indian, and Arabian cultures and in the past 600 years by the Renaissance and modern European cultures, although developments also continued elsewhere such as in China and India (Joseph 1991).

Including a historical dimension in the teaching of mathematics can serve to counter the received Eurocentric view, and promotes elements of a multicultural and anti-racist mathematics. Likewise, attending to ethnomathematics can also promote these perspectives and indicate the broad and living informal cultural presence of mathematics. The unique and universal characteristic of human beings is that we all have and make cultures, and every culture includes elements we can label as mathematical. Ethnomathematics should be understood in a broad sense referring to activities such as ciphering, measuring, classifying, ordering, inferring, and modelling in a wide variety of socio-cultural groups (D'Ambrosio 1985). It also includes the basket and rug designs, sand and body patterns, quipu, etc. made by various groups and obviously relying on a sense of the possibilities of symmetry and form. Examples of socio-cultural groups include the different peoples studied in Africa by Gerdes (1988) and Zaslavsky (1973) and in the Americas by Ascher (1991) and the street mathematics (Nunes et al. 1994) and shopping mathematics (Lave 1988) of modern urban life. Ethnomathematics is not about the exotic conceptions of 'primitive peoples'. The power of the concept of ethnomathematics is to challenge the notion that mathematics is only produced by mathematicians. This can provide a healthy antidote to the received absolutist views of mathematics as an addition to schoolchildren's classroom diet.

Overall, what I have indicated is the range of cultural contexts that are relevant to school mathematics, but which are usually ignored or treated superficially. My claim is that this is not due to neglect, but a consequence of the received conceptualization of mathematics as neutral, value-free and timeless. Being aware of the historical development of mathematics and its varying social contexts in the present and past which underpin science, technology, art, craft and all aspects of human culture can help dispel the widely held and demotivating view reported in Cockcroft (DES 1982) that 'mathematics is not about anything'.

Teaching Styles and Outcomes

A second class of elements to be considered for the mathematics curriculum are the different teaching styles and outcomes distinguished by the Cockcroft Report (DES 1982) and discussed above, which are such powerful determinants of the learner's experience. As mentioned above, Bell et al. (1983) provide a breakdown of the outcomes of school mathematics. These are indicated and defined in Figure 2.2.

Figure 2.2: The outcomes of school mathematics, after Bell et al. (1983)

OUTCOME	DEFINITION
FACTS	Items of information that are essentially arbitrary (notation, conventions, conversion factors, names of concepts).
SKILLS	Well-established multi-step procedures whether involving symbolic expressions, geometrical figures, etc.
CONCEPTUAL STRUCTURES	A concept is a set or property, a means of discrimination – e.g. concept of negative number. A conceptual structure is a set of concepts and linking relationships – e.g. concept of place value.
GENERAL STRATEGIES	Procedures which guide choice of what skills or knowledge to use at each stage in problem solving etc.
APPRECIATION	Appreciation of the nature of mathematics and affective response (attitudes) to it.

The importance of this analysis is that it provides a psychological rationale for treating a range of the teaching and learning outcomes in school mathematics across the full range of cognitive demand. Mathematical teaching is thus directed at basic facts and skills, conceptual understanding, problem solving strategies, and attitudes to and appreciation of school mathematics. The last of these four composite categories, attitudes and appreciation, has always been regarded as an incidental outcome of school mathematics rather than something to be addressed directly. This is a weakness. Nevertheless, the assertion that the development of general strategies is an important outcome of school mathematics has helped to introduce and maintain the place of problem solving and creative mathematical processes in the school mathematics curriculum despite the continued carping of reactionary critics from the Black Papers to the present. For example, a recent expression of such views is the following:

> These ideas have done enormous damage . . . there is no such thing as 'problem solving'; every problem must be tackled on its own. (Deuchar 1996, p. 26)

The Cockcroft Report (DES 1982) on the teaching of mathematics adopted this analysis of educational outcomes as a cornerstone for their argument for extending the range of teaching and learning styles. The teaching approaches needed to develop the outcomes listed above at all levels of

TEACHING STYLE   **OUTCOME**

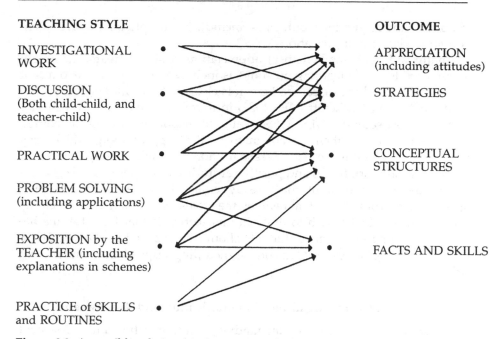

INVESTIGATIONAL WORK — APPRECIATION (including attitudes)

DISCUSSION (Both child-child, and teacher-child) — STRATEGIES

PRACTICAL WORK — CONCEPTUAL STRUCTURES

PROBLEM SOLVING (including applications)

EXPOSITION by the TEACHER (including explanations in schemes) — FACTS AND SKILLS

PRACTICE of SKILLS and ROUTINES

Figure 2.3: A possible relationship between teaching styles and outcomes

schooling, it concluded, should include investigational work, problem solving, discussion, practical work, exposition by the teacher, as well as the consolidation and practice of skills and routines. Figure 2.3 shows how these teaching approaches might contribute to the development of the outcomes.

The Cockcroft Report recommendation that students at all levels should learn by means of the full range of teaching styles indicated above has been widely accepted. It suggests a variety of experiences for students and also endorses the notion that all students throughout their learning careers should be developing all the specified outcomes (facts, skills, conceptual structures, general strategies and appreciation). This is an important suggestion, for all too often certain groups of students have received a limited or one-sided education in mathematics.

For example, recent reports by Her Majesty's Inspectorate and The Office for Standards in Education (OFSTED) indicate that the number-work content of average and above average attaining secondary school students decreases from less than 50% of the time at age 11 to 10% or less of the time for 15-16 year olds. However, for low attainers in mathematics the proportion of the time devoted to number-work never goes much below 50% of the time on average for secondary school students throughout the age range 11–16 years, and sometimes is considerably higher. Typically number-work will be at the level of facts and skills, with some low level applications, so it is very likely that these students are not having the opportunity to address the higher level outcomes, including conceptual structures, general strategies and appreciation.

Finally, although mathematical appreciation, which I treated at length above as a desirable learning outcome, is included among the outcomes of mathematics teaching discussed here, it is clear that it is understood by Bell et al. (1983) and Cockcroft (DES 1982) in a very limited sense. When Her Majesty's Inspectorate (DES, 1985b) came to elaborate on these outcomes, they retained all of them except mathematical appreciation, which they replaced by something called 'Personal Qualities', which they defined in terms of good work habits and positive attitudes to mathematics. This completed the withdrawal of the already emasculated aim of developing appreciation from their statement of the goals of mathematics teaching. The conclusion that I wish to draw in this section is that for a full mathematical learning experience, students should be exposed to the full diversity of teaching styles and outcomes, including appreciation understood broadly.

Modes of Understanding, Communication and Assessment

There are various modes of understanding, communication and assessment which have a powerful impact on the character of the mathematics curriculum, and on the nature of the learning experience. There are different cognitive styles, such as Pask's distinction between Holist and Serialist styles, with many analogous dichotomies, distinguished in the literature. There are modes of representation, both external and cognitive, such as Bruner's (1960) distinction between enactive, iconic and symbolic representations. Goldin (1987) in discussing the mental representations used in problem solving has proposed a more extensive model of representation in mathematics including the following (and other representations such as affect and metacognition not relevant here):

- Imagistic systems (including spatial, auditory and tactile)
- Verbal or linguistic systems
- Formal symbolic notational systems.

In developing a mathematics curriculum to suit the needs and preferences of all learners different cognitive styles and modes of representation, like those considered here, need to be incorporated.

However, the main distinction I wish to point up in this section is one which is more mathematics-specific. A widely used distinction is between the symbolic and conceptual aspects of mathematics. Of course these are in a sense inseparable, as acquiring conceptual understanding depends on the language and symbolism of mathematics, and vice versa. Nevertheless, it is useful to distinguish them to indicate possible deficiencies in learning experiences.

Thus, one aspect of mathematics is its symbolism. Typically, mathematical processes involve symbolic activity and complex manipulations of its notation, following the rules of symbolic transformation, such as applying formulas or performing the same symbolic operation to both sides of an equation. Mathematics is an archetypally symbolic activity and for many years there has been an awareness that mathematical operations can be performed by symbol manipulation alone.

> In Algebra, in which, though a particular quantity be marked by each letter, yet to proceed right it is not requisite that in every step each letter suggest to your thoughts that particular quantity it was appointed to stand for (Berkeley 1710, p. 59).

This reflects both a strength and a weakness of mathematics. The strength is that mathematics provides a structural symbolic language of immense power, which underpins modern thought throughout the sciences, technology, economics, business, administration, commerce, and other areas. Students are entitled to gain power over these and other diverse subject matters, which their developing symbolic mathematical capabilities bring. The weakness is reflected in the criticism that many students' experience is limited to that of pushing symbols around meaninglessly, following ill-remembered rules. Skemp (1976) and Mellin-Olsen (1981) term this ability to perform mathematical operations successfully without understanding why they work 'instrumental understanding'.

In contrast to the world of mathematical symbols is the conceptual world of mathematics, populated by numbers, relations, functions, structures, patterns, shapes, and so on. Some of the deepest and most abstract speculations of the human mind concern the nature and relations of objects found only in the virtual reality of mathematics. Infinities, paradoxes, logical deduction, perfect harmonies and symmetries and many other concepts are all analysed and explored here. Thus mathematics provides a realm of daring abstract thought, including both free-ranging speculation and the rock-hard certainties of proof.

Above, I referred to Platonism, which involves a belief in the existence and perfection of the objects of mathematics in some other-worldly realm. Ignoring the ontological problems of Platonism, which still trouble philosophers, there is an aspect of human experience which this position captures. This is the experience of, and belief in, the objects of mathematics, and their permanence, objectivity and enduring relationships and properties. Elsewhere, I and others have described how these features can be accounted for through viewing mathematical objects as cultural objects (Rotman 1993, Ernest 1997). The point I wish to make here is that the shared world of mathematical objects is part of the human cultural heritage, part of the lived truth of mathematical experience, and therefore should be seen as part of the school learner's mathematical entitlement.

Skemp (1976) terms the understanding of the ideas and relationships of school mathematics, and the conceptual underpinnings they provide for the symbolic rules, algorithms and procedures of mathematics 'relational understanding'. Other scholars have termed this meaningful, schematic, and conceptual understanding, e.g. Hiebert (1986). Of course, there are different types and scopes of relational or conceptual understanding: from the understanding of basic numerical skills and concepts to the appreciation of a wide and complex range of mathematical objects, concepts, relationships and structures. This latter notion is something that extends some way beyond the limited psychological notions of relational or conceptual understanding. For it represents much more than the meaningful or conceptual underpinnings of mathematical capability. I have argued that access to this domain is part of the student's mathematical entitlement, and that it should extend to the appreciation of big ideas and not just be limited to the conceptual underpinnings of utilitarian mathematical skills.

To appreciate and have access to the virtual world of mathematics, or even only a restricted corner of it, means to develop a robust mathematical intuition, to have appropriated and internalized mathematical objects, to have a sense of ownership over these objects and share in the sense of the perfection and inevitability of their relationships, structures and patterns. The world of mathematics in this sense is not something that can be entered in one step, for its population must be reconstructed piecemeal for each knower, based on the accumulation of the products of experience, knowledge and reflection. Many persons have already achieved this with number, with which they have an unselfconscious 'at-homeness'. I am suggesting that experience of a broader imagined world of mathematics should be part of the entitlement of all learners.

Curriculum Structure and Diversity

I have been exploring different areas of experience that might make up together the entitlements of students in a reconceptualized mathematics curriculum. I have argued for the importance of experiencing different mathematical contexts; teaching outcomes and styles; modes of understanding, including both symbolic and conceptual aspects of mathematics; and with mathematical appreciation as well as capability as dual aims of the mathematics curriculum. What I have not addressed is the question of what should be the shape and structure of the mathematics curriculum, and its relationship with different groups of students?

Above, I sketched a critique of the unique and rigidly hierarchical National Curriculum structure. The National Curriculum in mathematics, as developed over the period 1989-1995, and predicted to remain unchanged until the end of the millennium, imposes a monolithic curriculum model. Every student in the state sector must study mathematics defined as a set of decontextualized curriculum objectives concerned with skills, knowledge and capability. Progress is measured by statutory tests and examinations at the ages of 7, 11, 14 and 16, thus ensuring that students are kept on track. The only element of variation concerns the vertical levels which students attain in their progress up the curriculum framework. Thus there is no opportunity for choice, interest, variety or contextualization, beyond that permitted by the vagueness of the curriculum specification. None of the changing personal interests, career choices and vocational development plans of students, that emerge in the period from 13 to 16 years of age, can be accommodated, making the experience of learning school mathematics one of coercive uniformity, with almost inevitable social reproduction outcomes.

The antidote is not only obvious, but can be seen working successfully in a number of countries including Germany and Holland. What I am referring to is curriculum differentiation in secondary school mathematics. A strong case can be put that in primary school, and perhaps in the early years of secondary school, there should be a common curriculum in mathematics. For a broad experience of school mathematics including the diverse elements discussed above can be justified as forming a student's mathematical entitlement. If fundamental curriculum diversity and choice are brought in too early, some children may miss certain vital learning experiences and be mathematically disempowered as a consequence. However, such arguments must be thought through most critically, for there is a danger that they can be marshalled to deny the very rights and entitlement that I am arguing for here.

My argument is that a far-reaching differentiation in the mid and later secondary school mathematics curriculum is needed. The argument I have just offered for a shared entitlement in the earlier years of schooling is primarily based on a need for shared knowledge and skills, in providing an empowering set of capabilities. Of course appreciation and awareness should not be neglected, but my point is that this reasoning is largely based on cognitive dimensions of knowing. However, it is increasingly recognized that attitudes, affect, motivation, interest and commitment play a central role in learning. Whilst it is recognized that attitudes will play a vital role in learning throughout the years, a new set of motivations, interests and commitments will emerge or develop in the secondary school student as s/he approaches the end of statutory schooling and the beginning of further or higher education, vocational training or employment. If education is to contribute to the development of autonomous and mature citizens, who are able to fully participate in modern society, then it must allow elements of choice and self-determination. Currently this is permitted in state schools in that pupils are permitted to make some choices and partly specialize in their range of studies from the age of 14 to 16 years of age. My argument is that within a mandatory subject such as mathematics, there should also be elements of choice and differentiation which allow students to follow their interests and strengths and engage in learning activities and experiences which they feel are relevant to their choices, future plans and vocational leanings.

CONCLUSION

In reviewing aspects of the mathematics curriculum, a number of central factors have emerged. First of all, there is the paucity of the planned and realized aims for the school mathematics curriculum from 5 to 16 or 18 years of age. To rephrase them, the aims for the school mathematics might be stated as follows:

1. To reproduce mathematical skill and knowledge based capability.
2. To develop creative capabilities in mathematics.
3. To develop empowering mathematical capabilities and a critical appreciation of the social applications and uses of mathematics.
4. To develop an inner appreciation of mathematics; its big ideas and nature.

The argument I wish to put here is that an entitlement curriculum in mathematics requires that all of these aims are realized for students of school mathematics from 5 to 16 or 18 years of age. Given the centrality of mathematics in human history and in modern technological society, students have an entitlement to both mathematical capability and appreciation.

This chapter, then, engages with questioning school mathematics in two senses. On the one hand, it involves putting active questioning at the heart of the capabilities to be developed in school mathematics. Students, it is claimed, should be actively empowered by their knowledge and capabilities in school mathematics. However, questioning is to be incorporated as a capability which supports the appreciation of mathematics, not at its expense. On the other hand, this enquiry suggests the need to question the underlying assumptions about the nature of mathematics, the aims of mathematics teaching, and the nature and structure of the mathematics curriculum itself. This involves broadening the aims of school mathematics, to give a richer entitlement, as well as introducing real multiplicity and choice into school mathematics, at least in the secondary years. This chapter explored some of the rich and varying contexts and experiences that are possible for school mathematics and its learning and too few of them figure in the current provision.

NOTES

1. I shall return to the assumptions of Platonism when discussing the conceptual world of mathematics below.
2. It should be mentioned that a concern with gender and multicultural issues in mathematics could be interpreted as exceptions to this. However, the limited references to multicultural mathematics in the draft national curriculum documents in mathematics were patronising and disparaging, and no reference to social diversity occurs in the statutory specifications of the National Curriculum. What limited and peripheral references there were made to these issues represent a retrograde step from the position adopted in the Cockcroft Report

(1982), and this cannot be described as embodying the public educator perspective (Ernest 1991).

3. There has been some deeper criticism of the National Curriculum in mathematics, such as Dowling and Noss (1990). But this has been rare and rapidly marginalized.

4. It is appropriate to explain what is meant by a context here. By a context I mean either a domain of practice, which the student or others participate in or experience, or it is a domain of knowledge which while referring to others' practices becomes expressed in items of knowledge or textual resources (understood to incorporate the full range of representational forms) which can be imported into a domain of practice.

3

Scientific Experience

Daniel Davies

This chapter argues that, in the successive versions of science in the National Curriculum, schools have been subjected to an increasingly knowledge-based model of science education, drawn from a traditional secondary-oriented approach. This curriculum has adopted a view of science which is Euro-centric, absolutist and monolithic, treating scientific knowledge as objective and value-free. There is, however, a better alternative. In *Curriculum 11-16* (DES 1977a) Her Majesty's Inspectorate proposed a model of curriculum for secondary education which included science as one of seven 'areas of experience', which they warned teachers against viewing in subject terms:

> it is necessary to look through the subject or discipline to the areas of experience and knowledge to which it may provide access, and to the skills and attitudes which it may assist to develop (DES 1977a, p. 6).

As a primary specialist I recognize the relevance of such an approach, for many years at the heart of good primary practice, but now under political attack. This chapter will outline the rationale behind a science curriculum built on 'scientific experience', and review some of its implications. It will focus on primary practice, but I believe that the principles of such an approach are equally relevant to the secondary sector.

The chapter is written in four sections. The first of these looks at the nature of science itself, for, as Harlen (1992, p. l) states:

> like it or not, we convey through our teaching a view of science and so it is necessary to have a 'feel' for what this is.

This is an important starting point because as with any fundamental human endeavour there are several views which could be taken. The second section examines the relationship between scientific experience and other areas which might find themselves part of the curriculum. In particular I will examine the relationship between scientific and technological modes of understanding, since they are often so closely interrelated in public perception. Section three deals with the model of science implicit in the National Curriculum and concludes that there has been a shift to a narrower, more prescriptive view in successive versions. In section four I offer a set of principles upon which an alternative curriculum for scientific experience could be constructed, drawing on the insights from sections 1–3.

THE NATURE OF SCIENTIFIC THOUGHT

There are two contrasting views of scientific thought: that it is profoundly abstract and unrelated to everyday life, or that it is really just the extension of everyday thinking and 'common sense'. For a lay-person, the former view may express their perception of science as being incomprehensible and elitist, whereas scientists, for whom key ideas and concepts have become so familiar as to appear banal, may be tempted towards the latter view. As Karl Popper (1968, p. 19) observed:

> I agree that scientific knowledge is merely a development of ordinary knowledge or common-sense knowledge ... the most important way in which common-sense knowledge grows is, precisely, by turning into scientific knowledge.

According to Popper's view, scientific principles are ultimately derived from everyday thought, through the processes of scientific investigation. It is, of course, much more carefully structured and formulated, but retains its essential relevance through being grounded in the familiar:

> scientific knowledge can be more easily studied than common-sense knowledge. For it is *common-sense knowledge writ large*, as it were. Its very problems are enlargements of common-sense knowledge (Popper 1968, p. 22).

These are certainly words of comfort for the educator, because they imply that children will naturally extend their own knowledge into the scientific realm, given the necessary guidance. However, other commentators, such as Wolpert (1992), maintain that scientific thinking is qualitatively different from, and in many cases diametrically opposed to, common sense thinking:

> Generally ... the way in which nature has been put together and the laws that govern its behaviour bear no apparent relation to everyday life. The laws of nature just cannot be inferred from normal day-to-day experience (Wolpert 1992, p. 6).

Indeed many scientific ideas (e.g. that of constant acceleration due to gravity) directly contradict what would be expected from everyday life (that heavier things fall faster), and so can only be developed by breaking with previous thinking rather than extending it. Common-sense thinking is invaluable in solving the many complex problems of everyday life, but in proposing generalized theories which would account for a range of related phenomena it falls short, lacking the necessary information and rigour.

This is not to say that scientific thought does not entail assumptions about the nature of everyday experience. It is simply that these assumptions, together with those underlying the processes of scientific discovery and verification, need to be learned because they are not inborn (Polanyi 1964). We cannot see science as a natural progression and refinement of human curiosity, because it is a carefully transmitted set of orthodoxies, developed in a specific cultural context. For the dominant outlook at present is that of Western European and North American science, based on a comparatively recent legacy (two thousand years or so) of Greek, Enlightenment and Modernist thought which is broadly white, male and middle class. This is how scientific thought has been defined in our society, and 'it is this science which governs what scientists do, what problems they try to tackle, and what research they get funding for. And this in turn influences the kind of science taught in schools' (Watts 1991, p. 60). The roots of such a view, and the reasons for its predominance in science education, are outlined below.

Science as High-Status Knowledge

Although scientists themselves may have a relatively low status in our society (OFSTED 1994), the knowledge with which they deal has traditionally been accorded a high cultural value. Thus, when it is suggested that the school curriculum should take the form of 'a selection from the culture of a society' (Lawton 1975) it is generally assumed that this includes science. The definition of culture implicit here is that of 'high' culture – the canon of great art, literature and science accumulated by western society since the age of Plato and Aristotle.

Ancient Greek science was essentially rationalist and deductive in nature. It was based on the operation of the intellect on certain conceptions about the nature of the universe which were themselves considered to be transcendent and not open to question. Aristotle's reasoning about, for example, the rate of fall of bodies was deduced from his initial postulates rather than induced from experiment. His conclusion, that the rate of fall of a body was proportional to its mass, remained unchallenged until the time of Galileo because of its high status as 'natural philosophy'. This deferential attitude towards scientific knowledge persists to this day in the minds of politicians and curriculum planners. Science is seen as an 'intrinsically worthwhile activity', selected as a cornerstone of the curriculum because its 'cognitive concerns and far-ranging cognitive content give [it] a value denied to other more circumscribed activities' (Peters 1966, p. 66). However, the principal source for the model of science used in schools is the work of European scientists in the seventeenth, eighteenth and nineteenth centuries, the age of 'enlightenment' and 'modernism'.

Science as Modernist, Positivist and Empirical

Modernism can be defined as the prevalent world view of the Industrial Revolution, with its emphasis on the mastery of the environment through the study of the material world. Modernist science is characterized by its empirical nature: the primacy of the 'experimental method' which enables the scientist to 'arrive at truth by logical inferences from empirical observations' (Ziman 1968, p. 6). Hence the emphasis on observation and measurement in contemporary science education.

It can be argued that the values underlying Modernism grew directly from the dominant physical and mathematical theories of the 17th century (Newtonian mechanics and Cartesian geometry) which were themselves essentially deterministic in nature. Newton's laws allowed only the types of motion which accorded with them, whilst Descartes' rectilinear 3D space assigned precise shapes and dimensions to the Universe. 'Modern' culture placed great emphasis on scientific processes to explain every aspect of life, and to bring social progress and perfect society. This view, and the cultural arrogance which accompanied it, held sway until the beginning of this century, and arguably still dominates much of Western thought.

There are several characteristics of the modernist perspective. These have been summarized by Cohen and Manion (1994) and include *positivism*, which holds that 'all genuine knowledge is based on sense experience and can only be advanced by means of observation and experiment' (op. cit., p. 11), *determinism*: 'events have causes, events are determined by other circumstances; and science proceeds on the belief that these causal links can eventually be uncovered and understood; (op. cit., p. 13), *parsimony*: 'phenomena should be explained in the most economical way possible' (op. cit. p. 3), *generality*, and *objectivity*. Scientists' theories are presented as 'laws' governing nature, and science education is seen as the process by which these laws are transmitted to the next generation. This view, implicit in much school science, risks alienating many children and fails to take into account the revolution in scientists' perceptions of their field in the 20th century.

Science as Provisional and Uncertain – Twentieth Century Physics

With the advent of less deterministic, more uncertain views of the Universe, characterized in the world of physics by the theories of Relativity, Statistical Thermodynamics and Quantum Mechanics, and more recently by the mathematical concepts of Catastrophe and Chaos, new patterns of thought have emerged. The old order was seen to be flawed, both in the macro-scale (the curvature of space-time due to gravity breaking the laws of Cartesian geometry) and the micro-scale (the Uncertainty Principle in Quantum Mechanics breaking the Newtonian paradigm). Scientists have become less certain about the precise nature of the universe, and about their abilities to decipher it with any degree of precision:

> Our experience, both as individual scientists and historically, is that we only arrive at partial and incomplete truths; we never achieve the precision and finality that seem required by the definition (Ziman 1968, p. 6).

This is a post-modern view of science, with scientific knowledge seen as provisional and subject to change. Scientific theories are not seen as 'deduced from data but are constructions of the human intellect' (Driver 1983, p. 51). They are useful models to explain a range of phenomena, but essentially created by people rather than inferred from experiment by pure logical induction. The very concept of a 'scientific method' has been questioned and redefined as a range of approaches, varying in sophistication and dependent on the branch of science being studied. Polanyi (1964) has argued that scientific method can only be exemplified in practice, by what scientists actually do, rather than as a universal process:

> The rules of scientific enquiry leave their own application wide open, to be decided by the scientist's judgement (Polanyi 1964, p. 14).

Feyerabend (1978) had gone as far as rejecting the whole concept of a scientific method, arguing that science has historically progressed through a series of 'ad hoc hypotheses and ad hoc approximations' by creative scientists working in an 'anarchistic' way to question current concepts. He dismisses the idea that science can be run according to fixed rules as a 'fairy tale' and asserts that:

> Without chaos, no knowledge. Without frequent dismissal of reason, no progress (Feyerabend 1978, p. 179).

Once scientists are no longer seen as purely logical in their methodology, there is clearly room for intuition as a fundamental part of a creative scientific process. When scientists think, claims Polanyi (1964, p. 29), 'there is involved an intuition of the relation between observation and reality: a faculty which can range over all grades of sagacity, from the highest level present in the inspired guesses of scientific genius, down to a minimum required for ordinary perception.' This, once again, places scientific thought processes as part of a continuum which includes our everyday thinking; part of a much more 'user-friendly' view of science than that of modernism, likely to have a wider appeal because it no longer claims a purely objective and value-neutral stance. Indeed, science is seen as having moral responsibilities, an aspect explored further in the next section.

Science as a Sociopolitical Activity

> How can I save my little boy from Oppenheimer's deadly toy? (Sting, 1985, 'The Dream of the Blue Turtles')

> Is it not possible that science as we know it today, or a 'search for the truth' in the style of traditional philosophy, will create a monster? (Feyerabend 1978, p. 175).

Robert Oppenheimer's dismay at the linking of his name with the atomic bomb which was eventually dropped on Hiroshima and Nagasaki is indicative of the ethical crisis in 20th century science. Unable to escape from the perceived consequences of science (Thalidomide, global warming, genetic engineering etc.) many have been forced to admit that science cannot sit outside the realm of politics by claiming an objective, value-free position. Funding bodies, often major drugs companies or governmental research agencies, now set the scientific agenda by deciding on the types of research which will be supported. This reality should surely be reflected in any democratic curriculum, and was indeed incorporated by HMI in the *Curriculum 11-16* document:

> Science for citizenship is concerned with the role of science in the social, economic and political decision-making processes (DES 1977a, p. 28).

In parallel with the politicization of science has developed its sociology. The very nature of scientific knowledge is seen by many commentators as being socially constructed:

> *Science is Public Knowledge* . . . its goal is a *consensus* of rational opinion over the widest possible field . . . in other words scientific research is a social activity (Ziman 1968, pp. 8–9).

The traditional image of a scientist working alone in 'his' laboratory bears little resemblance to the ways in which scientists actually work: collaboratively in groups which are in competition with other groups; sharing information through continual publications and conferences. Feyerabend (1978) argues that the 'fairy tale' of scientific method helps protect the elite status of this 'scientific community' by implying that it holds knowledge to which the untrained have no access. Scientists do indeed constitute a community, with its own norms and processes by which novices are inducted into the 'code of scientific conduct':

> young scientists do not learn to do research by studying books about Scientific Method. They use their native wits, and they imitate their elders (Ziman 1968, p. 145).

In some respects, the scientific community is a very conservative social group, some members holding on to cherished beliefs long after they have ceased to accord with new evidence. However, the nature of science is to be self-critical and questioning, which sometimes results in huge swings in opinion across the whole community, a process Kuhn (1970) has described as 'paradigm shift'. Kuhn maintains that many aspects of physical science have undergone a series of revolutions over the last 300 years, as one paradigm, or dominant idea, has given way to another which appears to fit observations more closely and gains rapid acceptance by scientists working in the field. In the case of optics, Newton's 'corpuscular' model of light was supplanted by Huyghens' wave theory once this was seen to account for the phenomenon of diffraction (Young's slits). Wave theory was in turn

supplanted by Einstein and Planck's Quantum theory once the photo-elec-
tric effect cast serious doubt on its validity:

> The transformations of the paradigms of physical optics are scientific revolutions,
> and the successive transition from one paradigm to another via revolution is the
> usual developmental pattern of mature science (Kuhn 1970, p. 12).

The process of paradigm shift may be analogous to the way in which children develop scientific concepts: sometimes holding onto existing ideas
even when confronted with experiences which contradict them, sometimes
changing completely through discussion with each other or the teacher. The
social dimension of classroom science is clearly of vital importance, and has
many implications for children's broader development. I now turn to considering other ways in which science can enrich a curriculum seen as 'areas
of experience'.

THE RELATIONSHIP OF THE SCIENTIFIC TO OTHER AREAS OF EXPERIENCE

> Science stands in the region where the intellectual, the psychological and the soci-
> ological coordinate axes intersect (Ziman 1968, p. 11).

As we have seen, and as DES (1977a) acknowledge, not only does scientific experience have important concepts, skills and attitudes to contribute
to other areas of learning, but it too has creative, moral and even spiritual
dimensions. There is often a difficult line to draw between aspects of, say
cosmology, and philosophical or religious thought on the origin and destiny of the universe. If we consider the role of observation, hypothesis,
empirical testing etc. across the curriculum there does not seem to be one
characteristic which science can truly call its own. Indeed, 'the room
labelled Science is not sharply cut off from its neighbours but opens in every
direction to less specific, less "certain" apartments in the House of Intellect'
(Ziman 1968, p. 40). What scientific experience does seem to hold uniquely
is a combination of elements: theories which are generalizable and which
make predictions which can be tested, by many others if necessary, to confirm or refute the models proposed. Popper (1968) maintains that the characteristic of a scientific theory (as opposed to any other kind) is that it
should be refutable by observation or experiment, since in the last analysis it is not possible to conclusively verify knowledge which will be subject to change over time. Whilst recognizing this distinctive nature of
scientific experience, it is nevertheless worth exploring briefly the relationship of science with one of its near neighbours – technology.

Science and Technology – a Special Relationship?

There was once a time when Science was academic and useless and Technology was a practical art, but now they are so interfused that one is not surprised that the multitude cannot tell them apart (Ziman 1968, p. 24).

Popular media tend to use the terms 'science' and 'technology' interchangeably, or as one homogeneous phrase. Undoubtably the two are inextricably linked in the minds of politicians, who see the country's 'science and technology base' as the engine for economic growth, hence providing an 'industrial trainer's' (Williams, 1961) rationale for education in both fields. In fact, the relationship between the two may be more complex than this simplistic analysis. Gardner (1994, p. 3) defines four possible views of this relationship:

(i)   science precedes technology i.e. technological capability grows out of scientific knowledge; this position, often called the *technology as applied science* (TAS) view, is widely held and influential.

(ii) science and technology are independent, with differing goals, methods and outcomes (the *demarcationist* view).

(iii) technology precedes science; this *materialist* view asserts that technology is historically and ontologically prior to science, that experience with tools, instruments and other artefacts is necessary for conceptual development.

(iv) technology and science engage in two-way interaction; this *interactionist* view considers scientists and technologists as groups of people who learn from each other in mutually beneficial ways.

If we take the first of these views, it is tempting to believe that scientists generate knowledge for technologists to apply (as in the well-known catch phrase for Zanussi freezers) but the reality is that most scientific knowledge needs to be considerably reworked to make it useful in the highly complex 'real world' of technology with its multitudinous human and economic factors. As Black (1995), Wolpert (1992) and others point out, history is littered with technological advances which took little or no account of science, and inappropriate applications of scientific knowledge which proved disastrous because of lack of understanding of the human context of the technology.

Supporting a demarcationist perspective, Polanyi (1958) argues that scientific and technological modes of understanding are fundamentally different, and that to understand the physical or chemical concepts implicit within a piece of technology is not necessarily to appreciate its operational principles. A scientific analysis of, say, a mobile telephone would not tell us anything about its significance as a cultural icon, and hence 'the two kinds of knowledge, the technical and the scientific, largely by-pass each other' (Polanyi 1958, p. 331). Wolpert (1992) has concluded that scientific and technological modes of thought are clearly delineated, the latter drawing strongly on visual imagery and non-verbal expression, whilst scientific thought is largely expressed through the symbolic language of mathematics.

Gardner's third view (materialist) can be supported from a historical perspective: technology is very much older than science, and many fundamental advances (the wheel, agriculture etc.) were developed without reference to abstract, generalized theories:

> Not until the nineteenth century did science have an impact on technology. In human evolution the ability to make tools, and so control the environment, was a great advantage, but the ability to do science was almost entirely irrelevant. (Wolpert 1992, p. 25)

Although technology did not need science for most of its history, Wolpert argues, 'science by contrast has always been heavily dependent on the available technology, both for ideas and for apparatus' (op. cit., p. 30). It was by observing the workings of technology that scientists of the Enlightenment built up their picture of a 'clockwork universe' with every part having a precise, predetermined part to play. And how would Galileo have developed a model of the solar system without a telescope with which to observe the moons of Jupiter?

Few would claim, in a nuclear age, that technology still owes little to science. Those (like the author) adopting an interactionist perspective would point out that the roles of professionals in both fields are often intertwined, particularly in the area of research and development:

> Certainly at the level of individual scientists and technologists today, whether in industry or academia, their work may entail both scientific investigations and experimentation and the design and construction of new systems and instrumentalities of various kinds (Layton 1993, p. 41).

However, a simplistic view of the role of science in technological innovation and economic growth is not borne out by considering a country in terminal industrial decline (UK) which has produced more science Nobel prize winners this century than any other (Layton, 1993). The reality, Layton suggests, is that science is not a uniform activity, being composed of 'pure or fundamental', 'strategic' and 'applied' strands, each being distinguished by its degree of interaction with the world of technology. This complexity, and the degree of symbiosis it suggests, are not easily represented in the primary curriculum. However, let us now examine what we have at present – the National Curriculum for Science at Key Stages I and 2 – to see how it measures up to the models of scientific activity and thought set out above.

THE MODEL OF SCIENTIFIC THOUGHT IMPLICIT IN THE
NATIONAL CURRICULUM FOR SCIENCE

Now the National Curriculum has an enormous yawning gap between general principles stated in very few words and a list of ten subjects taken for granted; no philosophy connecting those subjects to those overall principles is laid down anywhere (Black 1995, p. 8).

With the exception of areas such as curricular planning for science and the need to improve the science subject knowledge of teachers, primary science can be counted a major success (OFSTED 1994).

There appears to be a complacency about the success of National Curriculum science in the primary school which is notably absent in the case of English or Mathematics. The content is seen as largely unproblematic, children apparently enjoy it and apart from a deficit model of teacher understanding, all seems to be going well. At first glance it would appear to be process-based, and to espouse many of the principles referred to above. Let us not forget, however, that it has undergone four major revisions, from the Interim Report of the Working Group to the Dearing 1995 version. With each of these amendments, a retreat can be traced from the fine rhetoric of early documents, to a reductionist model in which Attainment Targets 2, 3 and 4 (basically biology, chemistry and physics) have assumed a dominant role. Let us take some examples. The Science Non-Statutory Guidance (NCC 1989, para. 4.3) contains the following statement:

> Learning in science contributes to personal development ... Appreciating the powerful but provisional nature of scientific knowledge and explanation will bring pupils closer to the process by which scientific models are created, tested and modified. They will begin to sense the uncertain nature of even the most established explanations of scientific evidence.

The references to development and provisional knowledge echo the 'areas of experience' approach of HMI and the post-modern nature of 20th century science. Even better, there is within the 1989 Order an Attainment Target (AT 17) devoted to understanding the 'ways in which scientific ideas change through time and how the nature of these ideas and uses to which they are put are affected by the social, moral, spiritual and cultural contexts in which they are developed' (NCC 1989, p. 36). Admittedly this Attainment Target applies only to Key Stages 3 and 4, but nevertheless there is running through the document the understanding that science is one of many ways devised by humans for making sense of everyday life. There is also an emphasis on exploration and investigation (AT I) which in the overall weighting should make up 50% of children's experience of science.

Mismatch between Process and Content

This process aspect of science in the National Curriculum is seen as the vehicle through which scientific knowledge is delivered. In the Non-Statutory Guidance (NCC 1989, para. 6.3) it is acknowledged that:

> For the pupil learning science, as for the scientist, the way understanding develops depends both on existing ideas and on the processes by which those ideas are used and tested in new situations.

The exact form of the process is given a degree of flexibility; there being 'more than one scientific method', and 'imagination' having a part to play in children's investigations (ibid.). The emphasis is on children developing a scientific 'capability' (cf. technology), and the concepts to be developed are set firmly within an inductive framework.

As the National Curriculum came under increasing political pressure, we see the model for scientific process become more rigid, the word 'exploration' in AT1 being replaced by 'experimental', and a linear sequence of skills (question, hypothesize, plan, test, observe, conclude) emphasized, rather like a traditional secondary school chemistry write-up. The purpose of an experiment becomes increasingly that of arriving at the 'right answer' and 'proving' a piece of pre-specified knowledge, an outcome far less likely in an open-ended investigation. This notion of *process as the vehicle for content* represents a reversal of the model proposed by DES (1977a, p. 27) in which 'some content is essential to provide the vehicle through which scientific thinking can be developed, and there are important scientific ideas which every educated citizen should have met.'

Another feature of the successive versions is a stricter compartmentalization of, and increasing emphasis on, the knowledge component. In the 1991 rewrite we see the number of attainment targets reduced from 17 to 4 and the loss of AT 17 (though its content was said to be subsumed within other statements). The Programmes of Study are now directly linked to Statements of Attainment; in other words geared towards content delivery. Increasing criticism of cross-curricular, topic-based teaching by The Office for Standards in Education (OFSTED 1994. p. 7) applied pressure for the removal of overlap with other subjects:

> the rather tenuous connection of the science being taught with the wider topic content being studied means that learning is often fragmented and does not have intellectual integrity.

Hence the removal of references to weather and energy in Key Stages 1 and 2 during the further revision under Sir Ron Dearing (1994-5), a move portrayed as reducing the load on primary teachers by 'removing unhelpful duplication across related subjects, in particular geography and technology' (SCAA 1994. p. iii). In reality, it was a further move towards discrete subjects at Key Stage 2, taught by 'specialists' in a 'transmission' model, along the lines proposed by Alexander, Rose and Woodhead (1992). The purpose of investigation is now seen as the acquisition of 'specific' knowledge and skills, and science now provides 'explanations for many phenomena' (DfE 1995a), a clear modernist agenda.

The real coercive power of the National Curriculum is to be found in the assessment arrangements. For primary science education this has been felt particularly in the case of the Key Stage 2 Standard Assessment Tasks (SATs), or Statutory Assessment Tests as they have become. Introduced in 1995, only the knowledge component (Sc 2, 3 and 4) was to be tested, and little credence was given to Teacher Assessment of children's process skills (Sc 1). The result of this has been pressure on primary teachers to neglect investigational science, which is messy, demanding and does not always produce the 'right' answers. Instead there has been a strong temptation, particularly for Year 6 teachers, to implant 'facts' by rote if necessary, in preparation for the SATs. The nationally published results for 1995 show this to have been an effective strategy, for 11 year olds generally scored better in Science than in English and Mathematics. A triumph for memorization!

In 1996, there has been an attempt to set SAT questions in some sort of experimental and equal-opportunities context. For example, Test A, question 2, shows a photograph of a black girl apparently conducting an investigation into magnetism, holding different metal rods up to a suspended magnet. However, the question asks nothing about how to approach such an investigation: it is merely asking for factual knowledge: 'Which TWO of these metals will attract the magnet? (iron, aluminium, brass, steel, copper, lead)' (SCAA/DfE 1996). Here the reality of science in the National Curriculum is separated from the rhetoric. Although there are options for primary teachers to interpret the Order more broadly, the pressure to implant 'testable' knowledge (in the educational rather than scientific sense) will inevitably lead to an impoverished science curriculum.

PRINCIPLES UNDERPINNING A CURRICULUM FOR SCIENTIFIC EXPERIENCE

What then could replace the model we currently have? Teachers would undoubtedly wince at the thought of yet more curriculum change, especially with the current provision of a five year 'moratorium' in which to draw breath. However, it must be remembered that the turmoil of recent years has been caused by the attempt to impose a politically driven curriculum centrally, with a mismatch between educational rhetoric and instrumentalist reality. Real curriculum change is more gradual and evolutionary, driven by practitioners and research. And change must continue because, as Paul Black (1996) reminds us, science and technology, and their relationship with society and the needs of children, change with increasing rapidity. How can a curriculum 'set in stone' meet these challenges?

I have no quarrel with the stated principles of the National Curriculum. The concept of an 'entitlement' to science education is directly relevant within a democracy. However, an entitlement to chunks of scientific knowledge does not seem particularly empowering. The mantra of 'Breadth, Balance, Relevance, Differentiation, Progression and Continuity' (DES 1985a, NCC 1989c) also constitutes a worthy set of principles, but what are they actually to mean in practice? Several countries (Black 1996) are reviewing their science curricula, and the common feature appears to be a move towards a broader approach, with content less tightly specified and hence more flexible and responsive to rapid changes in science and technology. A good place to start in defining our principles for a real 'entitlement' curriculum would seem to be the purposes set out for science education by DES (1977a, p. 27):

> Any scientific subject can have three components, namely, science for the enquiring mind, science for action and science for citizenship.

I will take each of these in turn, to explore what they might look like in practice.

Science for the Enquiring Mind

> Science for the enquiring mind is concerned with the laws and theories – the disciplines of the subject. A great range of phenomena can be accounted for in terms of the nature of the particles of which all material things are made and of the forces between them which result in their being arranged in certain numerical and spatial configurations and in terms of the laws of energy to be followed in their transactions (DES 1977a, p. 27).

Conceptual content in science is, of course, very important. I am not advocating a 'content-free, discovery-learning' approach. It is simply that, in order to foster real understanding in children, there must be an emphasis on broad principles (such as that of 'energy transfer', mysteriously eradicated from the 1995 Order) rather than 'facts to be learned'. This will inevitably place greater conceptual demands on teachers, but places them in the role of 'co-researchers' rather than providers of 'the right answer'.

To be consistent with the weight of research opinion over the past thirty years this conceptual content must 'wherever possible, be related to the experiences of the children; it should, in accordance with their stages of development, provide them with knowledge and understanding of scientific ideas to help them to understand their own physical and biological environments and to understand themselves' (DES 1984b, p. 5). Much valuable insight into children's scientific ideas has been gained in recent years by researchers adopting a *constructivist* approach. Driver (1983) has proposed that children approach science lessons with their own 'alternative frameworks' for the concepts involved, which are very resistant to change by traditional methods:

> Pupils, like scientists, view the world through the spectacles of their own preconceptions, and many have difficulty in making the journey from their own intuitions to the ideas presented in science lessons (Driver 1983, preface).

Children (and adults!) often have a difficult conceptual leap to make in abandoning previously held frameworks and taking on new ones, even when experimental evidence contradicts the old ideas. This is often a slow and carefully planned process requiring considerable reflection and discussion, which is not helped by a teacher who is desperate to implant the 'right answer' for the SATs. Play also assumes a key role, because children can consolidate concepts by playing with resources once the teacher-led investigation is finished (Jarvis 1991).

The recent Nuffield Primary Science scheme (Wadsworth et al. 1993) is based on such a constructivist model, building on children's existing scientific concepts using a range of types of teacher intervention. It is academically rigorous, being based on the extensive SPACE (Science Processes And Concept Exploration) project research (Russell et al. 1991) into children's ideas, and consistent with the view taken by Harlen (1992) and others that the development of scientific concepts in children can only take place through the exercise of science process skills. The scheme is, for obvious reasons, directly linked to the current National Curriculum, but would fit more happily into a model whereby children receive credit for their progress in understanding, and in which investigations do not always have to produce the 'textbook' answer.

Science for Action

Science for action is concerned with the development of scientific skills, and the contexts in which those skills are deployed. Here again, the list of skills specified by the National Curriculum is relatively uncontentious (hypothesis, prediction, control of variables etc.) provided they are not set in a rigid, sequential framework. It should be remembered that they are not the exclusive preserve of science, and may 'arise in many parts of the curriculum and in pupils' experience out of school' (DES 1985a, p. 31). Particularly in primary schools, science must not be separated into a little box, decontextualizing the knowledge taught and rendering it irrelevant. It should be as 'concrete' as possible, related to real situations and problems (DES 1985a). One such productive context is Design and Technology (DT).

Whilst stressing that the outcomes and processes (both educational and conceptual) of science and technology are very different, there are a number of pedagogic models through which the contextualization of science learning could be achieved:

1) Using DT activities as 'interventions' to develop children's scientific concepts.
2) Applying the concepts developed in 'science lessons' in a DT project.
3) Using short science investigations as 'resource activities' for a DT project.
4) Teaching scientific concepts where they arise in the course of a DT project.
5) Using a 'problem solving' or cross-curricular activity to develop Science and DT learning simultaneously.

The above list obviously contains some overlaps, and is not exhaustive. What is interesting to note is that models 1 and 2 are 'science-led', with technology seen as a vehicle for delivering the science curriculum, or as simply 'the appliance of science'. Models 3 and 4 are, conversely, 'technology-led' with scientific concepts seen as service knowledge for a DT project. The fifth approach involves 'problem-solving' which is arguably common to both areas, but risks confusing the specific scientific and technological concepts and skills which it aims to develop. Although a popular approach, research has found 'little to support the general nature of problem-solving abilities, or the transfer of these skills into everyday life' (McCormick and Murphy 1994, p. 4). A problem which all the models share is that of 'situated cognition' (ibid.) whereby children are unable to transfer learning between contexts.

A further model, proposed by Black and Harrison (1985) is a science and technology curriculum based on 'Task-Action-Capability' in which tasks, conceived in terms of science investigations and technology projects, would draw interactively on resource studies containing both process skills and knowledge from each area:

> pupils should really use and extend the knowledge and skills that they develop in resource areas and . . . Tasks should form a progression to develop use of resources, exploration of wider implications, and development and practice of value judgments (Black and Harrison 1985, p. 26).

This model embodies Gardner's (1994) 'interactionist perspective' and acknowledges that scientific knowledge has to be extensively deconstructed and reconstructed in the light of other knowledge and judgments to make it useful for practical action in specific situations (Layton 1990). Also implicit within this view is the social dimension of science, involving children working in multi-disciplinary teams and negotiating meanings between themselves, so that:

> scientific knowledge becomes as much a resource for the construction and maintenance of personal identity, a sense of 'who they are', as an external instrumentality of understanding and manipulation of the material world (Layton 1990, p. 130).

Science for Citizenship

In a democratic society all citizens have a right to understand the scientific issues behind decisions which affect their lives, such as energy and transport policy. The Committee for the Public Understanding of Science (COPUS) has done much in the last ten years, through the media and interactive museums, to raise 'awareness of the multi-faceted, creative and qualitative aspects of science' (Johnston 1995, p. 2). Indeed Millar (1996) has proposed a curriculum based on the public understanding of science. However, according to Durand (1995) there are deeper issues connected with public distrust of science and scientists, which can be characterized as a debate between 'top down' and 'sociological' schools of educational thought:

> there are two views on the nature of the problems surrounding the 'Public Understanding of Science'. The first of these suggests that there is a large scale ignorance of science within the general public and that this should be addressed by more and better science education to ensure that students have a greater factual knowledge of science. The alternative view is that science is becoming set against the public and that this is resulting in an erosion of public confidence in science (op. cit., p. 45).

According to Layton (1990), the way lay people come to understand scientific principles can be viewed using either a 'cognitive deficit model', characterized by downward transmission, or an 'interactive model' in which people view scientific knowledge 'as a quarry to be raided, a repository of resources which might further their particular endeavours and assist the solution of specific problems' (op. cit., p. 124). The problem is not necessarily that the public do not understand science, but that scientific knowledge is seen to be 'inseparable from its social and institutional connections' (ibid.), and less important in specific situations than personal judgments. It is the social processes by which science ideas come to acquire general currency which need to be made more transparent:

> The 'black box' of theory needs to be transformed into a 'glass box' which exposes its inner workings: it also needs to be located in the wider context of a social world which has contributed to its making and is, in turn, shaped by it (op. cit., p. 132).

In conclusion, a curriculum based on scientific experience would aim to demystify the workings of science. It would focus on moral and ethical issues, opening these up to informed debate. It would foster scientific attitudes: 'curiosity, honesty in observation . . . willingness to make predictions, and the readiness to record observations' (DES 1977a, p. 27). Cultural diversity would be strongly reflected, 'illustrating that science has different implications for individuals in different parts of the world' (Watts 1991, p. 136). Teaching and learning styles would be participative, enfranchising girls and children with special educational needs. The content would need to be intellectually rigorous, both from a scientific and sociological point of view. An appropriate form of assessment, along the lines of that used by the Assessment of Performance Unit (APU 1989), would be required, using interviews and observations of process skills in different contexts.

Such a science curriculum would need to make its epistemological stance clear. It would reflect a view which sees scientific knowledge as provisional and socially constructed. Whilst teaching investigative process skills which are clearly contextualized, it would acknowledge the debate around the concept of 'scientific method' and stress the role of intuition and creativity in the scientific process. It would pay attention to the strong moral, aesthetic and creative dimensions of science, acknowledging its links with other areas of the curriculum (particularly Design and Technology) whilst asserting its distinctive contribution to children's holistic development. This model for science education would give real meaning to the concept of an entitlement curriculum.

4

Design and Technology: Creating New Futures

John Saxton

> The tendency to separate the cognitive from the affective is reflected in our separation of the mind from the body, of thinking from feeling, and the way we have dichotomized the work of the head from the work of the hand. What might seem at first to be abstract distinctions that have little bearing upon the real world in which we live turn out to shape not only our conception of mind but our educational policies as well.
>
> Elliot Eisner (1982, p. 30).

Elliot Eisner succinctly captures the essence of the separation of human capacities that has influenced many of the prevalent attitudes about education. The purpose of this chapter is to attempt to reconstruct these capacities into a holistic concept of design and technology as an area of educational experience.

Design and technology is concerned with our capacity as human beings to intervene in the world and effect change. From the dawn of civilization, we have been interacting with the environment and discovering increasingly more sophisticated and complex ways of changing it for our purposes. We have succeeded in this by utilizing the capacities of our mind and hands to manipulate tools and materials to create products and systems to meet our needs. Design and technology is the application of our understanding of what can be achieved in an endeavour to improve the human condition.

Design and technological capability in today's advanced technological society is, however, more complex than this. All members of our society live and interact with, and depend upon, technology in a variety of forms, and will do so throughout their lives. At work, the ability to operate competently with current technology, and to have the skills to adjust satisfactorily in a continuous technologically changing environment, are important concerns. As generators and consumers of technology, we need to be able to make critical judgements of value about its products and effects. To be aware of the potential of technology to affect our lives is the concern of all humankind, and developing technological 'literacy' in this respect is important for every citizen in a democratic society. Technology has the power to achieve tremendous good for the benefit of all: equally, it has the potential to inflict tremendous harm to people, to the other inhabitants of the earth, and to the planet itself. Ignorance is not an option.

Developing the competence to live, to work, and to have influence in a technologically advanced society can be construed as the instrumental aims of capability and literacy in this area of experience. The framing of the original National Curriculum orders in technology very much reflects these instrumental objectives, and many of the criticisms levelled against schools following its implementation concern their apparent failure to 'deliver' these. A significant lobby was mounted to 'tighten up' the perceived weaknesses of the original conception and delivery of the National Curriculum, not least by the Engineering Council (Smithers and Robinson 1992), and substantial pressure was applied to address these particular instrumental concerns in the revised orders.

Developing the competence to live, to work and to have an influence in a technologically advanced society are important features of the educational processes being considered here. But, the major goals of capability in design and technology are concerned intrinsically with the *development of the competence to learn and to be able to apply that learning in practical and ethical ways*. This will involve the acquisition of the qualities and attributes that will provide not just the capacity to operate effectively and have influence in the current situation and in that of the immediate future, but equally, to acquire those qualities and attributes that will enable members of our society to continue to learn and develop understanding, and to utilize this throughout their lives. This educational goal, in a paradoxical way, might be regarded equally as both vocational and democratic.

The principle of conceptualizing design and technology as an area of experience concerned with the development of the competence to learn and apply that learning in creating new futures is consistent with my view about the purpose of education in general, which is one that places the learners and the development of their individual capacities and capabilities firmly in the centre of the endeavour. This is achieved through a developmental and experiential educational process (Kelly 1989, Chapter 4), and design and technology, as an area of experience, should be consistent with such a process. Importantly, the principle of developing the capacity for further 'growth' (Dewey 1916, Chapter 4) is consistent also with the concept of design and technology. Design and technology is ever-changing as new understandings are achieved, or innovative interpretations of existing understanding are developed. The combined needs of: making a contribution toward future developments in design and technology; developing understanding of the impact and consequence of new or improved products; being able to operate competently with technology; and having control and influence over its development and use; all require the capacity to continue to learn, understand, adapt and utilize. In our lifetime there have been unimagined technology developments and we have all needed to learn how to use new technologies as they have appeared and influenced our lives. How many of us have felt competent and confident enough to do so satisfactorily? And how satisfactory will the current National Curriculum be in ensuring the development of such capacities in the present and future generations of pupils? I can hazard a guess at the response to the first question, but I am convinced that the outcome of the second will leave much to be desired.

DESIGN AND TECHNOLOGY AS AN EDUCATIONAL AREA OF EXPERIENCE

Design and technology, framed as an area of experience, would provide a powerful teaching and learning medium. Within a curriculum determined by areas of experience, it would make an important and unique educational contribution. It is not just the technological knowledge, skills and processes developed through engagement in an active and reflective experiential process of learning that make it so. Nor is it just in its relationship with, and to, the other areas of experience: both of which are significant. Its unique contribution lies within the nature of its learning methodology, at the heart of which lies the formidable combination of *the mind and the hand acting in concert*.

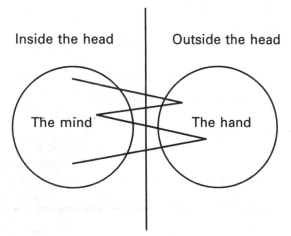

Figure 4.1

Design and technology is an activity that unites the abilities of our species as homo sapiens and homo faber ('man' the understander and 'man' the maker respectively) to effect change in the world. The capacity of the mind and hand to interact with the environment and effect change is achieved through a combination of human attributes working in harmony to facilitate *conceptualization and representation.*

Elliot Eisner argues that conceptual organization and its manifestations are achieved through a variety of complex 'forms of representation' (Eisner 1982, Chapter 3) which aid and abet learning by making them public. The formulation of these conceptualizations he believes 'depends upon experience, either the kind that emanates from the sentient being's contact with the qualities of the environment or from the experience born of imagination' (op. cit p. 37). *In the design and technological area of experience these two factors – experience and imagination – are combined with reason to facilitate learning.* It is the capacity of the mind to conceptualize, imagine and visualize 'what we have never experienced in the empirical world' (op. cit p. 31) and our ability to interact and intervene in the real world that provides the unique and powerful opportunity to learn through design and technological activities.

A coherent programme of experiences in this area of the curriculum would build from this central tenet. But there are a number of other important features that combine to make design and technology a particularly significant teaching and learning vehicle. The learning environment itself; the partnership between the teacher and the student in the learning process; the motivation of designing and evaluating 'real' products; the accessibility and relevance of learning experientially in an appropriate context; the opportunity to work as an individual, as a member of a team, or both; engagement with a problem and its resolution; the combination of intellectual capacities (both cognitive and affective) and motor skills – *all* contribute towards: the development of higher order intellectual skills; the acquisition of knowledge; the development of the understanding of concepts, principles, and applications; the development of personal qualities and interpersonal skills; and the fostering of motor skills through the use of tools and techniques to manipulate materials. But, it is *the capacity of the mind and hand to interact in concert and effect change* that invests the endeavour with such potential. And it can be a hugely enjoyable, challenging and rewarding experience.

The interaction between the mind and hand would epitomize the nature of this area of experience for all ages – and at all stages and phases of development – from the earliest years through to maturity. Unfortunately the educational value of this sophisticated capacity has been somewhat diminished by the emphasis in the National Curriculum on other features of design and technology. Attention in recent years has focused on teaching and assessing the knowledge and skills determined in the programmes of study, and there has been a heavy emphasis through legislation and funding (the National Curriculum, the Technical and Vocational Education Initiative (TVEI), the Technology Schools Initiative, and City Technology Colleges) on a vocational training perspective.

An alternative view which has evolved over the last thirty years has focused on design and technology as a *process*. There have been numerous attempts to capture and describe this 'process of design'. Although many of these have been flawed conceptually, they have been helpful (to an extent) in furthering understanding about this area of experience and in promoting an experiential, procedural learning activity in the curriculum. Unfortunately, they have also been damaging through the restrictive way in which they have been translated and applied in the National Curriculum and in examination syllabuses. Overall, they have probably done more harm than good because of their structural simplicity. And the appeal of the security they appear to offer has distracted attention from the true nature of design and technology both as a process and with regard to its substance and purpose.

The main problem that has arisen is that interpretations of design and technological activities have managed only to succeed in communicating an understanding of a dynamic and interactive process of learning in a mechanistic and prescriptive way. One of the most influential 'models' proposed (Figure 4.2) portrays the activity as a process with a logical, systematic development of stages that are completed in sequence – a technical procedure that relies on the adherence to a pattern of prescribed actions and behaviours for successful completion. This is an industrial model of production – an engineering model – which perhaps reflects the narrow vocational purposes desired by some. In the educational context it has

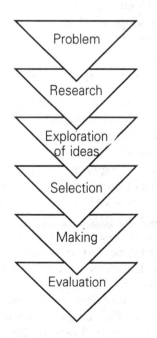

Figure 4.2

served its purpose – by providing a vehicle for the development of process-led learning. But, unless our understanding and practice in the classroom develop beyond this, the progress made so far, along with the current opportunities to develop further this area of human endeavour as a powerful teaching medium, will be wasted.

Current practice in schools does little to enhance the view of design and technology as a valid and powerful educational pursuit, and reflects in most instances – particularly at secondary level – poor exploitation of its educational potential. All too often it offers, at best, an indifferent educational experience and, alas, in all too many situations it is without educational merit or benefit, and is more akin to 'training' (and inappropriate training at that) than to 'education'. The design 'process' being employed is educationally prescriptive and restrictive, and is inappropriate to both the nature of design and technology and to the learning needs of our children and young people. The structuring of experience for progression and continuity is often piecemeal, if evident, and lacks coherence. We need to move on. And quickly.

This chapter will explore the concept of design and technology as an area of educational experience founded on learning through the interaction between the mind and hand working in concert and undertaken as a family of processes, perhaps best described as *'a process of processes'* – a flexible sequence of tasks and pupil-orientated, experiential learning activities, comprising a complex of sub-processes. Experienced progressively within a programme of structured learning activities, these sub-processes build cumulatively to develop capability in design and technology, and contribute to understanding in other areas of experience.

DESIGN AND TECHNOLOGY AND THE NATIONAL CURRICULUM

The framing of both the original and revised orders for technology in the National Curriculum differ in many respects from the other core and foundation subjects. This is, in one sense, the result of its conception as a 'new' subject, and even, to an extent, as a new concept. Developments in this area of the curriculum – beginning with Schools Council 'Project Technology' in 1969 (Schools Council, 1975) – embraced a concept that does not conform readily to that of a knowledge-based curriculum, and, in consequence, it has struggled to gain recognition. If it has achieved any 'academic' respectability it has been achieved by being regarded as a 'field' (Hirst, in Peters 1973, p. 105), served by contributory 'disciplines', framed in terms of knowledge. It has been regarded therefore, if regarded at all, as an interdisciplinary subject.

There is, however, an important distinction to be drawn between the conception of interdisciplinary in the context of a subject-defined, content-led curriculum, and that of a curriculum based on the areas of experience being considered here. The concept of interdisciplinary in this view of design and technology is one that reflects combining *ways of thinking* and *areas of experience* rather than combining knowledge-based subjects. In a subject-based, content-led curriculum, the concept of interdisciplinary is often construed as meaning several subject 'disciplines' contributing toward a 'field of knowledge'. In the context of the model of curriculum being presented here, however, interdisciplinary is concerned with the ways in which 'modes of thinking' (Peterson, in Peters 1973, p. 96), in the various areas of experience are integral to the concept of technological enquiry and to the families of processes that determine development. In other words, the ways in which the aesthetic/creative, the ethical/moral, the linguistic, the mathematical, the physical, the scientific, the social/political and the technological determine or inform on the nature of the activity and comprise the ways of thinking – through the families of sub-processes that facilitate learning.

THE ROLE OF THE TEACHER IN DESIGN AND TECHNOLOGY

Teaching is a complex human endeavour. There is massive evidence to support the fact that for effective learning to occur, 'the teacher's role is central and crucial' (Kelly 1990, p. 103). It is the teacher, through the application of professional knowledge, skills and judgement, who translates educational goals and transforms them into effective learning programmes, and who identifies and understands how to meet individual learning needs in the classroom.

For many years the role of the teacher in design and technology has been somewhat ambiguous. This problem is reflected in the difficulties associated with assessing performance wherein it is often recognized that the teacher has had a considerable, and sometimes significant, influence on the learning processes and outcomes. This sits uncomfortably with one of the main aims of the activity which is the development of autonomy: the capacity to have the necessary and sufficiently developed skills and understanding to be able to intervene effectively in the made world to effect change. Our understanding of the role of the teacher in the teaching and learning process has been to perceive his or her function as one that systematically changes, as the experience and capability of the learner develops, from being predominantly that of an instructor, guide and mentor in the early stages of development, to that of a being a facilitator and resource in the more advanced stages.

These functions may reflect the principal activities of the teacher in respect of the general needs of the learner within the process of learning in design and technology at different stages of development. But it is not a complete picture because individual needs will differ according to the task and the pupils' specific capacities and experiences irrespective of their stage of development. This may well require the teacher to adopt any combination of the functions, variously and appropriately, throughout the educative process.

To accommodate the flexibility implied requires the teacher to adopt a specific strategy in his or her relationship with the learner: that of *partnership*. The learning process requires, for it to be effective, that the teacher recognizes and responds to the activity as a *shared experience in learning*. The teaching and learning programme, the environment, and the task, all create the conditions necessary for learning to take place, but it is the crucial role of the teacher with the individual learner, *within* the learning process, that is the key to effective development in design and technology. All too often the teacher distances himself or herself from the learning process, believing that by setting up the learning context and intervening at appropriate points to meet either collective or individual needs effective learning will occur. This strategy does have some positive effects in fostering learning and in securing development. But it would be more effective and productive if the teacher consciously adopted the role of being a partner with the pupil in the learning activity. This perspective clarifies the role of the teacher in the learning process: he or she is 'a copartner, [and] would, in engaging in the conjoint activity, have the same interest in its accomplishment . . . He [or she] would share their ideas and emotions' (Dewey 1916, p. 13). Dewey believed that 'things gain meaning by being used in a shared experience or a joint action' (op cit. p. 16), and that participation in a shared enterprise enhances 'communication' which is 'a process of sharing experiences till it becomes a common possession' (ibid., p. 9). This concept is important because it recognizes that the process of the shared experience benefits not just the learner in the acquisition of knowledge, understanding and skill, but equally is of benefit to the teacher in revealing highly significant information and understanding about the pupil, and his or her ideas, capabilities and needs.

In design and technology, developing this partnership with the learner would create the conditions conducive to achieving the aims of each learning experience and to building on these cumulatively. The teacher, as a co-partner, would be in tune with the pupil's thoughts and intentions because the nature of a working partnership would enable him or her to have a significant understanding of the individual learning context and its needs in relation to the learner. An important point must be emphasized however. The teacher as a co-partner should not assume the role of a senior partner who takes control of the thinking. The role of the teacher in the partnership will fluctuate in terms of his or her influence on the nature, shape, and direction of development, but he or she should abdicate responsibility for the important 'thinking' that will go on within it. Although it is a truism, it is important that we recognize that the teacher, although involved in the enterprise as a partner, is there to facilitate learning by the learner and not to impose his or her own ideas and reasoning. As a partner, he or she may share in many of the decisions made, and in the thinking that informs them, but he or she should not determine them. The qualities that the teacher holds and is likely to transmit to the learner directly, as and when the need arises, are facilitative: they comprise and provide the necessary information, understanding and skill to enable the learner to identify, generate, develop, understand, appraise and communicate his or her own thinking and intentions. It is the development of the pupil's mind and his or her capacity to operate increasingly more effectively that is at stake, not the imposition of the teacher's own mind and will.

This important understanding about the role of the teacher in the partnership for learning can be exemplified by examining the role that he or she adopts when dealing with issues of *value* that will arise in design and technology activities. Valuing is an important and central feature of capability in this area of experience. The role of the teacher as a partner in the learning process is to facilitate recognition of the need to address issues of value, if they are not apparent to the learner, and then to enable him or her to derive his or her own resolution of them. This requires the teacher not to impose his or her own value system, but to facilitate the learner in helping him or her to recognize and derive his or her own position in relation to the issue(s) concerned. The art of the relationship in partnership with the learner requires the learner to recognize, assimilate and reconcile the issues relevant to the value judgement concerned, and then arrive at a *justified* position in relation to it. And, as mentioned before, this kind of interaction is not of benefit just to the learner. Engagement in the process of valuing with the learner as a co-partner is likely to alter or adjust the disposition of the teacher also.

The adoption of an effective partnership role as a principle in teaching and learning would accommodate other educational concerns. Differentiated learning needs would be more effectively recognized and catered for. Equality of provision and equality of opportunity for learning would be promoted. The efficacy of mixed-ability teaching would be enhanced. And assessment – both formative with regard to the pupil and evaluative in respect of the programme – would be improved. The adoption and development of the concept of partnership in teaching and learning would, I believe, constitute a significant advance both in the efficacy of the professional activities of the teacher, and in the fulfilment of the learning capabilities and potential of pupil. It denotes a further strand concerning the principles that should underpin the teacher's translation and interpretation of design and technology as an area of experience.

TOWARD A MORE DEVELOPED VIEW OF DESIGN AND TECHNOLOGY

Earlier in this chapter I claimed that many of the models purporting to represent the process of design and technology were in fact inappropriate and even damaging to the understandings they promote and to the curriculum practice that results from this. In this section I would like to examine one model that I believe did offer the beginning of a more conceptually appropriate view, but which needs developing further if it is to be of greater benefit to our understanding and practice. The model, first outlined by the Assessment of Performance Unit (APU) Design and Technology research team in their publication *Design and Technology Activity: A Framework for Assessment* (APU 1987), is consistent with the views that I am offering about design and technology in that it concerns the *'interaction between thought and action'* (p. 14).

The model describes the interaction between thought and action as the relationship between 'imaging and modelling activities inside the head' and 'handling tools and manipulating materials to confront the reality of design proposals' outside the head (ibid.). The concept had evolved from the ideas of Kosslyn's (1979) 'temporary spatial displays', Archer's (1980) concept of our ability to think visually 'in the mind's eye', and the human capacity to make these internal constructs (images and models) public. Importantly, these capacities – the ability to image and model in the mind's eye and the facility to express these thoughts in the real world – were seen not as being related in a simple, linear and sequential way, in which you 'think' and then 'act', but, were perceived as 'an interactive cycle of thought and action' (APU 1987, p. 14). Thus, the model portrays how the interaction between thought and action develops the learner's thinking 'through ever deeper levels of engagement with reality' (ibid., p. 13).

As a first step in developing our thinking about the relationship between the mind and hand, in a learning context, this is helpful. The research team realized, however, that there was a problem in 'defining' the concept at a time when understanding about such educational processes were still evolving because it could 'become a straitjacket' (SEAC 1991, p. 14). The model portrayed in the final report of the research (Figure 4.4) illustrating the interaction the mind and hand had evolved from the original in two important ways: the 'to-ing' and 'fro-ing' of the interaction between the mind and the hand increases in depth intellectually, and by way of the degree of engagement with reality, as pupils progress through the learning process; and there has been a significant development in understanding about the nature of this interaction, indicated by the change from the concept of 'thought *and* action' (APU 1987) to that of 'thought *in* action' (SEAC 1991).

The point I would like to make is that this model represents an *emerging understanding*, which, although far more valuable than what had preceded it, was nonetheless only a building block in the development of our thinking about the nature of the complex relationship between the mind and hand in learning. In my view, the strengths of the concept of learning and development presented in this work are contained in the notion of

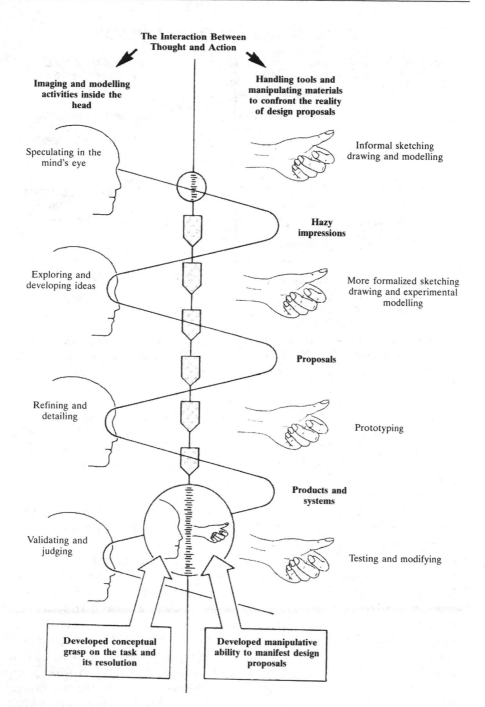

The Interaction Between Thought and Action

Imaging and modelling activities inside the head

Handling tools and manipulating materials to confront the reality of design proposals

Speculating in the mind's eye

Informal sketching drawing and modelling

Hazy impressions

Exploring and developing ideas

More formalized sketching drawing and experimental modelling

Proposals

Refining and detailing

Prototyping

Products and systems

Validating and judging

Testing and modifying

Developed conceptual grasp on the task and its resolution

Developed manipulative ability to manifest design proposals

Figure 4.3

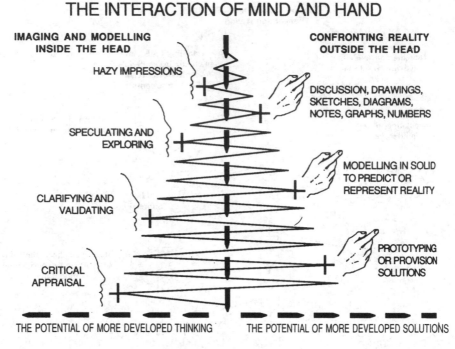

Figure 4.4

thought in action and in the consequences of this for learning and development through engagement in an *active and reflective experiential activity*. Both of these issues require further analysis and development because they are central to the concept of design and technology as an area of experience. We will return to them. But, before this, we need to examine the weaknesses of the model being considered. These, in the main, concern the *process* as it is described and illustrated, which does little to contradict the message of preceding models. Although the dilemma of explaining what is essentially an organic activity in a mechanistic way is recognized and addressed, it is not resolved. And, although the model proposed is concerned principally with the interaction between the mind and hand in learning in an active and reflective experiential activity, it *re-inforces* (albeit unintentionally) our understanding of the activity as one that systematically develops learning through a process that starts with the more abstract forms of representation (through drawings, sketches, diagrams, graphs, numbers), and which progresses by engaging the learner increasingly in more concrete forms of representation (through modelling in solid form before prototyping). In other words, it comprises a sequential and linear activity that begins in the abstract, symbolic world and develops to confront ideas in the concrete, 'real' world.

The implication that design and technology as an educational activity is driven initially by an intellectual, abstract process is somewhat topsy turvy to the more generally accepted view of learning in which a stage of 'formal operations' (handling ideas conceptually) follows that of 'concrete operations' (Piaget, in Kelly 1989, p. 95). The process illustrated in the model may be *a* way of working – and of learning – in design and technology, but it is not necessarily *the* way of working and, more importantly, of learning. Alternatively, it may be that it represents a way of demonstrating competence and capability in design and technology activities for the purpose of assessment. This does not mean, however, that it should be construed as the way, necessarily, of achieving design and technology capability, nor should it be considered as the most appropriate or effective way of developing contributory competences and capabilities therein.

Nevertheless, although pointing to what I see as weaknesses in translating the model as it stands into curriculum practice, the representation of thoughts and ideas in making them public, the intellectual activities that accompany such manifestations, and the families of processes that are engaged in so doing, are important aspects of teaching and learning in design and technology. My concern about much current practice is to do with how we understand, interpret and translate the processes embedded in this area of experience into effective curriculum programmes. And it is to our understanding of these that we must now turn.

THOUGHT IN ACTION

At the beginning of this chapter we began to explore the nature of design and technology as an educational activity. The formidable capacity of the mind and hand to act in concert was identified as a crucial component both of capability and the achievement of capability in this area of experience.

The conceptual shift evident in the research stance at the Assessment of Performance Unit (APU 1987; SEAC 1991) in describing the relationship between thought and action in design and technological processes – expressed initially as 'thought *and* action', and then subsequently as 'thought *in* action' – represents a significant development in understanding the nature of the relationship. The concept of thought and action suggests, literally, 'to think and then to act'. Perfectly reasonable. I think I will put my shoes on in order to go outside. I put my shoes on. Cognitive activity has identified a suitable response to a need which is then met by a sequential act – thought followed by action. But let us consider this again. I begin putting my shoes on when I notice that one of the laces is badly frayed. This provokes me to consider whether or not I should risk wearing them or take alternative action, such as selecting an alternative pair because it seems an easier option than fitting new laces. And I'd forgotten that this pair of shoes is uncomfortable. I wonder at this point whether or not I really need shoes after all and decide that I do because it is wet outside and that the decision to wear shoes in the first place had been determined partially by this. But I'm only going into the garden. Wellingtons would be fine. In fact wellingtons are . . . and so on. My point in describing something so inconsequential is to illustrate two points:

- First, that we do have a well-developed facility to engage in cognitive decision-making processes and then to act upon the outcomes. This feature of our capabilities is an important aspect of the place of cognitive decision-making determining action in design and technology. The relationship between thought and action is *sequential* in this respect.
- Second, the act described was determined by cognitive activity before the event, but, once engaged in, the act itself provoked further intellectual activity through *reflection* in the form of identifying needs, raising further issues, reconsidering the initial proposal and evaluating the reasoning in its regard, proposing solutions, considering alternatives, making decisions, etc. In short, predetermined actions in the real world provoked further intellectual activity that developed my original thoughts. This was *consequent upon the action itself* and provoked through reflection a more detailed analysis and consideration of the original situation. Further, it revealed issues for consideration that had not perhaps been recognized by the original cognitive analysis to determine the criteria for taking the action in the first place. The nature of the concrete experience provoked further, and perhaps deeper, thought. The relationship between thought and action is *interactive* and *reflective* in this respect.

The above example is intended to illustrate some of the potential in the relationship between the mind and hand through 'the interactive cycle of thought and action' (APU 1987, p. 14). I hope that it serves to highlight two of the features about the relationship between thinking and doing that are important to the nature of design and technology as an area of experience, namely, that thought can determine action, but equally, that action will evoke thought.

But the relationship between thought and action is more sophisticated even than this. In trying to express thoughts and ideas, as I am doing as I write this chapter, the operations described above pertain. I have made a decision about the issue l am attempting to communicate – to write about the relationship between thought and action. The act of writing down my thoughts, however, provokes me to reconsider not just what I want to say, and how exactly to express it, but to consider other possible issues for inclusion. So, the act is contributing by developing the thinking further through a cycle of action and reflection. It is *recursive* in this respect. But the relationship between the act of thinking and writing is even more dramatic because the *act* of getting my thoughts out by writing them *down* is contributing to that thinking *as I try to give it form*. When trying to give substance to my thoughts a dynamic fusion occurs at the point at which the thought is taking a manifest form. I can, perhaps, best describe it is a process of 'melding'. It is a consequence of the effect of thinking on the act itself, and yet, at one and the same time, it is the effect of the act on the thinking itself.

In the context of design and technology, this concept of thought in action is often concerned with the interaction of cognitive ideas with concrete, empirical form – sometimes graphic, sometimes solid – in a developmental model of education. Combined with the two other functions of the interaction between thought and action, it results in what I have described as 'the formidable interaction between the mind and the hand acting in concert'. In a coherent programme of development it would be utilized to develop capabilities progressively from that of more 'concrete operations' toward that of a more 'formal operations' stage. We will consider this in due course but initially let us look at the way in which the various functions of the interaction between the mind and hand work by considering a specific situation.

A pupil engaged in a technological task has determined – based on her experience, imagination and reason – that subjecting a material to a bending force will achieve the results she wants. In selecting the material to use she determines – based on her understanding of the properties of materials and aesthetic judgements about them in the context of the task – that a particular material of a specific size will achieve her purpose. As she is in the process of translating this into empirical reality – by confronting her reasoning with the empirical consequences – her thinking is further developed by engagement in the act itself: the material unexpectedly twists and deforms slightly. Her mind is spurred into further cognitive activity in seeking to understand the effect and to accommodate it within her conceptual scheme as she is attempting to realize her intentions. This is followed, perhaps, by a more systematic reflection on the event and could be accompanied by empirical investigation to determine a better understanding. The important issue is that the process of confronting her ideas with the 'real world' consequences provided direct insight into the properties of material. This information was received in visual and tactile form at the point when intellectual intent and empirical consequence met, and resulted in learning *at that moment in time*.

This example illustrates the main features of the interaction: thought determining action (sequential); action informing thought (reflection); and the effect of thought meeting consequence (melding). Consequent on this, a number of other issues need to be considered further: the role that the senses play in this process; the relationship between the rational, imaginative and affective domains; the implication that experiential learning is cognitively led; and the way in which experiential learning can be struc-

The Mind

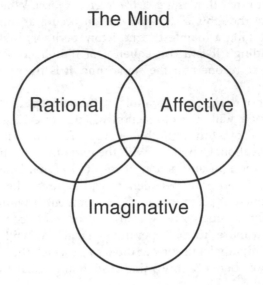

Figure 4.5

tured into design and technological activities and programmes.

The senses provide the means by which the intellectual world receives its information from the empirical world. However, 'which particular qualities the organism chooses to attend to and how he decides to respond are not completely influenced by the qualities themselves' (Eisner 1982, p. 33). The mind provides the vehicle by which we perceive and make sense of the physical world. But the mind exists in not just a rational state. It has the capacity to determine not just the logical or rational connection between things and to place this within a developing conceptual scheme, but also to value this connection for itself, and/or, against other 'understandings': to develop a perspective of 'feeling' in relation to it. Further, the mind has the capacity to translate and transform through the imagination what it perceives and to 'visualize' (op. cit., p. 31) this in ways that help develop understanding (i.e. through models) or in ways that construct potentially new meanings or arrangements (i.e. new designs, alternative futures). As Eisner (op. cit., p. 42) puts it, 'With visualization, complex relationships can be examined, the load on memory reduced, and forms of conceptual manipulation are made possible that would be very cumbersome if a linear, temporal mode of thought needed to be used'.

Much of my argument so far may have implied that the nature of this activity is cognitively driven (cognitive in the broader sense discussed). This is not the case necessarily. It can be our interaction with the environment and its effects on ourselves and/or others that leads us to develop our thinking in a design and technological way. Utilizing the capacity to engage thinking and development through this interaction with the environment is another feature of design and technology as an area of experience. We will consider this further when we examine the way in which thought in action might translate into the kinds of curriculum experience we design for our pupils.

DESIGN AND TECHNOLOGY: THE FAMILIES OF SUB-PROCESSES

There is, in my view, no single, discrete way of working in design and technology; the activities undertaken can be many and varied. There is, however, a coherent and recognizable format to these activities. The adoption of any single strategy for learning – similar to the one illustrated earlier as a common view of 'the design and technology process' – will inhibit or negate the potential of design and technology activities, and in consequence, the learning opportunities for pupils. The solutions are professional solutions, designed to meet specific teaching and learning goals.

The design and technology process is a process of sub-processes. The utilization of these sub-processes will be determined by the educational purpose(s) planned, the nature of the task, and the pupil's individual capabilities and response(s) to that task. Design and technology tasks should combine progressively both concrete and formal modes of thinking. They should seek to combine also, the physiological, the empirical, the rational and the affective, with the imaginative, in experiential learning situations. These situations should require pupils to work through active and reflective processes that utilize the capacity of the mind and hand to work in concert to achieve learning. The activities within, or composing, each task will vary according to the combination of factors described above, but they should involve pupils' developing capabilities in the following families of processes:

- creative activities of the imagination
- expressive activities through various 'modes of representation' (Eisner 1982)
- investigative activities
- evaluative activities.

Each family describes the purpose of the processes undertaken within and throughout design and technology activities. And each family comprises a category of activities that contain a wide variety of sub-processes. Each of these are concerned with achieving a particular goal but the underpinning purpose of the specific activity undertaken is driven by the nature of the family category concerned.

For example, if we take the family of 'evaluative activities', we can identify a variety of sub-processes that might comprise it. These can be categorized and described in various ways, but, they are all concerned with *making judgements*. These might be qualitative procedures, or quantitative

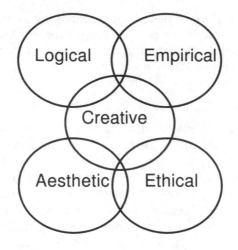

Figure 4.6

procedures, or both. They could be concerned with judgements about fact, or about opinion, or both. They can be concerned with ways of working. They could be moral, ethical, aesthetic or technical. What will determine their nature, form and degree in a design and technology task or sub-task, however, is the nature of the task itself and the pupil's individual response within the constraints or requirements of the learning environment. Similarly, creative, investigative and expressive activities can be described in terms of the types of sub-processes and concerns that comprise them. The important point here, however, concerns how they are determined in a design and technology task: they are decided appropriately by reasoning processes.

Reasoning comprises a family of processes that I have omitted from the list above. This is because it concerns the fundamental processes that learners should be engaged with and in throughout the approach to learning outlined here. It is reasoning which underpins and determines learning and development in all of the tasks and sub-tasks that constitute design and technology as an educational activity. In all aspects of their work pupils must be encouraged to reason in various ways to determine the nature and form of the processes needed to resolve the task being undertaken. By reason the pupil will determine what to do, where to do it, how it can be done, when it is needed, and why. He or she will do this by engaging in *ways of thinking* appropriate to the situation in hand. This can take the form, in any combination of thinking *logically, empirically, creatively, aesthetically,* and/or *ethically.*

Let us consider this further. The process of design and technology will involve pupils undertaking a complex of sub-tasks in order to develop understandings that will contribute to the resolution of a larger task. The nature, form and function of the sub-tasks will then be determined by the parameters of the task and the pupils' perception and interpretation of it (guided within the partnership of learning) through reasoning processes. The tasks they undertake will be concerned with *creative, expressive, investigative* and *evaluative* processes (Figure 4.7) determined by logical, empirical, ethical, aesthetic and creative concerns. These will be combined and integrated into a whole process to resolve a task and achieve learning and development.

For example, by reasoning in a logical way a pupil identifies that she needs to know how concrete will react to acrylic paints – this identifies the sub-task that will be involved: an investigation. The *nature and form* of this sub-task will be dictated by its specific purpose (reasoned by the pupil in relation to task need). She has in the event determined to do this empirically by designing experiments to investigate the absorbency and adherence characteristics of concrete when applied with acrylic paint and subjected to different environmental conditions. The achievement of this will require the pupil to think in a specific way, or combination of ways. And so, by reason she has determined both the nature and form of the activity necessary to her task, and consequently, the ways in which she will have to think in order to achieve her purpose – mathematically and scientifically (logically and empirically).

When she carries out the experiments she will need again to consider

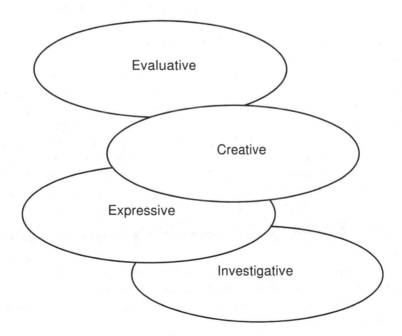

Figure 4.7

and evaluate the results. This will again require her to employ her reason in comprehending and utilizing the results of this sub-task in the context of the whole task. This will involve the employment of a variety of intellectual and expressive processes in order to achieve the desired purpose. This might include acts as varied as *transforming, translating, integrating, discriminating, manipulating, abstracting, composing, modelling,* and *optimizing.* The form that any one of these might take in any situation, however, will vary. The same process – for example, 'transforming' – will take on different forms according to the purpose and nature of the activity. It could be that the transforming activity concerns turning images in the mind's eye into representations on paper. It could be that it involves converting values calculated in number into components in a circuit.

As before, the important issue here is to do with the *principle* that should underpin the design of a curriculum programme or task in design and technology: namely that design and technology processes require reasoning to be at the heart of their operation, and that reasoning activities are dependent upon their purpose within the learning context.

Exactly how these processes and sub-processes come together in a design and technology activity might best be described, perhaps, by analogy. When walking along Porthmeor beach in St Ives, Cornwall recently, it seemed to me that the behaviour I was displaying in negotiating a route from Clodgy Point to 'The Island' might be appropriate to describe the processes and the reasoning determining technology activities. But in part only.

The tide had turned from full, leaving the foreshore newly washed. The small family group I was in shared a common purpose: to walk to the island. A few solitary walkers had preceded us, evidenced from footprints in the wet sand. What I found interesting was that they had followed a fairly common path through the rocks, around the rock pools, and over the tracts of sand toward the same goal as ourselves. And we, in the main, were following the same path. However, although the routes headed in the same direction with a discernible common pattern in the route chosen by most, there was also variation and occasional deviation from this norm. On reflection, I was aware that the route that I was taking was not simply that of following the 'path' before me but that I was in fact involved in fairly sophisticated mental activity in choosing my own path within the confines of being also in a party. We were well fed and not tired, fit and on holiday. There were no major biological needs driving us simply to reach the island as the only expediency. The tide had turned and we were not in danger of being stranded by an incoming tide. It was a fine day early in the year, windy but not unduly cold. There was plenty of daylight left. We could enjoy the journey.

Some of these things I had assimilated consciously and others unconsciously but they are important to the analogy because they affected my disposition about the walk. Had any or all of them been different the route I would have chosen would have been influenced accordingly. The conditions for the walk were, in this case, satisfactory and the journey itself, as an experience, was as important if not more important than arriving at the final destination. In choosing the path I was to follow I found myself continuously monitoring and evaluating information, concerns and thoughts, and, through a process of synthesis and reasoning, making short and long term decisions about my route. Information was sorted, interrogated, valued against experience, need, knowledge, desire and purpose, and assimilated for use in making decisions about the route I would follow. This continuous process was flexible to my short term intentions, sympathetic to the conditions that prevailed or might result, and set within the context of my longer term goal. I found myself following a route particular to myself within the framework of a common pattern of development. And my family, independently, did likewise.

The analogy may be weak in many respects in relation to the process of design and technology in the curriculum. But the reason that I offer it is to highlight the nature of decision-making and decision-taking processes in the short and longer term. Achieving my ultimate goal – in the form of a destination – was secondary to the experience of getting there. It did, however, provide me with a purpose and a direction. The conditions prevailing were sufficient to facilitate the need not to attend to other more pressing concerns, and there was a 'path' of sorts before me. My own interests were somewhat countered by the need to consider the individual wishes of the members of my own party, but in the main, gave me some freedom of choice. Some of the decisions I took were expedient, others more indulgent, some fruitful, others exasperating. But the process throughout was dynamic, continuous and flexible to the situation as a whole. I explored, experimented, took risks, experienced frustration and pleasure alike. Within the context of the purposes of the walk as a whole experience, the mental processes I engaged in were determined by my own will tempered by the needs of others and the overall intention of getting to the island. But, within this, I undertook creative, expressive, investigative and evaluative activities as and when appropriate. And for me, this describes, in some degree, the way in which processes are determined and combined in technology activities: determination through reason.

THOUGHT IN ACTION: TWO MODELS FOR COMPARISON

The final part of this chapter will compare and contrast the practice commonly found in many secondary schools with an alternative approach reflecting the issues previously addressed.

The first model typifies much of the current practice in design and technology education. The learner is engaged in a staged prescriptive process that begins with a task being set for the learner or identified by him or

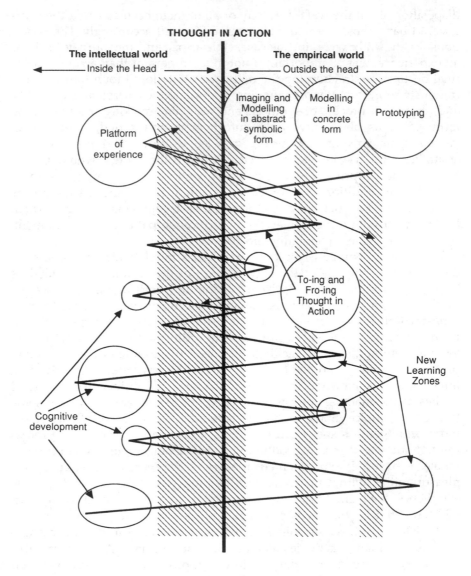

Figure 4.8

her. The first stage often requires them to draw up a 'specification' and to do 'research'; throughout this stage ideas are left to fester in their minds and their understanding of the task and its needs remains in the abstract and intellectual world. There then follows the second phase of 'designing' when the pupils are commonly required to design 'three alternative solutions' (sometimes more!) and then to choose and develop one idea. The final activity of the designing phase usually requires the production of a working drawing of the product 'designed', a cutting list of the materials/components needed to make or model it, and a plan of manufacture for its realization. The third stage is the actual realization of the design followed by evaluation of the finished product. The whole process undertaken is often recorded in a design folio but in many cases these contain only 'pretty nonsense' (Ive 1997).

In my view the interpretation of this as a process of design and technology leaves much to be desired. It works to a prescribed pattern of behaviour, with a rigid series of process stages, unsatisfactory products, and limited learning opportunities and outcomes. It involves pupils in little procedural reasoning and denies the flexibility to respond to the needs of the task and the designer's interpretation of it. It requires pupils to work in a procedural straitjacket that bears little relationship to design and technological capability. It works from the abstract and symbolic to the real and concrete, negating the opportunity to learn through engagement with the task from the outset. It depicts the activity as cognitively led and separates 'designing' from 'making' (when the making of models and prototypes is inherently part of the designing process). It is of strictly limited educational value and, unless rejected, could ultimately be the straitjacket that condemns design and technology to the curriculum dustbin.

A contrasting model illustrates the path a pupil might take as he or she worked through a task that involves engagement in a variety of forms of representation and cognitive activity. It also seeks to illustrate the way in which the learner initially engages with a task from within their own platform of experience (APU 1987, p. 18) and which provides a touchstone throughout. Finally it attempts to illustrate that which I see as investing design and technology with such power as a teaching and learning medium, namely its ability as a dynamic, experiential learning methodology to lead pupils into new, relevant and meaningful educational experiences.

CONCLUSIONS

National Curriculum design and technology represents an inadequate understanding of this area of the curriculum. But then again, the National Curriculum itself is an inadequate and unsatisfactory requirement for the current and future educational needs of our children, and our current and future society. The way forward is to review our understanding and practice within the context of a more developed view of educational needs in general and design and technological needs in particular. It depends upon, more than anything else, the understanding of our teachers about their educational goals and the principles that guide the translation of these into curriculum practice. A developmental view of learning, as well as a developmental view of curriculum practice, are the conditions *necessary* for success. The professional interpretation and commitment of our teachers to such an understanding would enable this to be translated into teaching and learning programmes that provided the conditions *sufficient* for success.

5

The Physical: A New Millennium, A New Beginning?

Dave Boorman

Most of us will remember our first experiences of 'PE' with emotions that vary from affection to shame-faced loathing, depending on the quality of that experience and our individual reaction to it. Thus, whether that first taste of the subject at school was swimming or games or dance or any other of the six areas now enshrined in the National Curriculum, we will have reacted not just physically but cognitively and emotionally as well. The point here is that although physical education has almost totally concentrated upon delivering a body of subject knowledge and skills, usually carefully prescribed in advance, the actual reaction of the individuals in receipt of this kind of programme is rarely, if ever, evaluated. As teachers, however, we know from experience that there is a multiplicity of responses to the provisions made. This is graphically illustrated by Harlen (1980, p. 60) who indicates that 'an obvious example of this is in children's reactions to swimming classes at school; generally reactions range from over enthusiasm to cowering resistance'.

But observations like this have done nothing to deter the curriculum planners in physical education from demanding the teaching of a balanced, planned core of subject material. It is, and indeed has been, the case throughout most of this century that physical educationalists have advocated or demanded the now legally enforced policy of 'same for all'. In effect, there has been an ongoing demand for a return to the good old days between 1904 and 1933 when the Board of Education issued detailed syllabi that were intended to provide uniformity of provision. Although the pattern of teaching the gymnastics, games, dance, and swimming established by these syllabi remained largely in place in the post war period, the increasing perception that PE was being badly taught gave rise to demands for the re-imposition of a standard curriculum (Whitaker 1984; Jones M. 1984). Initially, physical educationalists sought to encourage this by pressurizing primary teachers to follow the voluntary guidelines that were introduced by most Local Education Authorities during the 1970s. The lack of compulsion, however, and the perceived inadequacies of primary teachers were blamed for continued low standards of teaching (Mawer and Sleap 1984). This produced increasingly strident demands for the imposition of a standard, core, physical education curriculum long before the implementation of the present National Curriculum. Thus, although the basic content and teaching methods used in physical education have remained largely unchanged for the past thirty or more years, it seems to be generally accepted that a lack of teacher commitment combined with poor training are the main reasons for ineffective teaching.

The net result of this has been that although many people have school experiences of physical education which provide the entrance to a lifetime passion for physical activities of all types, these same experiences for others generate an ongoing aversion to anything remotely physical. In between these two extremes are a multitude of people whose experiences have given rise to a loathing for one activity and delight in another. Furthermore, although some activities have been derived from the formal education system, others have come from experiences or interests developed totally outside the parameters of a school curriculum.

The solution to this problem for most physical educationalists is to seek the imposition of a standardized programme of activities for all and ensure that it is properly taught. Thus, the present National Curriculum has been widely welcomed on the grounds that it will at least go some way to ensuring uniformity of provision for all. It is a policy which seems doomed to fail many pupils in that, no matter how effectively a subject is taught, we can never predict that it will generate the desired reaction. A standardized programme will never cater for all needs and interests and some pupils will inevitably be alienated by their experiences.

As adults, we make choices about our activities that are founded upon previous knowledge, past experiences or sometimes a simple desire to explore the unknown. People often take up a new activity sometimes quite late in life and discover a talent or enthusiasm for a particular physical activity previously unknown. At fifty, or even older, people who would regard themselves as totally non-sporting take up activities like skiing or jogging and find themselves captivated by all that these experiences provide. Eighty year olds have been known to undertake parachute jumps and discover the thrill of a lifetime. My point is that none of us really knows what will provide us with the key to enjoying physical activity and it is only through a process of trial and error that we find out what motivates us to participate. For some, it is the physical, emotional and even intellectual challenge provided by competitive sport in one or several of its many forms; for others, it is the opportunity for creativity and self expression afforded by some forms of dance. Yet others find satisfaction from the sense of well-being derived from arduous fitness training by whatever method or methods they enjoy most. For others still, the sheer exhilaration, excitement and speed of surfing the face of a huge wave is what offers the ultimate physical and emotional experience. In other words, as adults we acknowledge and take pleasure in our differences as individuals.

To elaborate on this a little, individual experience varies not just between various facets of physical education like games and dance but even within them. Hence, for some, the skill and speed of hockey is the ultimate sporting sensation; for others, it is the power and physical challenge of rugby. We can love ballet and loathe the kind of modern, creative, so called educational forms of dance usually taught in school. We may even enjoy some aspects of gymnastics but dislike others. Each and every physical activity, from snooker to downhill skiing, offers opportunities for a wealth of experiences that are not only physical; they are emotional and social as well. The actual experience itself is also unique to the day and the individual. Thus, for some, that first game of golf may generate a lifetime enthusiasm whilst, for others, it may seem a boring and pointless waste of time.

A further dimension to this theme is that many of the physical activities that people enjoy and gain great physical and emotional satisfaction from taking part in are not even part of that which is held to be the physical education curriculum. Walking is one such activity, gardening another; and both provide a wealth of opportunities for experiences which are not only physical, but emotional and intellectual as well. Similarly, although it is rare for classical forms of dance like ballet to be taught in school, or activities like 'twirling', which would probably be regarded as having little educational value, these and many others capture the imagination and enthusiasm of large numbers of people. Children who find little satisfaction or enjoyment in the activities they are compelled to undertake at school often become passionately committed to activities like fishing that can find no place in the school curriculum.

It would be rare for most teachers when evaluating children's development and performance in physical education to take account of the depth and breadth of the activities engaged in by children outside school. Yet, activities undertaken in the playground, or the street or elsewhere after school, or at weekends, are all part of children's overall physical experience. Even accepting that the majority of children in this modern era of television are more sedentary than their predecessors (Armstrong 1984), nevertheless physical activity to a greater or lesser extent is still part of their everyday experience. How much or how little is seemingly irrelevant to schools who provide the same programme for all children whether a child concerned is undertaking swimming training six days a week as a budding international or does nothing active at all outside school.

In view of the diversity of experiences that physical activities in all of their guises have to offer, it seems strange that there is such a strong emphasis upon the provision of a standardized curriculum. It is patently obvious, as I have endeavoured to indicate, that the kinds of universal inflexible programmes advocated by the current National Curriculum inevitably fail to cater for the needs or interests of many individuals, let alone respond to the multitude of different reactions that result from each and every experience. So why do we persist?

One possible explanation for the inherent resistance to change evident in physical education may be found in a brief examination of its genesis as a part of the school curriculum. The initial impression is that the subject, like Topsy, 'just growed' but this does little justice to all those people who, over the years, have fought so passionately to extol the virtues of physical education and enhance its status as a school subject. Nevertheless, development has the appearance of a somewhat haphazard and arbitrary evolution into the present six areas of gymnastics, games, athletics, dance, swimming, and outdoor activities.

Amongst the more important factors that have contributed to these activities being identified as the subject was the undeniable nineteenth century desire to impose discipline upon the potentially threatening urban poor. This led first to the introduction of military drill and then gymnastic exercises into the elementary schools. According to McIntosh (1968), the latter was promoted not just in order to gentle the masses, it was also seen as a means through which to raise standards of health and fitness for military reasons and to ensure the availability of a strong and healthy workforce. Similar reasons are often cited for the introduction of swimming as and where swimming pools became available. Significantly, discipline and control are still fundamental aspects of teaching the subject, although this is now ostensibly for reasons of safety.

Games, including athletics, derived from nineteenth century public schools and are said to imbue the values of competition, elitism, and individualism that are associated with the British upper classes in the age of *laissez faire* capitalism. Their popularity, first in the public schools and universities, and then in society as a whole, gradually led to their inclusion in the state educational system. Educationally, this was supported by the widely held views that such activities encouraged the development of such things as fair play, adherence to the rules and team spirit in addition to qualities of leadership and higher moral standards. Similar arguments regarding character building and team work were mounted in support of outdoor activities as an aspect of the physical education curriculum as these activities became popular and available to schools.

Finally, dance has traditionally been a part of our culture and has been part of the culture of the school since the early 1900s. Initially, this took the form of folk dance but since the second world war this has been increasingly replaced by 'modern' creative or expressive dance which is generally assumed to be more educational in that it provides for cognitive, aesthetic and emotional development in addition to pure physical skill.

These six areas then gradually emerged, or were promoted, as the 'subject' during the first part of this century and although teaching methods have changed in order to accommodate the move from 'training' (PT) to the more acceptable 'education' (PE) they have remained stubbornly unchanged. It is true that the content has expanded to embrace for instance a wider range of games and that teaching methods have altered in line with changing attitudes to education and a desire to be more 'child friendly'. Nevertheless, the basic content and general ethos of the 'subject' has changed little in the ensuing years. The transmission of the basic core of the six areas has remained the *raison d'être* throughout. Furthermore, it is almost universally held in physical education that this is best achieved through the medium of clearly prescribed programmes of study or syllabi. The National Curriculum demands for 'balance', 'continuity' and 'progression' simply reinforce the long standing view that this is the only way of ensuring that the subject is effectively delivered to all children. The ethos throughout is one of 'subject' and its transmission by the most effective means available. Traditionally, this has taken the form of an aims and objectives approach, mainly via didactic teaching of the prescribed body of knowledge and skills (Kirk 1988).

Physical education in its present form has been a part of the school curriculum for so long that it is difficult to conceive of it in any other way. As the subject evolved, however, so too a professional caucus of its exponents emerged through the departments of physical education in colleges and universities. This has resulted in an identifiable physical education profession which has become a distinct entity within education as a whole. Within this fraternity is an occupational hierarchy of teachers, lecturers, LEA advisers and HMI inspectors all with a vested interest in retaining and promoting their subject *vis à vis* others. There is within this fraternity a common identity and rationale which is reinforced through professional associations like the Physical Education Association (PEA) and the British Association of Advisers and Lecturers in Physical Education (BAALPE), and through their respective professional journals. The net result of this is that although there have, over the years, been debates and conflicts over teaching methods and strategies through which to advance physical education, there is little if any attempt to question the validity of the basic subject core which remains sacrosanct. Thus, there is an inherent conservatism and resistance to any form of change that may be regarded as potentially threatening to the subject and the vested interests of its professional elite.

One way in which this pattern is reinforced may be seen in the ideology that in order to achieve a degree of physical 'literacy' all children need to be given a basic grounding in the main components of the subject. It is simply accepted as a truism that the physically educated person must have been taught a core of basic knowledge and skills taken from gymnastics, games, athletics, dance, swimming and outdoor pursuits. Just as others (e.g. Peters 1966) have argued that the curriculum as a whole needed to initiate people into an essential core of intrinsically worthwhile activities, so too physical education is assumed to have a core of essential knowledge and skills of intrinsic worth. Effectively, this unquestioned shibboleth provides a convenient justification for maintaining the status quo.

There are various ways in which this mythology of an essential subject core is sustained in physical education. In primary physical education, for instance, the idea of child-centredness seems to have been interpreted in terms of 'need'. This, however, is a term which is very much conditional upon who is making the value judgement about what it is that children 'need': parents, educators or politicians. It is a concept that gives rise to a number of questions regarding for instance the distinction between what a specific individual child needs and the assumptions made regarding what all children need (Blenkin and Kelly 1981, p. 49). Similarly, there may be a fundamental conflict between what is in the child's best interests and what they as individuals are interested in. As Blenkin and Kelly (1988, p. 254) point out:

> It is an enormous fallacy to assume that the same kind of provision will offer truly educational experiences to all children. It is analogous to suggesting that they should all have the same diet or wear the same clothes or pursue the same hobbies.

The above statement reveals most starkly the difference between advocates of child-centred education and physical educationalists' interpretation of that concept. In the latter, it is generally argued that all children need a balanced curriculum comprising of the various core elements of the subject we have already identified and thus the concept of need is simply used in order to justify the maintenance of the existing status quo. It is seemingly assumed that children's needs can only be catered for through the medium of a balanced programme of gymnastics, games (including athletics), dance, swimming and outdoor pursuits. Wetton (1988) for instance, despite arguing that planning should be based upon individual needs, is equally adamant that the teacher should be committed to 'long-term planning' and the formulation of a 'syllabus for physical education'.

Typically, the demand for a preplanned programme takes precedence over individual needs and is so ingrained that everyone seems to accept it without question. Even Plowden (CACE 1967, para. 706) felt constrained to note that 'by the time they are ready to leave the primary school, however, the work and the teaching will be more closely related to specific ends; gymnastics, games, dance, drama and swimming will be the normal elements of a weekly or seasonal programme'. Here, and throughout physical education, the concept of 'need' seems to be generalized into the idea that all children need to be introduced to more or less the same core of activities.

Despite assertions that physical education makes provision for individuals' needs, the extent to which this is true appears to be extremely limited. Instead of a curriculum that constantly changes, and is different for each child as they develop at different rates and in different ways, physical education seems to a large extent to be predetermined by the experts' value judgements regarding the things that all children need for development. Given that the claims made come almost exclusively from subject specialists responsible for planning and promoting physical education, the idea that all children need this essential core of subject knowledge and skills requires a degree of scepticism. In fact, in view of the difference evident between this approach and that of those who genuinely base curriculum planning upon individual children's needs, there seems some doubt whether the things advocated are truly in the best interests of the child or, rather, are more concerned with fostering the interests of the subject.

In physical education the core areas of subject content are almost universally advocated for all children in order to ensure a balanced programme of activities. This assumption seems to follow Lawton's (1981, p. 118) suggestion that 'all children have a right to access to all important areas of experience'. From this perspective it is assumed that the curriculum would be planned so that it would provide all 'those kinds of knowledge skills and experience to which it is assumed all pupils ought to have access (ibid., p. 119). Clearly, this is an approach to curriculum planning that is derived from judgements either about the nature of knowledge or the needs of society upon which it is assumed we can base decisions about what ought to be taught. This approach originates from a very different philosophy of the curriculum than that espoused by advocates of a developmental view of education.

On those few occasions when alternative possibilities for conceptualizing the curriculum have presented themselves the reaction from those in physical education has been to reinterpret these in subject terms. Thus, although it is possible to view the areas of experience outlined by HMI (DES 1977a) in a very general sense and outside the usual subject-based curriculum, it is equally possible to see them in precise subject terms thereby reducing the whole concept of areas of experience to a traditional subject-based notion of curriculum.

In physical education, it is quite clear that the subject specialists' response to the concept of areas of experience is simply to associate them with particular elements of subject content. The supplementary paper produced by PE HMI (DES 1979b, p. 12), for instance, attempts to identify the physical area of experience in terms of the following aims:

- the development of skilful body management
- creating or being involved in artistic experience
- competition between groups or individuals
- body training for strength, stamina, endurance and a general feeling of well being
- meeting challenges in varying environments.

It would be easy to interpret these in very general terms in that any of the five aims outlined could be achieved via experiences in a multitude of different physical activities. Dance or swimming, or indeed any other aspect of physical education, could be used to make provision for any or all of these experiences. This would allow for a much more flexible approach to curriculum planning for physical education than has hitherto been the case. Unfortunately, whatever the intention of PE HMI, many in physical education were quick to point out that the first two are obviously intended to refer to gymnastics and dance and the others may equally be identified in terms of games, athletics, swimming and outdoor pursuits. Similarly, the reference to 'body training' undoubtedly reflects the concerns of the time for 'health related fitness' as a cross-curricular theme within the subject. Significantly, PE HMI go on to illustrate ways in which the various aspects of the subject in themselves 'encompass areas of experience beyond that of the purely physical' (op. cit., pp. 11–13). Not surprisingly, it is argued that dance provides aesthetic/creative experiences and games social and ethical ones but they also go on to cite many other ways in which these and other aspects of the subject contribute to the 'scientific' or the 'mathematical' areas of experience.

The whole document provides a neat legitimation for the six aspects of physical education, and negates any attempt to see curriculum planning in anything other than subject terms. In essence the 'physical area of experience' has been reinterpreted in terms of a common core of physical activities or skills to be presented to all children through the medium of a preplanned programme to ensure that all receive their 'entitlement'. This illustrates how the attempt to include 'the physical' in the developmental approach to education is subverted by subject considerations. The physical education specialists' desire to safeguard or promote the subject seemingly results in the interpretation of all new initiatives in subject terms. In this case the attempted break with the subject-based curriculum by HMI (DES 1977a) is quickly reformulated by PE HMI (DES 1979b) and the 'areas of experience' are used as yet another means of promulgating physical education as a 'subject'.

Parry (1988), in noting the way in which the areas of experience as interpreted by the PE HMI may be identified in purely subject terms, goes further in rejecting the concept of 'areas of experience'. For him, it is simply a woolly idea which potentially waters down the subject's identity because it opens physical education up to areas not traditionally part of the subject. This, he argues, threatens the subject's role as a clearly identifiable part of the school curriculum. The whole debate is a clear indication of the confusion in physical education in that there is a fundamental dichotomy between the ideas inherent in the original intention of the 'areas of experience' as expressed by HMI (DES 1977a) and the interpretation subsequently placed upon them by those in physical education and other subjects. As originally conceived, the areas of experience offer at least the potential of a curriculum unfettered by narrow subject considerations and permit planning based upon individual children's needs.

It seems clear, however, from the reaction of Parry (1989) and others that any attempt to either broaden or reduce the basic parameters of physical education is immediately perceived as a threat to the subject and its status as a discrete aspect of the curriculum. Thus, the attempts by some within the dance fraternity to extract dance from the physical education curriculum and relocate it as part of the arguably higher status expressive arts were fiercely resisted by the majority of physical educationalists. From this perspective, the reaction to the idea of a curriculum based upon the eight areas of experience identified by HMI in *Curriculum 11-16* (1977a) is typical of the desire within physical education to retain its territorial purity and integrity. In effect, the concept of 'need', similar considerations of 'entitlement', and even the 'areas of experience', seem to be used by physical educationalists to justify a core subject.

Another example of this tendency is that of Almond (1984) who offers his own reinterpretation of the 'areas of experience' as an entitlement curriculum for all children in primary schools. In brief, he argues that a group of 'core experiences provide us with principles for selecting what we might include in the physical education curriculum [and] as a result, there is more likelihood that we can achieve balance, continuity and coherence' (op. cit., p. 9). The experiences he identifies – body management; games; outdoor living and learning/adventure challenges; artistic; aesthetic – in fact seem little different from those cited by PE HMI (DES 1979b) and thus may be regarded as yet another convenient argument for continuing to impose the traditional aspects of the subject.

The temptation to reinterpret concepts like the areas of experience in subject terms seen in both PE HMI (DES 1979b) and Almond (1984) is even more starkly revealed in the claim made by the authors of Dance (Staffordshire C. C. Education Committee, 1985, p. 9) that 'dance has perhaps a unique contribution to make to the eight essential "Areas of Experience" as defined by HMI'. In this document it is argued that although 'clearly dance makes its major contribution to the aesthetic, creative and the physical areas concepts and ideas in the other areas can also be explored' (ibid.). This is illustrated by showing how dance explores 'mathematical concepts of spatial awareness' or 'scientific concepts of balance' (ibid.). Similarly, it is argued that a dance theme like 'Fire' can contribute to other areas of experience like the social/political – 'History: the Gunpowder Plot' – and the spiritual – 'Religious Education: Moses and the Burning Bush' (op. cit., pp. 9–10).

These extravagant claims, and the artificiality of some of the cross-curricular linkages cited, once again highlight the problems of planning a curriculum on the basis of criteria like the 'areas of experience'. In order to justify a place on the curriculum, subject areas like dance immediately endeavour to show how they might contribute to all of the criteria. In fact, dance is by no means unique as a subject area in being able to claim a contribution to the eight areas. Gymnastics might, music might, design and technology might, as might many other discrete subject areas. Thus, there seem to be no good reasons why dance any more than any other subject can argue that it has a special right to be included in the curriculum.

Nevertheless, the claims for dance once again reveal the preoccupation of those within physical education to justify their place on the curriculum, no matter the basis upon which it is made. This is illustrated by the claim that:

> included as a subject of study in its own right, dance can develop a child's aesthetic awareness, creativity and skilful use of the body. It can embody the use of language and music as well as stimulating the imagination. It is an art form in its own right and, as such, offers a three stranded activity of creativity, performing and appreciating' (Staffordshire C. C. Education Committee 1985, p. 11).

Although it may be argued that many of the methods advocated for teaching dance or gymnastics or, to some extent, games, can provide opportunities for cognitive and affective – as well as physical – development the whole enterprise is underpinned by subject considerations. Thus it may be argued that dance like other aspects of physical education is really concerned with promoting itself.

If one accepts the basic premise that all children need to have access to common 'areas of experience' this does not in itself prescribe a common curriculum in subject terms because the experiences may actually be obtained in a variety of different ways. There are, for instance, a multitude of ways in physical education for gaining aesthetic experiences other than through dance. Eric Cantona, for example, argues that artistically he has never found 'any difference between the pass from Pele to Carlos in the World Cup in 1970 in Mexico, and the poetry of the young Rimbaud' (quoted in *The Daily Telegraph*, 25.6.1994). Almost certainly, many of Cantona's own following would similarly regard his performances to be infinitely more aesthetically pleasing than those of Rudolph Nureyev. Furthermore, Carr (1979) points out there is no guarantee that exposure to certain experiences like dance or games of themselves lead to the desired outcomes. The ballerina may be a complete Philistine, the games player totally amoral.

Indeed, the whole argument is specious in that it might be suggested that aesthetic experiences are actually much more effectively facilitated by participation in a variety of other activities like art and drama. Thus, from this perspective, there is no need for physical education at all other than its unique contribution to the physical. Conversely, if one accepts the view that dance, in itself, provides for all of the essential areas of experience

(Staffordshire C.C. Education Committee 1985, p.11) one wonders why it is necessary to include anything else in the curriculum.

In practice, similar claims might equally well be made by all of the other curriculum subjects and the net result is that these arguments do little to advance the debate about curriculum content and planning. In effect, the idea of an 'entitlement' curriculum based upon the 'areas of experience' may be used to justify many different activities or subjects. In physical education, as we have seen, the whole concept is simply used as yet another means by which to justify the continuation of the traditional six areas of subject content.

As already indicated, there are inherent problems with this whole approach to physical education as a core of knowledge and skills which need to be transmitted to pupils via a planned programme in order to ensure that they are physically 'literate'. First, it is inevitably inflexible and fails to respond to individual needs. Second, many areas of physical activity are not even considered because they are not regarded as legitimate aspects of the subject. Thus, many children are either alienated by their school experiences or simply fail to find anything that captures their interest or enthusiasm.

The idea that the 'physical' should embrace much more than the traditional activities of physical education will, no doubt, be regarded in some quarters as heresy. Nevertheless, in view of the criticisms outlined in this chapter, I would like to argue that the only way forward is for us to undertake a fundamental reconceptualization of the curriculum not only in terms of content but also with regard to its structure and organization. If we accept the idea of the 'physical' as a valuable area of experience and address the constraints imposed by the subject then it seems to me that there is at least the possibility of making physical activities accessible to all. However, in order to pursue this enterprise it seems important to challenge some of the seemingly unquestioned assumptions that dominate current thinking.

In the first instance, the six areas of physical education are generally justified on the grounds that each is unique not just in terms of providing some particular dimension of physical experience but also because of its particular contribution to other areas of learning. From this perspective, gymnastics provides the development of body management, dance for aesthetic development and games for moral or social development. If this is looked at a little more closely, however, it might be argued that body management or control might just as easily be promoted through dance or yoga or soccer. Similarly, aesthetic development for some might come from gymnastics or from outdoor education or, as Cantona indicates, from some of the undoubtedly beautiful experiences which games provide. And moral, personal or social development might be derived from any of the six areas, or indeed from other activities drawn from outside the school programme. In fact, since teachers rarely if ever check, we simply do not know what the experiences provided actually achieve. Thus, as already indicated, far from promoting the attributes that are usually assumed to accrue from participation in dance the dancer may become a Philistine and the games player experience constant humiliation and/or the development of immoral behaviour. In practice, the educational aims of each of these areas might or might not be attained and there is certainly no guarantee that mere participation in a preplanned programme will in itself ensure the desired outcomes. We cannot even assume that the activities undertaken will enhance physical skills or wellbeing since as we know reluctant children find all kinds of ways to avoid exerting themselves. Sitting out, feigning illness or injury or simply volunteering to play on the wing are all strategies through which to minimize the extent of physical involvement. There seems to be little merit in persisting with a standard preplanned programme if, as suggested here, it fails to achieve its own avowed educational aims with many children.

The argument that everyone needs the same programme is based on the assumption that unless we learn the basic physical skills of gymnastics, games, athletics, dance, swimming and outdoor pursuits whilst at school we will be unable to function as adults. However, although it is probably true that unless we take part in gymnastics whilst of school age we are unlikely to achieve the standards of performance necessary for competition, there seems no other good reason why gymnastics should be essential for all. In fact, only competitive gymnasts really need pure gymnastic skills and for the most part these are usually obtained from gymnastic clubs rather than school. For everyone else such things as flexibility, mobility and general body control might easily be obtained from a multitude of other physical activities. Similarly, dance skills may be derived from any of the different forms of dance including those not taught in the school programme, or even through gymnastics. Arguably, few if any basic physical skills *have* to be taught in school and these might be achieved in a variety of different ways.

A stronger case might be made for games in that they are clearly such a large part of our culture, and many of the basic skills are much more easily learned when young. It seems to be assumed that a progressive development of basic skills followed by a gradual introduction to certain selected games will produce both a love of games and a level of competence that will facilitate continued participation. This assumption remains unproven and I would argue that the present approach of imposing the same games programme upon all pupils alienates as many as it captivates. It is lamentable that for many people their experience of school games has merely produced a hearty dislike of all physical activities. However, it is also clear that many function perfectly well without ever playing games, or successfully take up some new and enjoyable activity after leaving school. If games is an essential experience for school, and I do not believe the case to be entirely proven, then it seems to me that this might be achieved in a multitude of ways. Any programme offered has to be flexible enough to make provision for the individual needs, interests and state of readiness of the pupils involved in a way that the present system patently fails to achieve.

One further argument for a compulsory programme of school physical education is that schools provide the basic raw materials for the nation's sporting talent. The recent moves by government to promote school sport and encourage the identification and nurturing of talent clearly has this in mind. Arguably, it is only the few who aspire to the highest standards who actually require regular involvement in games or sport, and the few who do are probably better served by participation in club activities. Furthermore, even if we disregard the dubious morality of encouraging young children to participate in high level competitive sport, it is difficult to see how the present system actually caters for the physically talented. Gymnasts and swimmers, for instance, are likely to have been involved in their respective sports before entering school and their training will be undertaken in the sports clubs rather than school. For these pupils the compulsory school programme is almost certainly unchallenging and largely irrelevant to their needs. In reality, much sporting talent is identified and nurtured outside school and pupils themselves develop their own sporting interests irrespective of the school programmes.

The case for a compulsory swimming programme on the grounds of safety alone would seem to be the strongest of all. However, in view of Harlen's observation regarding the variability of children's reactions (1980, p. 60), there is a grave danger that the usual standard approach when presented without reference to the needs and state of readiness of the individuals concerned merely results in totally negative experiences. Thus, rather than developing the desired skills and confidence in the water it is possible that the reaction might take the form of a total antipathy towards all forms of water-based activities. Conversely, there seems little point in taking the junior international swimmer for an introductory swimming lesson when they have just finished a two hour pool session prior to school.

My point is, that since the arguments for including all of the various elements of physical education are at best tenuous, a more flexible approach is essential. There seems to be no absolute case for any one particular aspect of the subject to be included on the curriculum let alone all of them. If, however, we view the 'physical' in its entirety as an essential area of experience the possibilities for making provision for the specific needs and interests of individuals are almost endless. Clearly, this would have profound implications for teachers who would need to base curriculum decisions upon a good understanding of children's physical development and state of readiness. They would also need to keep much more detailed records of the totality of children's physical experiences in and out of school and, indeed, of the children's reactions to those experiences.

I should make it clear at this point that I am not making a case for voluntarism nor do I wish to negate the potential value of any physical activity to the development of an individual. Quite the reverse. I would argue that everyone needs and indeed ought to engage in some form of physical activity for the reasons cited in this chapter. The difficulty is that a traditional compulsory programme, however well it is taught, simply alienates a significant proportion of people. Gymnastics, for example, in whichever form, may be considered wonderfully good for people (rather like castor oil) but we have to recognize that many pupils will dislike it as an activity. No matter how talented and committed the teacher, the compulsory programme will merely aggravate a basic antipathy. Thus, using gymnastics as a medium through which to develop body management skills is likely to be counter productive for many pupils. The good teacher would acknowledge this fact and seek an alternative medium like dance or yoga in order to encourage learning, rather than continue to impose an unwanted activity.

I am thus arguing for a flexible, ever-changing programme that emerges as the result of an ongoing process of negotiation between pupils and teachers. Only in this way can teachers, using their professional knowledge and understanding of children's physical, emotional and cognitive development, provide experiences that genuinely meet the real needs and interests of individual pupils. The key to this exercise, it seems to me, lies in the ability of teachers to first identify physical activities which genuinely stimulate pupil interest and enthusiasm, then to use these as a medium through which to expand learning. As I have tried to indicate, any activity may be used to provide all kinds of different learning experiences including those identified by PE HMI (DES 1979b). Furthermore, a starting point that builds upon a genuine interest in even one particular activity is more likely to stimulate learning and progression than any compulsory programme. It may also be used as a basis through which to encourage a gradual broadening of experience into other aspects of physical activity or an understanding of the value of exercise in all its forms. At present, we do not build on interests. We simply seek to impose them via a somewhat arbitrary programme and the net result is that we fail many individuals.

I would argue that the much advocated 'broad', 'balanced' programme is neither essential nor desirable. Balance, even supposing it were necessary, and again I would argue that it is not, may be much better achieved by a gradual widening of physical experiences to include the whole spectrum of activities including those outside the usual physical education curriculum. Similarly, real progression is much more likely to be achieved if the individuals concerned are involved in an activity for which they have a genuine interest and liking. The compulsory participation in activities that are often disliked is far more likely to alienate many pupils and inhibit any desire they might have to learn or improve.

The change proposed here clearly has profound implications for the way in which the curriculum is currently planned and structured. It would require, for instance, a much more flexible approach to planning, timetabling and grouping if individual needs and interests are to be met. Indeed, it is astonishing given the clear evidence of the variations in size, maturity, aptitude and ability amongst children in the same year group that the practice of class teaching persists. The kind of differentiation implied here would, however, necessitate detailed analysis and recording of pupils and their development as a basis for selecting appropriate activities. From this perspective, physical experiences both in and out of school need to be seen in their entirety and evaluated with due regard to their total effect upon the individuals concerned.

In essence, I am arguing for a cafeteria style of provision with pupils being obliged to make guided choices from a jointly planned menu. This might easily be arranged through an extension of the after school clubs and the wider use of taster courses or coaching clinics provided on the basis of the children's interests. Potentially, this offers the exciting prospect of utilizing the talents of teachers, parents, local sports clubs, or national sports organizations as and where the class teacher deems it appropriate. In particular, this offers the possibility of altering the traditional role of primary teachers who are currently obliged to teach physical activities for which they frequently have little aptitude or enthusiasm. Freed from these restraints it would be possible for them to either match their own enthusiasms to that of groups of pupils or seek expertise from outside. Similarly, pupils would be able to explore their interests in new activities and/or develop their skills in known ones either in or outside of the school programme. From this perspective, the role of the teacher is crucial in evaluating pupil development and responses to the provisions made in order to plan for future progression.

It seems to me that the kind of flexible provision advocated here is essential if teachers are truly concerned with the growth and development of the whole person. Indeed, there is no alternative if we are to provide physical, emotional and cognitive experiences that genuinely relate to individual needs and interests, rather than simply impose an unnecessary and frequently irrelevant programme of activities.

The overall conclusion that may be drawn from this chapter is the unsurprising one that physical education is unique only in that it focuses upon the provision of physical experiences. In themselves each and every one of these is different. Thus, although there may be similarities, the experience of playing rugby is totally different to that of tennis, which is different to tap dancing, which in turn is different to disco dancing. Each and everyone of these, and a multitude of others, many outside of the normal school curriculum, has something special to offer. Furthermore, because the actual experience itself is inextricably tied to the emotional, social and intellectual experiences which go with it, each can only be judged in terms of the way in which the specific individual responds. From this perspective, the standard physical education programme is totally inadequate. The wider concept of the 'physical' as an area of experience argued for in this chapter at least holds the potential of providing an education that truly satisfies the needs of all rather than the lucky few whose interests happen to coincide with the standard offering.

I recognize the somewhat negative analysis of the present state of physical education presented in this chapter. My concern is that an area of experience that holds the potential to offer so much to all has, for far too long, contrived to alienate so many children. Furthermore, this is a problem which cannot simply be laid at the door of teachers who of late have been blamed for far too many things beyond their control. The real difficulty lies in the maintenance of an imposed, narrow physical education curriculum which will continue to fail many children no matter how well trained or talented the teachers. It is my contention that there is need for a much more fundamental reappraisal of the structure and content of the curriculum and our whole approach to providing meaningful and valuable physical experiences for children. As has been argued, the alternative approach advocated here has profound implications not just for the way in which we traditionally think about physical education but also with regard to the whole way in which the curriculum is currently organized. It may be that a leap of faith is required if we are ever to step outside the narrow confines of the traditional subject and see the 'physical' in much broader terms. Nevertheless, unless we do so it seems certain that the standardized programme of activities currently imposed will continue to alienate large number of pupils well into the twenty-first century.

6

English, Fetishism and the demand for change: Towards a Post-Modern Agenda for the School Curriculum

Alex Moore

My intention in this chapter is to argue that English teaching, in schools in the United Kingdom, continues to be bound by an essentially 'fetishistic', culturist, approach to both literature and language, despite the partially successful efforts of English teachers to de-fetishize and to liberalize it. I shall suggest that this fetishistic approach to English, which has done little to educate large numbers of students, has always sat comfortably with an equally fetishistic – and equally outmoded – model of curriculum. Consequently, the urgent need to re-address what the subject 'English' is – and what it is *for* – cannot be divorced from an equally urgent need to inter-rogate in a radical way the nature of the school curriculum as a whole. It is the underlying view of the chapter that, in spite of appearances to the contrary, the time may still be right for such interrogations to be made and for appropriate curricular and pedagogical changes to be initiated: indeed, for all the regressive measures and policies continuing to be foisted upon schools and English departments by central government, I shall suggest that something of a start has already been made in this area.

The context for my argument is the set of questions raised by Doyle (1989, p. 2) and addressed by all serious educators at some point in their careers: 'Why did such institutions [as schools] come to exist in the first place? What was, and is, their cultural significance? Are alternatives to these institutions desirable or possible?' I shall suggest that 'official' government-underwrit-ten answers to these questions, and to parallel questions related specifically to English teaching, not only contain internal contradictions and deceits, but have habitually differed from – and continue to differ from – the 'unof-ficial' answers often voiced by practising teachers. This difference contin-ues, even in times of local management, to present a major source of difficulty for schools striving to put into practice models of teaching and learning in which they passionately believe (for example, teaching that pri-oritizes group work, oracy and continuous, formative assessment), only to find themselves perpetually thwarted by contradictory directives from on high.

In mounting this argument, I shall not be suggesting that all schools, or indeed all departments within schools, are united in a joint effort to oppose 'official wisdom'. On the contrary, there is ample evidence (e.g. Halpin et al. 1993) of schools themselves – though not necessarily all teachers within schools – colluding quite comfortably with such wisdom in, for example, shifts back towards setting by 'ability' or check-list assessment procedures. Neither am I suggesting a simplistic, 'one-to-one' link between government policy on education on the one hand and the needs and demands of capital, in the form of government-focused pressure from the domains of business and industry, on the other (see also Hargreaves 1994; Gewirtz, Ball & Bowe 1996). Such pressure clearly exists, and it would be equally naive to overlook or to underestimate the strong, essentially utilitarian influence of such domains upon the content and style of educational systems, both as it is filtered through government policies and agencies and as it reaches the domain of 'commonsense wisdom' through media agencies. What I want to suggest, however, is that these essentially *utilitarian* demands, which may, in the past, have coincided very closely with official governmental views as to what formal state education is for and what it should look like, have, as we move towards the twenty-first century, become far less unified, and in some instances have come to coincide much more closely with the essentially *humanitarian* aims and intentions of a large number of practising teachers. (An obvious example of this is the demand for increased social and oracy skills made by a burgeoning service and leisure industry, for whom such skills are bound to be perceived as more useful than, say, the ability to talk at length on certain items of pre-twentieth century literature.)

In such a kaleidoscopic scenario, the persistent demands of business and industry for 'basic literacy and numeracy', still widely reported via the mass media, sit side by side or even in competition with these developing demands, in ways that often transcend traditional class boundaries and expectations. Whereas there may once have been a major perceived need, for example, for non-literate labourers, for functionally literate clerks, typists and shopworkers, and for 'more-than-literate' (or even 'other-than-literate') managers, an increasing prioritization of customer relations and customer care, with its own very specific notions of what education is for and about, begins to permeate the entire workforce, regardless of positionings within persistent hierarchical and remunerative systems. While we might choose to adopt a cynical stance towards such changing demands, suggesting that their roots lie not only in the demand for a different kind of workforce but also in a different approach to keeping such a workforce obedient and functionally contented, the resulting implicit and explicit support for (for example) increased task- and experience-based group work in the classroom remains encouraging for teachers wishing to pursue such activities for often very different reasons.

It is precisely this convergence of agendas – however tenuous and uneasy it may be – which leads me to suggest that the time for effective change is right, and that, despite appearances to the contrary, schools and teachers are relatively well placed to discredit (if indeed they want to) the outdated models of education that are still trumpeted loudly by both major political parties in this country. They need to do this, I would argue, not through acceding to the ideology of a marketplace which may well offer them some significant measure of support in their project, but (Giroux 1990) by seizing opportunities to re-argue the case for a movement away from curricula and methodologies that have often interfered detrimentally with the development of their students, towards new methods and a new concept of curriculum that are both more effective and helpful from the student's viewpoint and more appropriate to the world in which we now live. If, in this particular enterprise, there is a central role for English teachers commensurate with the centrality of the subject English itself (Donald 1989), it is a role that may well, ironically, lead to the abolition of the subject-based curriculum as we now know it, and with it (Green 1995, p. 405) the abolition of the subject 'English' itself.

MODERNISM AND THE MONOLOGIC CURRICULUM

I have described English and the curriculum as 'fetishistic', and governmental education policy as 'outmoded'. What do I mean by these terms?

The outdatedness of the content and process of the present UK school curriculum, in terms of how we perceive learning, of the ways in which we conduct our everyday lives, and of whole-world changes (for example, the effective end of British colonialism and the growth of the phenomenon known as 'globalization'), is not an entirely new concept. Giddens, for example, has suggested that school students are increasingly experiencing a world and a methodology within the school classroom that offers less and less of a fit with the worlds and the methodologies that they experience outside it, arguing that the persistent *school* discourses of Authority and Tradition stand in direct opposition to the 'post-Authority', 'post-Tradition' world into which we are moving (Giddens 1995; see also Hargreaves 1994). Others (Levin 1987; Hamilton 1993; Reid 1993), have chosen to describe similar mismatches in terms of essentially 'postmodern' approaches to education as hampered and harried by the persistence of an essentially 'modernist' discourse.

'Modernism', like 'postmodernism', is, of course, something of a problematic term, not least in its continued openness to interpretation both within and across the different domains within which it is used (Callinicos 1989; Harvey 1990). I want to argue, however, that it is precisely within the general framework of the modernist-postmodernist debate that the difficulties with our current school curriculum can be most effectively defined, and that this is partly the result of a certain level of accord as to what these terms signify within the educational setting.

Hamilton (1993, p. 55) has offered one definition of the modernist view as perceiving and seeking to represent the world as 'an ordered place', and of the 'elements of the world of knowledge [as] topologically invariant'. It could be argued that this representation of 'modernity', if we accept its authenticity, happily embraces the model of curriculum that is still very much in place in United Kingdom schools. It is, as we shall see with reference to English in the curriculum, a view that reifies and itemizes knowledge and skills, strips them of cultural or ideological content in the quest for essentials and universals, and then offers them to students through an over-structured 'cover-all' programme, in the belief that (provided the student plays their own part properly as learner) they will provide everything the student needs to know or be able to do. Even in the face of more recent educational initiatives, such as the promotion of investigations in mathematics and science, the interrogation of sources in history, or the development of cross-curricular projects within the arts – initiatives all geared towards challenging the sanctity of the fact while at the same time forcing re-interrogations of what the subject-based curriculum should look like – the outdated 'modernist' discourse persists both in and through the school curriculum. Its rationale resides within a belief that education needs to be organized along lines which prioritize knowledge over process, and which promote the individual's skills and development over group skills and development – a view crystallized in the 'back to basics' agendas of both major political parties in the UK, and in the persistence of assessment through individual, end-of-course examination. It is an approach that represents the dominant educational wisdom of the past hundred years and more, and that has brought us, among other things, the whole-class, teacher-led lesson, the emphasis on the 'what' and the 'when' of education rather than the 'how' and the 'whether', and the fragmented, knowledge-dominant curriculum in which knowledge and skills are (in Bourdieu's and Apple's sense of the word) arbitrarily selected, prioritized and taught *through* subject areas *by* teachers (Bourdieu & Passeron 1977; Apple 1979: see also Lankshear 1993; Hargreaves 1994).

This particular approach, currently enshrined in the National Curriculum for England and Wales, represents what we might call the essentially monologic, monolithic model of schooling: monolithic in that it presupposes a body, equally resistant to development and decay, of 'essential' knowledge and skills; monologic in that neither its content nor its process are open to negotiation: that is to say, examiners and governments unilaterally decide what is to be learned; teachers teach it. Such a model, I want to suggest, incorporates a central, fundamental act of what is, essentially, a form of commodity fetishism (Marx 1872), in which particular skills, items and areas of knowledge, as well as styles of learning and representing learning, are invested with a value – over and above other skills, knowledge, and styles of learning and representation – that exceeds the sum of their parts. Furthermore, I want to suggest that such a fetishization becomes absorbed, hegemonically, as 'common sense' or 'received wisdom' through what Zizek (1989), after Lacan (1979), calls the 'transferential illusion': the illusion, that is, that a quality or a value which we have ourselves invested in an object (such as an 'item' of learning, or a set of facts) actually does reside in the object itself. It is just such an illusion that results in the hands-up-in-horror reaction to geography teachers' suggestions that naming and locating may be of less importance than analyses of global power relations, or to complaints that students successfully completing intellectually demanding English degrees 'still can't spell'.

FETISHISM IN THE TEACHING OF ENGLISH

In English, which is often perceived as a central plank of the school curriculum (Board of Education 1921; Donald 1989; Medway 1990), the particular form of fetishization that I have attributed to the curriculum in general operates in two distinct but related areas. The first of these is the study of literature (or Literature as it is often known, in an effort to distinguish it from mere 'writing'). In the monolithic, monologic curriculum, Literature – essentially, the writing of identified Others – is reified and presented as something of enduring, intrinsic value and wisdom: truly (Arnold 1909, pp. 10–11) 'the best that is known and thought in the world' (see also Doyle 1989, p. 25). In English, the study of Literature continues to take priority, not only over speaking and listening but also over the writing of 'other Others' of lesser repute, and over non-literary texts which might also reward study *as texts*. Furthermore, a great deal of examined *student* writing is itself undertaken in response to the reading of 'Literature'. (This is true both of public examination assignments and of formal assessments undertaken by 14-year-olds.)

   In this model, Literature is identified according to its 'timeless qualities', its 'eternal', 'enduring' values and themes, even (Arnold 1932) its power to humanize and ennoble. The greatness with which each work of Literature is invested is viewed not as an investment at all, but as emanating from the work itself. Its study, consequently, becomes a matter of excavating and displaying exactly what its timeless qualities, values and themes are: in short, what makes it great. The emphasis is not on how the student responds (or students respond) to a text, but on how the text 'works' in itself.

   Should we be in any doubt that this view of 'Literature' and this approach to its study still dominate the English classroom (despite teacher successes in extending the range of what counts as Literature), the revised National Curriculum Order for England and Wales (DFE 1995) provides us with a salutary reminder. The Order not only advises secondary-school teachers that their students must be 'introduced to major works of literature from the English literary heritage in previous centuries . . . literature by major writers from earlier in the twentieth century and works of high quality by contemporary writers' (DFE 1995b, p. 20), but also provides them with lists of writers as indicators of what 'major works of literature', 'major writers' and 'works of high quality' are. As to the study of such 'major works':

> Pupils should be encouraged to appreciate the *distinctive qualities* of these works through activities that emphasize *the interest and pleasure of reading them,* rather than necessitating a detailed, line-by-line study. (1995, p. 20, my emphases).

The wording of the Order here is interesting, providing an example of what Jones K. (1992, pp. 17–18) aptly refers to as 'a tactic of half-recognition' in which, 'within the shell of the new discourse, new restorationist meanings are accommodated'. To translate this in terms of the above National Curriculum reference, we can say that the instruction reads initially – and superficially – as evidence of support for new, non-fetishistic attitudes towards literature teaching, that emphasize the student's 'interest and plea-sure in reading' rather than, for example, the more 'scientific', awe-inducing kind of study that led millions of public examination candidates to suffer on the altar of the infamous context question. A closer reading, however, quickly reveals a fundamental acceptance of the monolithic, monologic English cur-riculum, in which students do not decide for themselves which of a range of works they 'enjoy' and 'find interesting' but are presented with works which they cannot help but find interesting and enjoyable, since they are intrinsically so. What the teacher has to do is to help the student towards an enjoyment of and interest in such texts. If the student's study of such work does not necessitate 'detailed, line-by-line study', that is only because one does not want to put them off the 'major works' and so deprive them of that enjoyment and interest or of the noble and ennobling qualities that such works possess. The student's own fundamental task remains the same as it always was: to describe what it is 'in' the works that makes the works great – or, as the Order puts it, to:

> extract meaning beyond the literal, explaining how choice of language and style affects implied and explicit meanings; analyse and discuss alternative interpre-tations, unfamiliar vocabulary, ambiguity and hidden meanings; analyse and engage with the ideas, themes and language . . . ; reflect on the writer's presen-tation of ideas, the motivation and behaviour of characters, the development of plot and the overall impact of a text; distinguish between the attitudes and assumptions displayed by characters and those of the author; . . . appreciate the characteristics that distinguish literature of high quality . . . (DFE 1995b, p. 21)

The 'half-recognition' in this second extract lies in the acceptance of 'alter-native interpretations', engagement with 'ideas', and 'distinguish[ing]' between the attitudes and assumptions displayed by characters and those of the author' – implying, perhaps, support for a more critical analysis of the text as text, embracing such matters as its cultural context, its ideological base, and the ideological basis upon which it is selected for study in the first place. This suggestion, however, is swiftly undermined by the persistence of the fetishistic discourse, demanding that students learn to 'appreciate the characteristics that distinguish literature of high quality'. Once again, we are pulled smartly back to the monologic and the monolithic: in this instance, the notion that 'literature of high quality' exists 'in reality' rather than as a human construct; that it is definable by certain 'qualities'; that it is up to somebody other than the student to define what it is or what its qualities are; and that the student's job is to learn to enjoy and be interested by it, largely through an identification of what its inherent qualities and characteristics are. The possibility that a student's analysis and engagement with 'the ideas, themes and language in literature', or their distinguishing of the 'attitudes and assumptions' of the author, might lead them to dismiss a 'major work' on the grounds of (say) racism, sexism or the promotion of poverty and inequality through an unquestioning promulgation of dominant class ideologies is not allowed for in this 'restorationist' bottom line. Political and ideological questions – that might suggest a vastly alternative model of literature study (along, for instance, the lines argued by cultural materialists such as Dollimore and Sinfield 1985) – simply do not apply: except, that is, in the case of 'information sources', in whose study students 'should be taught to sift the relevant from the irrelevant and to distinguish between fact and opinion, bias and objectivity', and of 'media texts', which students are invited to 'analyse and evaluate' (DFE 1995b, pp. 20-21).

The second principal area in which fetishism in English works is through the reification and praise of standard English over other forms of English. Standard English has always presented something of a conundrum for English teachers working with students from backgrounds in which standard English is, effectively, a second dialect. On the one hand, there has been a recognition that such students need to acquire and develop expertise in standard English if they are to have the opportunity of, for example, doing well in public examinations and gaining access to prestigious, well-paid jobs. On the other hand, English teachers have often been reluctant (Raleigh 1981; ILEA 1990) to allow such a recognition to indicate that they see an inherent 'superiority' in standard English, or to pass on such a view to their students. One solution to this has been to adopt what we might call, after Bakhtin, a 'repertoire extension' model of language teaching (Bakhtin 1929). Such a model values all forms of English, encouraging the study of standard as well as non-standard texts and inviting students to write and speak themselves in standard and non-standard forms as the situation and subject-matter dictate. Such an approach does not view non-standard English as incorrect, any more than it perceives standard English as correct. Rather, standard is presented as a socially useful dialect (Trudgill 1983, Stubbs 1976) which has no *intrinsic* superiority over any other form of English, but which, for clearly definable social and historical reasons, has come to be invested with a particular status. Standard, in this model, has its grammar, its vocabulary, its rules, in just the same way (Labov 1970) that non-standard dialects do: the user of non-standard English is, thus, not an incorrect user of English, whose language represents a deviation from some correct, prototypical norm, but one whose language already operates according to the same kind of grammatical and generic rules upon which standard English is structured. The development of standard English with such students becomes a matter of the application of language skills and knowledges they already possess in, effectively, the continuing develop-ment of a second (though already not unfamiliar) dialect.

This perception of and approach to the teaching of standard English with non-standard users is plainly at odds with the fetishistic approach to stan-dard English as exemplified in the National Curriculum English Order (see, for instance, DFE 1995b, p. 3). Here, standard English is clearly perceived as grammatically 'correct' English, with the obvious corollary that non-stan-dard English must be grammatically incorrect. In the past, such a view might have led, logically, to attempts at the eradication of non-standard forms and practices and their replacement with standard ones. The more recently developed discourse of cultural pluralism, however, has clearly taken sufficient hold for such a view to be publicly unacceptable. Instead, therefore, the National Curriculum offers us another 'tactic of half-recogni-tion': Of course we must allow non-standard speakers, in addition to teach-ing them how to use standard forms, to use their non-standard forms in appropriate situations; of course we must not tell them that non-standard English is 'wrong'; and of course we must recognize that the 'richness of dialects . . . can make an important contribution to pupils' knowledge and understanding of standard English' (DFE 1995, p. 2). However, standard English remains fetishized as 'distinguished from other forms of English by its vocabulary, and by rules and conventions of grammar, spelling and punctuation' (ibid., p. 3). The disappearance of the 'its' from the second part of this sentence is not insignificant. It signals very clearly a belief that stan-dard English has rules and conventions, while other forms of English do not.

'OLD' AND 'TRANSITIONAL' ENGLISH

It is easy to see how each of the two fetishisms I have described operates in terms of the monolithic curriculum as a whole, and how they suggest a certain form of monologic pedagogy. Both 'Great Literature' and 'Standard English' are reified, their 'inherent' qualities and characteristics identified and described. This is how they are to be received by students, whose task is to learn how to enjoy and profit from the former and to gain expertise in and profit from the latter. Both Great Literature and Standard English are stripped of any cultural or ideological history or content: they are, as it were, timeless, beyond the touch of variables, godlike in their fundamental rightness and in their immortality – monarchs by divine right. Students are to stand humbly before them: to offer criticism through dialogue is pointless and unthinkable. Since they cannot be expected to come to school with all the appropriate critical, aesthetic and cognitive tools to be successful in their study either of 'language' or of 'literature', they must, furthermore, be given these tools by those who have them – the guardians of 'the knowledge'. In order to discover and record how successful this process has been, the students must be independently assessed. Any credit given, in this assessment, for expertise in non-standard linguistic forms, in knowledge of and sensitivity to non-recommended texts, or in non-standard ways of responding to texts, must remain peripheral.

Does the persistence of the monolithic, fetishistic English curriculum imply, however, that talk of radical change, both in English teaching and in the curriculum as a whole, is no more than mere idealistic optimism? I want to argue that it does not, and to suggest that in order to locate possible areas of radical development we need first to take a closer look at what exactly has been happening in the field of school English teaching over the past twenty-five years, both in terms of government interventions and in terms of developments undertaken by radical English teachers themselves often in the face of stiff governmental opposition. This must clearly include, as Donald has suggested, 'a self-critical assessment of which elements in radical English teaching should be defended, and which need to be transcended' (Donald 1989, p. 16).

Selleck (1968) has written of the 'New Education' and Green (1995) of the 'New English'. My own view is that we are still waiting for the New Education and the New English, but that as practising teachers we should be – and indeed have been – pro-active in hastening their arrival. When Selleck talks of the 'New Education', he is referring to developments that took place from around 1870. What I want to talk about are rather more recent developments, involving what I shall call 'Old English' and 'Transitional English' – this latter being the English which, I want to suggest, we still have in place in the school curriculum, regardless of central government's persistence in seeking to remove it.

By the Old English I mean the English that held relatively untroubled sway from the end of the Second World War (and indeed from long before then) until a period of change and development that spanned the end of the 1960s and most of the 1970s and 1980s. This Old English was founded on the twin rocks of the Literary Canon and the Development of Standard Written and Spoken English. Significantly, it was an English which, despite local subversions, remained largely unquestioned in the individual and collective minds of English teachers themselves, and indeed which may have remained unquestioned but for the efforts of such bodies as the National Association for the Teaching of English and the Inner London Education Authority's English Centre.

In terms of how the Old English broke down into lesson content and organization (Figure 6.1), it was characterized by the following common key ingredients:

(a) The study of decontextualized comprehension exercises, with an emphasis on demonstrating basic understanding and basic appreciation of 'style' – usually with ancillary exercises focusing on grammar, punctuation, and parts of speech: typically, a once-a-week activity, in which students progressed through a series of ever more 'difficult' books.

(b) Writing essays, stories, poems, descriptive pieces and plays to pre-set titles ('a summer's day', 'my views on television violence', 'my most embarrassing moment') – usually with little stimulus, often timed, 'supervised' and in silence.

(c) Precis writing (that is, the summarizing of decontextualized pieces of writing, reducing them to a specific number of words, often within a time limit).

(d) Writing formal responses to literature ('Describe the character of so-and-so', 'Write about so-and-so's poetic style'), typically preceded and followed by little or no whole-class discussion.

(e) Reading out loud round the class: all students reading the same 'set' text, with marks given for 'reading performance'.

(f) Formal language study, focusing on the mechanics of standard English spelling, grammar and punctuation, often through decontextualized exercises.

The emphasis on classroom organization and pedagogical style in this model of English emphasized very firmly the importance of the individual student working alone and being tested alone, with speaking generally discouraged unless in answer to a teacher's specific invitation, and listening skills rather taken for granted (the student who had done their homework inappropriately had, for instance, simply not listened properly). Leaning for support in its later years to relatively liberal, Piagetian views as to how learning and development took place – that is to say (Piaget 1926), the notion that learning is an active, meaning-making process and that normal development takes place in a relatively orderly, universal, incremental fashion – English teachers were generally content to adopt such philosophies to promote, justify or accede to a number of key features of English as it then was. These included:

Figure 6.I: 'Old' and 'Transitional' English

Old English	Transitional English
Decontextualized comprehension exercises	Emphasis on interpretation/multiplicity
Composition-writing to titles	Compositions arising from stimulus/discussion
Summaries to word limits	Note-taking skills
Formal responses to literature	Creative and formal responses to literature
Reading round the class	Encouragement of private and group reading
Formal standard English language study	Growth of 'socio-linguistics'
Formal assessment by final examination 'coursework'	Formal assessment continuous
Students work alone	Groupwork valued and encouraged
Classes organized into 'ability' sets	'Mixed-ability' groupings
Emphasis on reading and writing	Speaking and listening skills encouraged
'Piagetian' model of development	'Vygotskyan' model of development
'Transmission' dominant	More student-centred
English perceived as 'service industry'	English asserts its own curriculum

- the setting of students according to their current perceived developmental achievement (often referred to, erroneously, as their 'ability');
- a broadly 'transmissional' model of teaching (developmentally, it was the teacher's prime concern to decide what input a student needed and when they needed it – which, in the setted situation, more often than not meant deciding what input the whole class needed and when they needed it);
- an incremental approach to the English curriculum, that extended the shelf-life of graded comprehension books and books providing step-by-step guides and tests to standard English grammar, spelling and punctuation.

This itemized, teacher-led approach to English sat comfortably within the monologic, monolithic curriculum as a whole, where knowledge generally was reified and parcelled up in the same kind of way and taught according to notions of its appropriateness to an age-group or 'ability range'. However, it also resulted in a certain kind of perception of the subject English on the part of many other subject teachers within the curriculum: that is to say, the perception of English as a 'service industry', whose primary rationale, apart from putting on school plays and mounting attractive wall displays, was to teach students the essential literacy skills they would need if they were to succeed in other academic subjects such as history, geography or the sciences. Such a view of English-teaching may have been questioned by the notion of Language Across the Curriculum, first publicly promoted in the Bullock Report (DES, 1975); however, it was one that remained persistent even after the Old English had been replaced by Transitional English.

Towards the end of the 1960s, English teaching began, quite perceptibly, to change and to be in the forefront of a number of other changes that affected the school curriculum as a whole. Chief among these changes in literature study were a broader view of what counted as literature (embracing, for instance, students' own writings, works in non-standard English, and 'media texts') and a parallel broadening of permitted ways of responding to texts (including, for instance, a development in so-called 'creative response', whereby students were invited to demonstrate their understanding and appreciation of texts through activities such as writing in the role of particular characters or devising newspaper reports of key incidents). In language development, meanwhile, the changes incorporated a new valuation of non-standard as well as standard English (including the encouragement of students to write in non-standard forms), coupled with a new approach to the teaching of standard English that introduced sociolinguistics into the classroom through explaining to students not that standard English was essentially 'right English' (useful though it was), but how it had come to achieve the status it had and why it might be a useful dialect to own.

Such developments – which were matched by examining boards softening their own monolithic, monologic approach to the English curriculum through, for example, giving credit for work produced in non-standard forms and formats, or through the active encouragement of creative literary response – emphasized pleasure above duty in reading and writing, and stressed the importance of interpretation, and a multiplicity of interpretations, over the excavation of fixed meanings. In terms of curriculum content, compositions arising out of a range of stimuli – including discussion – began to take precedence over compositions to set titles; classroom discussion was encouraged as the status of speaking and listening skills was raised and as teachers thought in more complex ways about their nature and about how best to help develop them; flexible note-taking replaced the formal precis (which had worked on the pseudo-scientific assumption that any text – or fragment of text – could be reduced meaningfully and usefully to a third of its original length); the value and importance of group-work became recognized, resulting in collaborative writing enterprises, shared readings, and an increased use of Drama within the English classroom; formal round-the-class reading became challenged by the encouragement of private and small-group reading, with teachers devising ways of assessing reading that did not require the student to have to read out loud in often intimidating situations; and a more student-centred approach to learning emerged which, among other things, saw a dramatic increase in assessment by coursework rather than by end-of-course examination, along with an increased valuation of what the student already knew, thought, believed in and could do rather than what the teacher felt had to be 'got through'.

These developments represented, I would argue, a vigorous re-valuation and reassertion on the part of English teachers as to what English was, what was unique about the English curriculum, how it related to other school subjects, and how it was not to be simplistically identified with 'language' (the medium of instruction for all teachers) or with basic literacy. Theoretically, they found strong support in the psychological-linguistic writings of the Russian educationalist Lev Vygotsky (1962; 1978), whose work built on and simultaneously critiqued that of Jean Piaget. Whereas Piaget's work had appeared to prioritize the individual, 'intrinsic' development of the child, for example, Vygotsky appeared far more concerned with education and learning as social processes undertaken by individuals *only in consort with other individuals*.

Many of Vygotsky's ideas impacted on or supported developments in both pedagogy and assessment in the English classroom. The notion of 'setting' pupils according to ability, for instance, sat less well with Vygotskyan social dynamics than the notion of 'mixed ability', while the notion of the isolated individual always working silently and alone at their desk (when not listening to the teacher 'delivering') seemed to make less sense than the development of small-group activities and oracy skills. Meanwhile, the famous Vygotskyan diktat that 'what a child can do with assistance today she will be able to do by herself tomorrow' (Vygotsky 1978 p. 87) suggested a development in the teacher's role away from predominantly 'front-loaded', whole-class teaching followed by summative assessment, towards a far greater emphasis on classroom mobility accompanied by formative assessment, involving working with individuals and groups of students on task and paying as much heed to what students manifestly brought into the classroom with them as to some 'universal' developmental template.

To introduce a Lacanian note (Lacan 1977; 1979), we could say that the Old English had represented a modernist project, in which 'essential' skills and knowledge were neatly separated out and imparted to passive, unified subjects. Though the good of society as well as of the individual may have been touted by the public voice of such a project (see, for example, the 1944 Education Act and preceding [1943] White Paper), competition between individuals had clearly been at the heart of the English curriculum, as indeed at the heart of the whole-school curriculum. Transitional English, on the other hand, may be said to have represented something of a 'post-modern turn' (Green 1995), recognizing the multidimensional nature not only of the subject English but also of the subjects studying it – a perspective which resisted separating out the individual's needs and wishes from those of 'society', through mounting and inviting a challenge as to what our social needs and wishes are, where they have come from, and what they might be in the future.

RESISTANCE AND CHANGE: (I) THE PERSISTENCE OF DOMINANT IDEOLOGIES THROUGH FORMAL ASSESSMENT PROCEDURES

Since I have now argued (i) that 'transitional English', with its 'post-modern turn', has represented a radical break with 'old English', (ii) that 'old English', with its modernist perspective, continues to dominate the English curriculum through its fetishization of certain forms and items of oral and written expression, a word of explanation seems in order.

The first thing that needs to be said is that during the late 1980s and into the 1990s there has been a concerted attack by central government on most if not all of the changes initiated by English teachers during the 1970s and early 1980s. This attack has resulted in much – but not all – of the ground gained by those teachers being significantly eroded. Comprehension exercises and writing to titles have been resurrected, for example, through standard tests for 14-year-olds; the 'literary canon' has been re-affirmed through the National Curriculum Order; and continuous formal assessment has been pruned back again (despite the newly-popular term 'formative assessment': another 'tactic of half-recognition'), in favour of re-prioritized end-of-course assessment by written examination. In any resistance to these reversions, moreover, teachers now face the rule of law. The National Curriculum is not a 'guidance document': it instructs teachers as to what, broadly, they must teach and how they must organize their priorities.

The second thing that needs to be said is that, arguably, most of the changes allowed to take place during the 1970s and 1980s were not at all radical in one very important respect (indeed, it may not be unreasonable to speculate that if they had been radical in this respect, they might not have been allowed in the first place). That important respect concerns the general criteria by which students are assessed and which continue to act as the prime indicators of their 'success'. Despite all the changes that took place within English teaching during the 1970s and 1980s, including changes to the format and style of public examinations, the examination system itself has never radically changed: it is still there, still emphasizing written over oral or practical performance, still overly memory-dependent, still predominantly 'end-of-course', and still offering most students the best route into better-paid work. Furthermore, although its style may have changed – increased emphasis on coursework assessment; the ratification of creative responses to literature; the recognition of pieces of creative work presented in non-standard forms – its priorities and its biases arguably have not. As Green (1995, p. 405) argues of English in general:

> [T]he emergence of a more radical and socially-critical version of English teaching . . . is still linked to a particular, and arguably limited, understanding of culture and society. . . . [It is] still consistent with the larger cultural logic informing Western capitalist societies, and still contextualized therefore by a particular system of ideological and metaphysical assumptions. Even in its more socially-critical emancipating forms, it has still participated in the enlightenment project of modernity, which has come to be described as modernism.

If changes to the English curriculum such as I have mentioned represent, potentially at least, some of the more 'socially-critical, emancipating' forms of this particular subject area, it is in the examination system, despite its own developments, that the 'larger cultural logic informing Western capitalist societies' continues to dominate: not so much in the how of examining, as in the criteria by which the examinee continues to be judged. Within such systems, non-standard English, non-standard genres and what might be termed non-standard texts may be granted some measure of acceptability, but only as long as they remain peripheral and as long as the examinee can additionally display abundant expertise in and knowledge of standard English, standard genres and standard texts. Meanwhile, the criteria underpinning the assessment of those standard written performances remain 'as contextualized . . . by a particular system of ideological and metaphysical assumptions' as they always were – assumptions, for example, that there is only one 'right way' of telling a story (characterized by 'rounded characters', 'background detail' and so forth), only one right way of presenting a case (introduction, arguments for, arguments against, conclusion) and only one right way of responding to a standard text (recognizing its enduring, inherent qualities and articulating what they are through detailed reference). That these criteria might, in Apple's (1979) and Bourdieu's (1977) sense of the word, be 'arbitrary', and that in cultures other than middle- and upper-class English different criteria might be prioritized, has no place within the misleadingly-titled 'public' examination system. When one learns to write a story, one does not merely learn to write it in 'appropriate English', one learns to write it in 'the proper way'. Teachers may be free to encourage non-standard forms and styles of English with their students knowing that they do so with the apparent (if limited) sanction of the National Curriculum Order. They will also know, however, that in assessment terms it is still standard grammar, spelling and punctuation, as well as standard genre reproduction, that will mark the essential difference between students who do well and students who fail. They will also know that in the area of Literature study it is still the positive criticism – an 'understanding' and enjoyment (however feigned) of the 'great works' – that will be prioritized over negative criticisms of those works, and that it will still be an 'understanding' of how characters operate and develop, how plot is structured, and how literary effects are achieved that will be prioritized over an approach which comes to texts via the much wider socio-historical contexts in which they are situated.

RESISTANCE AND CHANGE: (2) TWO 'RADICAL ELEMENTS'

If the above suggests a certain pessimism regarding radical developments in English teaching it is not meant to. Not every gain has, as I have already suggested, been eroded, and there are, I believe, at least two radical developments in this area that have taken root and that continue to thrive within the National Curriculum English Order. These two developments are (i) a prioritization of co-operation over competition, (ii) the development in students of 'critical literacy' alongside 'basic' functional and cultural literacy. Neither development exists in isolation from alternative pressures to prioritize competition at the expense of co-operation, or basic literacy at the expense of critical literacy: but both developments have established a firm foothold which still offers the best hope of mounting an effective challenge to the traditional curriculum that continues to dominate.

I have already indicated that the struggle between genuinely new developments in education and 'traditional' education can be conceptualized in terms of a struggle between postmodernist and modernist thinking (for an alternative but not dissimilar contextualization, in terms of philosophical pragmatism, see Crump 1995, esp. 207-208, 210-212). Postmodernism remains, as has already been indicated, a very fluid and open concept, having attached to it different meanings and purposes not just according to the context in which it is used but also among different social actors operating within broadly the same context (Green 1993, p. 8; Hargreaves 1994, p. 85). A broad consensus as to what postmodernism might mean in terms of curricular and pedagogical development, however, is emerging among commentators who perceive the concept positively, and the term is rapidly becoming descriptive of more radical advances in English teaching that look beyond Transitional English towards what might more confidently be called New English – beyond that, too, to a New Education, in which the identification of individual subject areas like English might, eventually, cease to have relevance.[1]

Green (1995, p. 402) has distinguished 'new', 'post modern' English from old (modernist) English in terms of 'its commitment to notions of process, experience and pleasure; its fluid and dynamic sense of disciplinary and other social boundaries; and generally its attitude to concepts of difference and marginality'; while Hebdidge (1986, p. 81) introduces postmodernism as a term 'used to cover all those strategies which set out to dismantle the power of the white, male author as the privileged source of meaning and value'. In the same vein, Levin (1987, p. 2) talks of postmodern thinking as problematizing 'what was once unquestionable: the paradigm of knowledge, truth and reality that has dominated the whole of modern history' – a sentiment echoed by, among others, Giroux (1992), Ulmer (1981) and Reid (1993), who equates 'modernity' in education with the notion of fixedness, non-negotiability and a corresponding attachment to the development of a very limited version of *literacy*.

The relation of postmodernism in education to the need for an elaborated version of *literacy* is a recurrent theme in the writing of these 'postmodern' educators. Willinsky (1993, p. 59), for example, suggests that a central need for such educators is to develop an interest in literacy 'that goes beyond "personal growth" and the like', and, in so doing, seeks to 'find, with some insistency, the social situation of a reading and writing that also makes a difference in people's public lives'. Lankshear, meanwhile (though not necessarily a postmodernist by persuasion), argues against the notion of a 'literacy first' model of curriculum planning and presentation, in which literacy is perceived as the basic 'prerequisite' for students' introduction to and coverage of the curriculum, suggesting instead that curricula should 'help to induct students *into* literacies of *one form or another*, and that we need to understand curriculum as very much an initiation into literacy' (Lankshear 1993, p. 155 my emphases). Lankshear's 'literacies' comprise not only the basic literacy required of students to translate print into speech and thought, or speech and thought into print, but demand of schools the promotion of a literacy 'conducive to keeping the ideal of social justice alive and equipping citizens with the capacity and commitment to pursue it' (op. cit., p. 158).

Lankshear's call for a re-defining and broadening of the notion of literacy in this way finds support in two overlapping areas of radical development in English teaching in the UK. The first of these relates specifically to the notion of education as 'keeping the ideal of social justice alive and equipping citizens with the capacity and commitment to pursue it' (1993, p. 158) – that is to say, an ethical dimension focusing on the importance of cooperation. Nationally-contextualized 'competitiveness' is still a watchword for business and industry, as well as within official government publications, in elaborating the requirements and the rationale of State education (see, for example, DFE 1992, p. 1). However, schools have done much to extend and challenge such demands, helping develop in their students a sense of collective concern and partial responsibility for what takes place in the world, and promoting a model of education for citizenship that goes far beyond a simple 'respect for people and property' (DFE 1992,

p. 7), towards equipping students with the voices, the confidence and the desire to militate for a safer, more just and more equitable *world* (see also UNESCO 1982; Masterman 1992; IPPR 1993). Such developments have taken place partly through the 'content' or substance of the Transitional English curriculum – through, for example, the selection of works of literature that deal with major social *issues* such as homelessness, racism and environmental catastrophes – and partly through its pedagogical style: in, for instance, promoting group activities that develop discussion skills and collaboration, or focusing on the issues of a literary text as well as or instead of the manner in which its characters are 'drawn' or in which its rhyming scheme operates.

One of the ways in which, in the English classroom, the importance of co-operation over competition has been most effectively promoted is through the second radical development to which I have referred: the development, principally through language awareness programmes and the study of Media texts, of the role and importance of critical literacy in the English curriculum. McLaren (1988, p. 213) has defined critical literacy as literacy that involves students and teachers in 'decoding the ideological dimensions of texts, institutions, social practices, and cultural forms such as television and films, in order to reveal their selective interests'. Unlike 'functional literacy' (the back-to-basics literacy of simple decodings and translations between thought, print and speech) or 'cultural literacy' (that is, 'educating students to be . . . the bearers of certain meanings, values and views'), the purpose of critical literacy is 'to create a citizenry critical enough to both analyse and challenge the oppressive characteristics of the larger society so that a more just, equitable, and democratic society can be created' (op. cit., pp. 213-14). To put this another way, the prioritization of critical literacy sets out not merely to achieve basic literacy or the straightforward replication of mainly dominant cultural forms and genres, but to challenge the status of those dominant genres and forms as a way towards both a better understanding of existing social power relations and inequities, *and* to some idea as to how those relations and inequities might be overturned. By way of a postmodern, 'not-only-but-also' elaboration, we might say that the development of critical literacy is a matter *not only* of helping students from de-privileged backgrounds to do better within the system, *but also* of mounting a challenge to the system itself through, for example, recognizing – and helping students to recognize – that such students *are* de-privileged and not merely 'under'-privileged (as though this were their natural condition).

This relation of versions of literacy to versions of curriculum seems to me to be critical. While I would not want to argue that the three versions of literacy described by McLaren are mutually exclusive, their discursive *domination* clearly is. It is equally clear that it is 'functional' literacy and, to a lesser extent, cultural literacy that have continued to dominate both curriculum and pedagogy for as long as there has been compulsory State education in the UK, and furthermore that they continue to dominate the English curriculum: indeed, there is a sense in which the development of cultural literacy and functional literacy work in harness in their resistance to the development of critical literacy. We could argue, for instance, that cultural literacy offers an *endorsement* of the importance of *functional* literacy: i.e. it is (culturally) understood and agreed that the 'basics' of functional literacy are of greater importance and value than, for example, the ability to work together as a decision-making team, or the ability to argue coherently and effectively against injustices in current social structures.

The domination of the functional literacy discourse is well suited to rigidity and fixedness of meaning, to a modernist world-view in which all is orderable if not ordered, and to an emphasis on the individual student individually developing and individually tested. Critical literacy, on the other hand, represents something else – an alternative way forward that demands new ways of looking at what education is for, and new definitions of standard, 'mythic' meanings (Barthes 1972) attached to the everyday words through which education is described: not only asking questions like Is citizenship a principal aim of education?, but What do we mean by citizenship? Is the term open to other meanings than those with which it is habitually invested? Clearly, there are considerable implications here for the *purposes* of education in the terms we have already considered. To refer back to comments made earlier in the chapter, under the postmodern perspective the growth and development of *social beings* is prioritized, in terms of agenda-setting, over the more utilitarian demands of merely (re)producing an 'appropriate' work-force.

TOWARDS A NEW CURRICULUM: SOME KEY PRINCIPLES AND SOME INEVITABLE OPPOSITION

English teachers who have already started working in the radical directions to which I have referred – prioritizing issues and contexts in textual study; linguistic and cultural pluralism in language awareness programmes; deconstructive activities in the study and production of a wide range of media texts; group discussion and joint decision-making in text production – are, along with radical teachers in other subject areas, among the advance party not only in terms of key developments within their own subject area but of parallel developments in what could become the New Curriculum and what is already, arguably, the Transitional Curriculum.

If the New Curriculum does materialize, its approach and its rationale will be underpinned by the same key principles and styles that have underpinned Transitional English and that continue to offer the only real alternative to the persistent modernist agenda. To summarize those principles and styles as they manifest themselves in what we might call transitional curriculum activity, we can say of such activity:

1. It is fundamentally and actively political, in a way that the development of functional and cultural literacies or the 'handing down' of selected skills and facts is not. By consequence, it demands (Freire 1972, 1974; Giroux and Simon 1988) a 'critical pedagogy': one, that is, which challenges existing curricula and pedagogies *as well as the cultural-ideological assumptions that underpin them.*

2. It resists a linear, 'hierarchical' literacy and knowledge development in which 'the basics' precede the complexities and in which the complexities only come much later (and then not to everyone).

3. It encourages development not merely along what Jakobson (1981) and others (Walkerdine 1982; Lacan 1977), have called the metonymic axis, but also along the metaphoric axis. That is to say, it does not simply encourage development within the current dominant educational discourse (the monolithic, monologic curriculum, with its emphasis on 'basic skills'): it also encourages the consideration and understanding that there may be other, equally valid discourses through which to examine, express and make use of our experiences of life.

4. It celebrates cultural, linguistic and perceptual difference – and promotes pleasure in that difference – rather than pathologizing it.'

5. It promotes a specific view of citizenship and democracy that has at its centre informed, radical criticism. Its persistent question is not 'How can education make this country (whatever that may mean) more prosperous?' but 'What do we need to learn – and to learn to do – in order to make the world a happier, safer place for all who inhabit it?

6. It calls into serious question, often through cross-curricular projects, the fragmented, subject-based curriculum, which offers such 'a poor basis from which to frame courses of transforming social action that stand a reasonable chance of being effective' (Lankshear 1993, p. 55). Through questioning definitions of subject areas, and focusing on making sense of the world through interrogations of the representations by which we experience it, it focuses less on 'what is?' than on 'what might be or what ought to be?' (ibid.; see also Green 1993). In this, it promotes the defetishizing of texts themselves, focusing not so much on the business of treating certain selected texts as more valuable or significant than others, as on fostering 'a radicalizing mentality, both intellectual and political, which is applicable to all texts' (Brooker 1987, p. 27) .

If the above represents an agenda for radical change, what hope is there for such an agenda becoming, even in current teachers' lifetimes, anything more than an elaborate clarion-call? In answering this question, we need to be clear about what the 'official' education agenda is all about, and to be unapologetic about articulating that clarity.

For as long as formal, compulsory state education has existed – and from before its inception – official, government-sponsored views on the importance of universal education have prioritized its 'life-quality-enhancing' benefits both to the individual and to the nation state. This is evident in Arnold's (1932) and Ruskin's (1898) claims for the soothing, civilizing effects of 'high culture'; it is evident in the 1943 Government White Paper on Educational Reconstruction, with its references to the 'happier child' enjoying the 'better start to life' and enriching 'the inheritance of the country whose citizens they are'; it is evident in the 1944 Education Act, with its talk of the 'spiritual, moral, mental and physical development of the community'; and it is evident in the recent UK Government's White Paper *Choice and Diversity* (DFE 1992, pp. 1 & 7), with its talk of 'happy', 'rounded', 'balanced' and 'qualified' children with 'a respect for people and property' contributing to 'our future work-force and the foundation for the economic development and competitiveness of this country'.

All this seems, at first glance (with the possible exception of the reference to the 'competitiveness of this country'), uncontentious, reasonable, and even altruistic. But is it mere rhetoric, concealing a less defensible purpose? What I want to suggest – and I am aware that the suggestion is not new – is that far from wanting education to produce more 'morally aware', 'fulfilled', 'well rounded', even more literate individuals, central government has persistently feared and interfered with ethical and literacy development in the school curriculum. It simply does not want education to foster the kind of citizen promoted in, for instance, Masterman's model of curriculum development (Masterman 1992), that questions the impact of one person's wealth upon others within a community, or of one nation's wealth upon other nations, or that links crime to arbitrary social conditions rather than to internal, personalized 'goodness' or 'badness'. When central government talks of the promotion of morality, it means a very particular kind of morality, that precisely does pathologize the individual actor while underplaying or overlooking the collective responsibility of communities and of the governments that manage them. Similarly, when central government talks of the empowering advantages of literacy development, it means very specifically the empowering advantages of functional and cultural literacy development, which only offer at best a very limited empowerment within an essentially disempowering social system. Indeed, the prioritization of literacy (and, for that matter, numeracy), which for centuries was considered by the ruling classes to be totally irrelevant for the vast majority of working people, is very easily traceable to changes in the socio-economic structure of the country rather than to an enlightened, altruistic awareness of education's life-enhancing powers. Put bluntly, 'basic', functional literacy and numeracy skills have been prioritized in the school curriculum not because literate, numerate people will be happier, more fulfilled people with better job opportunities (though that may well be a desirable side-effect for some), but because, in post-industrial Britain, capital's needs have moved from requiring a labour-dominant workforce to requiring a clerical-dominant workforce and increasingly (Medway 1990, p. 31) from requiring 'producers' to requiring 'consumers'.

Should we be in any doubt that such a hidden agenda underpins the 'official' one, we could do worse than refer to some of the relatively honest expressions of fear, concern and rationale expressed by politicians during the debates immediately preceding the instigation of universal state education. We might consider, for example, Robert Lowe's (1862) suggestion to Parliament that '[w]e do not profess to give these ["labouring class"] children an education that will raise them above their station and business in life ... but to give them an education that may fit them for that business' (quoted in Selleck 1968, p. 15); or Playfair's (1870) articulation of 'a lurking, though inexpressed fear, that the lower orders may be too highly educated' and that the state has done its duty 'when it imparts the *rudiments* of knowledge' (Selleck 1968, p.15, my emphasis); or, indeed, Tory-led opposition, more than half a century earlier, to proposals for the establishment of parish schools, on the basis that 'instead of teaching [the labouring classes] subordination, [education] would render them factious and refractory' (cited by Simon 1974, p. 132, and Willinsky 1993, p. 68).

The governing classes' persistent difficulties with education are nowhere better articulated than in the these early debates (see also Maclure 1986): a more educated workforce was required in order for the nation to be more competitive and for its domestic inequalities to be perpetuated – but only a very limited kind of education would do. Too much learning – what we might call 'more than literacy' – was potentially a very dangerous thing, which meant that State education itself was potentially a very dangerous thing that would need to be very carefully regulated. Depending on what definition of education we adopt, we might, indeed, argue that central government's allegiance *to* 'the basics' is, simultaneously, a reaction *against* education.

Once we have grasped this central difficulty, it becomes a lot easier to understand – and to articulate an effective response to – the back-to-basics agenda that currently seeks (and is very effective in reaching) the high moral ground in its battle against critical change. No one, of course, is naive enough to suppose that this battle will be easily won. The gravitational pull of the fetishistic curriculum inhibits the trajectory of the 'postmodern turn' with all the force a large, monolithic body commands: everyone knows that central government is not going to decide overnight to instruct schools to prioritize co-operation over competition, critical, collective morality over uncritical personal morality, or non-standard forms of expression side-by-side with 'standard' ones – and indeed unless such a course of action were taken by governments around the world, such a decision might not, in itself, achieve a great deal. It is important, however, to recognize that a start has to be made somewhere, that there may already be some common ground of sorts between the perceived needs of capital and the preferred pedagogies and curricula of radical teachers, and to keep rational, alternative arguments alive through pro-active as well as re-active initiatives of the kind I have already described. The context for this must surely include a strenuous, reasoned evaluation of post-war developments in education, that measures the present situation not against the status quo of 1990 or 1980, but against attitudes and practices that were still prevalent fifty, forty, or even thirty years ago. Such an evaluation may not only offer a far clearer indication of the developments that have actually occurred within English teaching and other curriculum areas, but will also help to map out the ideological battlefield in which we now find ourselves. Who knows? It may also suggest that radical, forward-thinking teachers are not at such a huge disadvantage as sometimes seems the case in these days of 'levels' and 'basics' and the reassertion of dominant cultural preferences in our schools: that what might appear, at times, the irresistible resurgence of the modernist discourse may, in the due course of time, be seen to have been nothing less than its death-rattle.

In an epoch characterized by one humano-ecological catastrophe after another, much will depend, of course, on the alacrity with which the proponents of the monolithic, monologic curriculum arrive at their own understanding (even if, initially, on the level 'no people, no profit') that it is only through an alternative, understanding-centred, co-operation-focused education that the future of the human race – indeed, of the planet itself – is to be secured. Working together as informed pressure groups, a central role for teachers is still – as always – to help to ensure that this understanding occurs sooner rather than too late.

NOTES

1 In making these observations, I am aware that a complete consensus remains elusive. Lather (1991), for example, has argued for a distinction between the postmodernism of *reaction* and the postmodernism of *resistance*, while Blake (1996) has positioned postmodernism in opposition to, and simultaneously as a viable alternative to, neo-Marxism. Cole, Hill and Rikowski (1997) have argued most passionately that postmodernism of any hue supports, in one way or another, not left-wing but right-wing radicalism in terms of educational theory and practice. While adopting a stance roughly in line with Lather's, I see no fundamental contradiction in bringing both a postmodern and a neo-Marxist perspective to an analysis of educational development. It will also be evident to those who read their article that I do not find Cole et al.'s interpretation of postmodern thinking on education unproblematic – an interpretation which also posits postmodernism in opposition to [neo-]Marxism rather than to certain forms and manifestations of modernism.

7

The Aim is Song: Towards an Alternative National Curriculum for the Arts[1]

Malcolm Ross

Before man came to blow it right
The wind once blew itself untaught,
And did its loudest day and night
In any rough place where it caught.

Man came to tell it what was wrong:
It hadn't found the place to blow;
It blew too hard – the aim was song.
And listen – how it ought to go!

Robert Frost (The Aim was Song)

I am sitting with the Deputy Head in his office. We have just returned from chatting with one of the art staff in her relaxed and colourful design studio. The alarm phone rings. The next moment he is rushing away to a classroom that has been invaded by a gang of skinheads bent on racist assault.

I am sitting with the Head in her study. I have been watching a group of sixth formers improvising a contemporary version of *The Country Wife* – set somewhere in the city. We are talking about Philip Lawrence and she describes a recent incident at the school gates when she herself was threatened by a young man with a knife.

I am sitting with the Head in her study. On the preceding evening I had attended the school's Christmas concert. She is telling me how, when one of her students was murdered on her way home from school, it was to the arts teachers that the girl's friends turned the following day in their effort to cope.

These are all moments from my research diary and cover three consecutive days in December 1995. I place them here simply as markers. Whatever I try to say about the arts in education in what follows I want to be sure to hold on to this reality.

In January 1995 the revised Orders setting out the Programmes of Study

126

and Attainment Targets for National Curriculum Art and Music were published and distributed to all schools. The 'slimmed down' specification represented the outcome of the review of the National Curriculum undertaken by Sir Ron Dearing, Chairman of the Schools Curriculum and Assessment Authority. Following years of argument over the weight of the National Curriculum as a whole and various intermediate moves to ease the load on teachers and children – including the making of the arts optional at Key Stage 4 – educators in England and Wales have been promised five years respite from any further changes to the curriculum: a period of 'consolidation'.

Given that the revised Orders are to shape curriculum design, practice and assessment for some years to come it seems reasonable to take a look at what all the formulation, consultation and revision have achieved. In this paper I shall be considering a number of questions. I want to establish if I can what view of the arts – what view of art and music – emerges from the Orders. Closely connected with that question would be one concerning the view of arts education embodied therein. I want to look at the Orders in terms of the guidance and support given to teachers in the shaping of children's experience in the arts and, particularly, at how the notions of 'progression' and 'development' – the conceptual main-stays of the assessment-led National Curriculum – are handled. I shall further consider whether the publishing of separate Orders for the different arts would seem, on the evidence, to have been justified. These questions are very much in order I feel since the publications are intended, presumably, to provide, among other things, the framework for school inspections and individual teacher assessment. They will also no doubt be used to communicate a child's educational entitlement in the arts to parents. They are not of course full blown guidelines on Art and Music teaching. An avalanche of such material may now be expected. What we have here are the bare conceptual bones of the arts curriculum. I want to see how much faith we should have in them as supporting a body of work that we might feel was appropriate, and that was congruent with our own sense of the role of these subjects in the experience of children at school. How ready should we be to 'consolidate' around the specifications as now decreed?

THE NATIONAL CURRICULUM FRAMEWORK

If we are to grasp the 'logic' of the way the Orders for Art and Music have been structured it is sensible to refer back to the 1983 publication by the Assessment of Performance Unit (APU) entitled *Aesthetic Development*. Whilst apparently making little impact at the time, the framework developed by the team responsible for the study is plainly evident in the revised Orders – as indeed it was in the earlier, fuller prescriptions. This would seem to suggest that the thinking which informs the new Orders might fairly be said to represent some kind of professional consensus about what constitutes the curriculum in these subjects, thereby avoiding any further, unhelpful controversy and, indeed, lending an added sense of legitimacy or authority to the formulations. Even in their leaner manifestation they derive after all from the deliberations of groups selected by Ministers from among experienced Art and Music educators but also representing the interests of parents, arts institutions and employers. If we are to take issue with what is set before us we should not perhaps expect to be universally persuasive, despite the fact that the experts recruited for the purpose of advising the government were not necessarily always representative of the whole range of interests and orientations within specific disciplines. As we shall see in what follows, the notions of Art and Music officially now sanctioned bear a distinctive and consistent bias. We can assume that government had an ear tuned to its own music.

The earlier APU framework for the arts curriculum had two dimensions. The first dimension distinguished three principal activities which were felt to embody the participatory roles associated with experience in the arts: forming, performing and audience/critic. The second dimension itemized the 'elements' or content of the arts curriculum: 'knowledge of context', 'skills of handling', 'artistic appraisals' and 'personal values'. A glance at the Attainment Targets (ATs) for Art and Music is sufficient to indicate the significant presence of the APU's first dimension: the participatory roles. Music has Performing and Composing as AT1 with Listening and Appraising (standing in for audience/critic) as AT2. Things don't look quite so obvious with Art. However, Investigating and Making are activities obviously associated with forming in art and craft, and the way Knowledge and Understanding are translated into specific activities makes it clear that here too we have the notions of 'responding to' and 'evaluating' works of art (and craft) – however understood. Meanwhile a number of the elements (the second dimension) established by the APU as constituting the content of the curriculum figure one way or another in the detail of the two sets of Programmes of Study. I say 'a number' because there are some significant omissions and a degree of weighting which does distinguish the present Orders from the model (APU) formulation. I shall come back to consider this matter of emphasis later but in the meantime I would simply point out that the Orders make more use of the APU 'Knowledge of Contexts' and 'Skills of Handling' aspects of arts practice than they do of 'Artistic Appraisals' and 'Personal Values'.

Given such a pronounced, shared identity of formulation in the two sets of Orders – and I leave aside the obvious and superficial similarities of layout and Attainment Target specification (seemingly a decision based upon presentational rather than conceptual considerations) – I am tempted to ask why more was not made of the common ground in the documents themselves, and, indeed, whether there might not have been a case for providing a combined set of Orders in which the measure of overlap was pointed up constructively, whilst at the same time demonstrating the special character of the elements distinguishing one discipline from the other. By my reckoning only elements a and b in the Programmes of Study seriously differentiate Art from Music, whereas there is considerable identity across all the remaining elements, including matters such as control of media, realization of artistic intentions, ability to refine and modify work in progress, awareness of the range of artistic experience, understanding artistic communication, recognizing historical and cultural contexts, possessing a vocabulary of artistic discourse. In similar vein, the End of Key-Stage Descriptions for both subjects echo each other at almost every point. Both are concerned to build pupil confidence, to encourage accuracy in performance, to improve crafting skills and motor control, to enhance powers of discernment and discrimination, to require self-assessment and the readiness to modify work in the light of criticism, to promote communication skills and independence, to build a solid foundation of knowledge of the 'elements' characteristic of each medium, to teach the use of a specific vocabulary of discourse and the relation of form to function – and so forth. I can only discern one major omission from Music of a consideration prized in Art: imagination. And that surely was simply an oversight.

All of this suggests to me that were the people responsible so minded – and they were not – there was no inherently rational point in treating these two subjects separately. We must assume that government and those specialist advisers charged with drawing up the Orders had their own reasons for wishing to keep the subjects apart. It goes pretty much without saying that the degree of congruence evident between Art and Music as presented in these documents would be replicated for the other arts: the verbal arts, dance and drama. Some arts educators – and I would certainly be one such – see the present dispensation as a lost opportunity, even a serious tactical mistake in the struggle to maintain a significant arts presence in a tightly packed curriculum. There is evidence dating back a number of years[2] that students much prefer to experience the arts in schools through inter-disciplinary projects than as single subjects – a preference amply justified in terms both of their experience of the arts outside schools and indeed of the practices of many of today's professional artists. There is also evidence that teachers working in schools offering such interdisciplinary curricula in the arts benefit hugely from the sharing of resources, the blocked time-tabling and the general sense of collective enterprise and mutual support associated with such schemes.

Perhaps we should formulate our First Alternative Proposal:
The arts in schools should be expected to work together.

CONTINUITY AND PROGRESSION IN THE NATIONAL CURRICULUM

Here we have two principles absolutely central to the whole National Curriculum project. The paraphernalia of Key Stages, Attainment Targets and Programmes of Study aims above all things to persuade teachers (and parents) that it is possible to *teach* the arts and to teach them in an ordered and coherent fashion which clearly conforms to a model of learning we are all familiar with: the more you study the more you know; the harder you practise the better you get. Whether such a model is in fact appropriate for the arts is never considered. The whole fabric raised upon the framework we have just been examining – a framework, as we have said, claiming considerable authority – assumes the common-sense accretive, gradualist model of learning that assimilates bits to whole and equates more with better. Where such a conception of learning might be appropriate in some subject areas – in Physical Education for example (I don't say it should be but it might be) – it might not sit so very well with the arts – with dance for instance. Let's examine the substance of the material that such a model gives rise to.

It will perhaps be argued by the National Curriculum supporters that a blow has been struck for 'continuity' simply by having the Orders available for primary and secondary teachers to consult and work to. A common framework of elements and objectives should lend coherence to the curriculum. Everyone will be talking about the same things and using the same terms. But what about distinguishing work and expectations at different ages? Two observations are in order here: (i) the sequencing principle that informs the consecutive stages is not always immediately apparent in the new Orders, and (ii) the notion of progression as presented is virtually impossible to translate into actual criteria of achievement or attainment. What are we to make, for example, of the following developmental sequences:

'improvise musical patterns' > 'improvise rhythmic and melodic ideas' > 'improvise and arrange in a variety of styles';
or,
'rehearse and share their music making' > 'rehearse and present their own projects/performances' > 'plan, rehearse, direct and present performances';
or,
'recognize images and artefacts as sources of ideas for their work' > 'record observations and ideas, and collect visual evidence and information, using a sketchbook' > 'select and record observations and ideas, and research and organize a range of visual evidence and information, using a sketchbook';
or,
'identify in the school and locality the work of artists, crafts people and designers' > 'identify in the school and the locality the materials and

methods used by artists, crafts people and designers' > 'recognize the diverse methods and approaches used by artists, crafts people and designers'?

My question in each case is simply, What is the *pedagogical* notion of progression which informs the sequence? I maintain that there is none whatsoever – certainly none that would help a teacher at any particular key-stage to distinguish her work – on the basis of her particular place in the sequence – from that of her colleagues operating elsewhere on the scale. What we have instead is a layout, a design that *looks* as if it makes sense. Again, it might be possible, honestly, to translate certain learning activities in certain subjects into sequences like the ones we have just been looking at, but the very banality of what is given us in the Orders for Art and Music is proof if proof were needed that the whole project where the arts are concerned is not simply misguided but dishonest. It is damaging as it serves to inhibit speculation and experimentation which might actually provide a realistic and appropriate model of progression in the arts.

Second Alternative Proposal:
Progression/Assessment in the arts is qualitative rather than quantitative.

In almost every case the specification of elements in the programmes as stages in a sequence of learning in the arts is a blatant sham. The intended effect of the typographical lay-out is to persuade by impression rather than substance. The intention is to create an illusion of progression – in other words, to fabricate a fiction. It is my belief that the whole project translates into a fiction – a set of inscriptions that are no more than that. They rely for their force upon the mere fact of having been written down. They claim the authority of a financial spreadsheet. Not only might the exercise be misconceived, as we have said above, because learning in the arts is not like this; it fails even on its own terms because when it is rendered as articulate statement, it is self-evident (and pretentious) nonsense.

We are no better off when we look at the sequence of statements for guidance over Levels of Attainment. There is no indication of what it might mean to be performing any one of the activities at a level appropriate to the child's age. We are left simply looking for greater accuracy, more refinement, more self-confidence, a more developed 'vocabulary', better motor-control, more awareness of more musical or artistic 'elements'. What is required is a coherent conception of aesthetic experience that would allow for individual, qualitative profiling of each student. I shall be suggesting a possible approach to this difficult assignment a little later in this chapter. Meanwhile, the revised Orders, claiming to present a developmental account of teaching and learning in the arts, ignore entirely all research, all theoretical models available to inform such a scheme[3] and end up imposing a specious structure upon mere ignorance and confusion. It might not really be too extreme a judgement to see the whole exercise as one enormous con trick designed to maintain the status quo and leave the reigning barons in Art and Music education firmly at the helm for the foreseeable future, their credentials now beyond question.

THE NATIONAL CURRICULUM IDEA OF AN ARTS EDUCATION

It is not difficult to see what notions of Art and Music inform the Orders. It is, in fact, one and the same notion – and perhaps that should not surprise us. There are several clues. If we look at the language used in the two documents, particularly if one does so with some experience of writing and reading in the arts, it immediately becomes apparent that the vocabulary is strangely restricted. There would appear to be a cluster of favoured or legitimate words, notable for the regularity of their recurrence; by the same token, there are certain words for which one looks more or less in vain: words that are strictly taboo where the National Curriculum in the arts is concerned. Let's take the OK words first: words such as *identify, recognize, record, select, describe*. Using Donald Schön's (1983) terminology I would say that these words signal the world of Technical Rationality (rather than art); shifting to the writing of Maurice Merleau-Ponty (1973), these are the words of the 'prose of the world' (rather than its poetry). The taboo words are: *create, feel, express, imagine, play*. Where these words do occur – and words from the same family such as *improvise, explore, intuit, experiment* – they are heavily outnumbered by the more 'correct' vocabulary. These words that I have called 'taboo' are words one might certainly have expected to find, not least because most arts teachers still use them definitively to talk about their work (Ross 1991). An on-going study of the language used by arts teacher trainers to describe their professional priorities[4] endorses this finding. No matter how constrained by pressures on time and resources in the present situation in colleges and departments of education, these lecturers in the arts all acknowledged 'expression' and 'creativity' as major principles in the experience of the arts in education. Why, therefore, are they not to be found – or not to any significant degree – in these documents? The answer has to be that the Orders were drafted by (and/or for) persons with an idea of Art and Music education for which such words had little or no significance. What kind of an idea would that be?

We have already made mention of Schön's distinction between the language and practices of what he calls Technical Rationality and those characteristic of an artistic mode of action. Schön is not exhorting art teachers only, but all teachers to adopt creative and expressive ways of teaching. He favours a dialogical and improvisatory approach to teaching, with the teacher's expertise manifested in a capacity for intuitive judgement within the teaching-learning encounter. That judgement arises in the teacher's perception of the student's approximation to an imagined possible performance. Teaching thereby comes to rest upon the teacher's imaginative powers every bit as much if not more than upon mere management skills. Again we are in direct conflict with the spirit embodied in National Curriculum thinking which would see teachers as those whose job it is to deliver the prescribed goods – the goods that together constitute the curriculum. For the true artist teacher the curriculum is the child, not some externally prescribed agenda. Socrates was allegedly a sculptor and perhaps that is where his strength as a teacher lay. As an artist he knew about dialogue and about tuning into the emergent image latent in the stone. He followed a similar process in his intuitive approach to teaching – an approach elaborated by, for example Martin Buber (1965; 1966) in his writings on education. There is a description by Herbert Read (1931, p. 217) of Henry Moore's way of working with stone that catches the notion we have been examining.

> If you are translating from one material form into another material, you must create that form from the inside outwards. Most sculpture – even, for example ancient Egyptian sculpture – creates mass by a synthesis of two-dimensional aspects. We cannot see all round a cubic mass; the sculptor tends to walk round his mass of stone and endeavours to make it satisfactory from every point of view. He can thus go a long way towards success, but he cannot be so successful as the sculptor whose act of creation is, as it were, a four-dimensional process growing out of a conception which inheres in the mass itself. Form is then an intuition of surface made by a sculptor imaginatively situated at the centre of gravity of the block before him. Under the guidance of this intuition, the stone is slowly educated from an arbitrary into an ideal state of existence. And that, after all, should be the primary aim of every artistic activity.

To answer the question, What notion of art informs the revised Orders?, I shall turn to someone once thought of very highly in the realm of art education, the English philosopher R.G. Collingwood. In his original and challenging book *The Principles of Art*, first published in 1938, he was at some pains to distinguish between what he called 'misconceptions' about art and 'art proper'. For Collingwood the most pervasive misconception about art was to confuse it with craft – as in the Greek *techne*. He listed six different versions of the craft account of art, 'of art', as he put it, 'falsely so called': amusement, magic, puzzle, instruction, advertisement or propaganda, exhortation. He elaborates his position by examining art as amusement and art as magic at some length. It would be fair to say that for Collingwood the crucial concepts for understanding 'art proper' are *expression, creativity, feeling, play* – precisely those words we described as 'taboo' within the National Curriculum. His account places art in the realm of language – though not 'language' understood simply as a system of 'expressive' signs and codes requiring translation from one medium into another (e.g., the visual into the verbal), but as the formative act of reciprocal speech – the impulse to become articulate with another. As many readers will no doubt be aware, for Collingwood art served a moral purpose – a purpose which was only incidentally to do with crafting skills or production techniques but was rather psychological: to serve as 'the community's medicine for the worst disease of mind, the corruption of consciousness'. I cannot resist the temptation to apply Collingwood's stricture to the documents under discussion – indeed to the whole National Curriculum enterprise, with its coercive and impositional ethos. Children and teachers are actually subject these days to a reign of terror – I believe that to be no exaggeration. It is disguised by talk of parental choice and consumer rights, by league-tabling and endless testing in the name of Quality Assurance, as if children were manufactured artefacts and teachers production-line operators. Meanwhile, the very choice of Attainment Targets for the arts stresses practical skill and productivity, rather than profiling arts experience as such.

What we have in these Orders is not simply a very one-sided view of art – art as craft, technique, product, knowledge, know-how – we have a kind of travesty, a mockery. It is not informed by a wrong or an inadequate rationale. It is informed by no rationale at all. Even on its own technical-rational terms the offering fails because it does not deliver on either of the counts which purport to vindicate it. In as much as it ignores the issues deemed essential by Collingwood, and not without provenance in much other writing on art and music both ancient and modern, it renders itself hopelessly irrelevant. The squeamishness of the authors is difficult to understand outside the political in-fighting which bedevilled the whole process of National Curriculum formulation. The 'expressivist' tradition in arts education was deemed at the time to be inimical to government thinking. Visual Art educators had long since made their peace with the craft and design wing of their outfit, reckoning that their's was the future. Music, having acquired its own 'product-based' profile by including 'composition' in its specification, was well placed to survive by additionally appealing to other craft-type roles under Collingwood's categories of amusement and magic.

Our Third Alternative Proposal:

The arts must figure in the curriculum as creative and expressive experiences, nurturing and extending individual critical perception.

AN ALTERNATIVE FRAMEWORK FOR THE ARTS

In the Leverhulme Assessment Project (Ross et al. 1993), my co-researchers and I found we could make no progress together until we had an agreed way of conceiving of the creative process in the arts and some mutually acceptable terms for talking about our experience as teachers and assessors. Together we came up with a framework based upon the writings of Rom Harré – especially his book, *Personal Being* (1983). Harré describes the arts as projects in the formation of personal identity – and it should be clear by now that I see the arts in schools instrumentally in terms of the student's personal enrichment, integration and self-definition. Harré's account consorts well with the idea of the arts giving access to personal voice, personal speech, personal 'style'. What was important about Harré's description was the model by means of which he articulated the different, complementary elements of the process he was interested in. He proposed a two-dimensional matrix crossing the experiential domain (public-private) with action (individual-collective). In Figure 7.1 it will be seen that the matrix yields four quadrants: Harré gives to each a particular designation, namely: (1) Conventionalization, (2) Appropriation, (3) Transformation and (4) Publication.

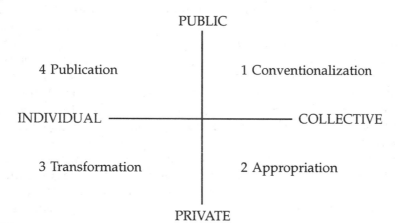

Fig 7.1

In essence Q1 (Conventionalization) refers to the public/collective field of language. Here what is meant is not so much the notion of language or convention or tradition held in some kind of cultural limbo or never-never-land, but all these things understood as living and operating in the on-going experience of the culture. So this is the living language, these are the practical codes and conventions regulating the present, on-going discourse of the people. Here are the synaesthetic origins of all expressive speech: 'universals' of utterance and gesture. Here too, if you like, in Q1, we have the conversation of mankind (Oakeshott 1959) as a living possibility: a living repository of practice. Conversation is not generated here: this area marks the possibility of conversation as a constantly evolving system and a constantly renewing tradition. This is the cultural context, the symbolic order, into which the uninitiated is propelled at birth and by means of which she or he must find their way. It follows that each must become, as the phrase goes, 'a member of the wedding', and that means accommodating the mores and traditions of the tribe. For anyone interested in using the model as a way of rationalizing curriculum provision in the arts, Q1 represents the (evolving) heritage, the culture in which we must become literate. There is no contradiction between becoming a creative artist in one's own right and learning the language of the tribe. In fact of course there can be no creativity outside the context which makes shared meaning possible in the first place.

Q2 (Appropriation), the collective/private domain, is the movement in assimilation by which the individual makes the language their own. It means, of course, taking over the language as personal speech as personal voice – the apparatus or personal material from which personal speech is generated. Without this act of appropriation there can be no personal speech – merely the mechanical reproduction and replication of the voices of others. The words in the mouth of the other (Q1) remain alien to the tongue of the individual until voiced by her or him in their own right and as their own speech articulating in a particular way their own experience. To have one's own speech is to be at home in the world.

Q3 (Transformation), the domain of the private/individual, is the realm of the creative imagination, the realm of creative symbol use. This is where 'thinking' in the arts takes place. This is the realm of Gardner's 'multiple-intelligences' (Gardner 1984) – of what we might prefer to call our own multiple-imaginations. Here consciousness is transformed, and kept whole and holy. This, to pursue the connection with Collingwood, is where the special 'making that is not the making of material things' takes place.

Q4 (Publication), the domain of the public/individual, sees the presentation of authentic conversation with the world. Here personal style manifests itself as does public voice. Here is the site of trial (experience) and of validation, of the surrendering of the work of imagination and its reflecting back in the act of meeting, in the encounter with the other. This is the site of living conversation, of company, communion, of the breaking of bread, the practice of ritual, the festival. Here the word is spoken, articulated, deployed transactionally and in the service of the sacred. Here authenticity and integrity are sacrosanct: good-faith and good-will are the rule. Here hope is possible. Here too, alas, the rules are bent, false-seeming and false-dealing practised and the word broken. This is the place for vigilance.

In Harré's version, the four quadrants are traversed as an invariant cycle and sequentially, the cycle repeating itself as experience in Q4 converts to an alteration and/or increase in the cultural stock as represented by Q1. I am not sure that, for the purposes of modelling the arts curriculum, we should be too concerned with the regularity of the progression through the quadrants. Art may not be a circle dance. I think it does help to think of the operations involved in making personal meaning through the arts by means of this comprehensive model. I suspect the movement around the matrix when we come to consider particular projects might be more irregular as the private experience weaves in and out of the public, and individual action alternates with the collective. The most significant feature of the model is the way it balances the various polarities: the way we are bound to recognize the claims of the private as well as the public aspects of the experience of art; the way the actions of the collective are balanced against the actions of the individual. The characterization of the four quadrants is also equally enlightening, giving us a clear sense of the different targets or operations which, as teachers, we need to take account of in providing and managing a personal experience of the arts for any particular child. 'Comprehensive' and 'balanced' come to mean not so much a 'representative' experience involving dipping into and sampling all the arts on offer, including as many of the arts of other cultures as might be heaped upon the student, but rather a curriculum which places equal stress upon the tradition, upon the student's acquiring a personal voice, developing an effective imagination as a means of 'thinking' intelligently in at least one (albeit multi-) medium, and then being able to participate in the conversation of mankind using her own or his own authentic voice. This is the project of the creative and expressive arts.

Harré (1983) and Gadamer (1975, 1986) can be understood as coinciding to a significant degree: Gadamer's concern with Tradition meets Harré's Conventionalization; Gadamer's Play is Harré's Appropriation; Gadamer's Symbol is Harré's Transformation; Gadamer's Festival is Harré's Publication.

Our Fourth Alternative Proposal:

Arts education is an identity project which brings together public and private experience, individual and collective action in the making and handling of 'feeling' forms.

SEEING THINGS

What is also noticeable in the revised Orders is the emphasis placed by both subjects on the concept of 'literacy'. This is perhaps more surprising in the area of Art than in Music, where being able to read and write has long been thought a mark of distinction. To expose the gravity of the mistake made by the Art group I turn to Merleau-Ponty. In the final chapter of his enigmatic book already referred to, *The Prose of the World* (Merleau-Ponty 1973), he exposes the flaw in the debate about children's art which focuses achievement upon the mastery of two-point perspective. He argues that this is part of the Enlightenment project and is consonant with removing the particular, human element from depiction. Children's drawings, he argues, retain this element by seeing a drawing not as something to be read but as something to be 'received'.

> The aim is to leave on the paper a trace of our contact with this object and this spectacle, insofar as they made our gaze and virtually our touch, our ears, our feeling of risk or of destiny or of freedom vibrate. It is a question of leaving a testimony and not any more of providing information. The drawing is no longer

to be read the way it was until recently. It is not to be dominated by the look. We are no longer to find in it the pleasure of embracing the world. The drawing is to be received. It will concern us like some decisive word. (p. 150)

Where, in the Programme of Study for Art at Key Stage 1, is the spirit of Marion Richardson (1948) to be found?

The concept of 'visual literacy' given such prominence in National Curriculum Art threatens the whole undertaking. It is not that the notion has no meaning in a total art curriculum. It is simply that it must not be allowed to become the determining principle. Apart from wishing to respect the ideas identified with Collingwood's work, it seems to me that no account of either music or art could be deemed comprehensive unless it addressed what he says about works of art being 'things of some other kind, and made in some other way'. To do so, room would also have to be found for H-G. Gadamer's key notions of *play*, *symbol* and *festival*, as well as for Merleau-Ponty's idea of speech. What the National Curriculum represents is an overt strategy for rendering the arts acceptable in schools provided they function either as crafts or as quasi-academic disciplines rooted in the traditions of reading and writing, i.e., literacy. If this is an offer we cannot exactly refuse, it is certainly one we should subvert. We shall glance at this principle before we conclude.

Gadamer has written extensively on the nature of art and of aesthetic experience. A discussion of art forms the basis of his principal work in hermeneutics, *Truth and Method* (Gadamer 1975). Gadamer outlines his theory of art in his extended essay entitled *The Relevance of the Beautiful* (Gadamer 1986). In this essay he identifies three concepts as essential to understanding the function of art in the modern world. I cannot spend long elaborating his position here, so I shall merely sketch in his main ideas. In the first place he singles out the notion of *play*. For Gadamer play is identified not with the notion of playfulness and as a realm of experience at the opposite pole from what most people might call 'work' or 'reality' (see for instance D.W. Winnicott's *Playing and Reality*). Play for Gadamer is a mode of perception. He refers his reader to various uses of the term – the play of sunlight upon the sea, the play in a gear-box, the play of gnats on a summer evening. He has in mind such notions as the play of ideas, of feeling and imagination essential to the 'making' process in the arts but found in all those moments of intuitive reflection when we allow the mind to drift, thought to wander and unconscious forces to direct our attention and our purposes. At such times we 'think' holistically, with attention moving to-and-fro upon the surface of consciousness itself, much as Yeats in his poem *Long Legged Fly* describes the inspired moments in the careers of Caesar, Michaelangelo, and Helen of Troy, 'practising a tinker shuffle' –

Like a long-legged fly upon the stream
Her mind moves upon silence.

Silence is probably one of the most prized elements in the creative process. Gadamer associates this account of play with what he calls the moment of 'self-presentation'. It is to be open to the presence of the other, to what Walter Benjamin (1992a) called its 'aura'. Whereas as we have seen this mode of perception might not be exclusive to the arts it is essential to what artistic experience is about.

Gadamer's second concept concerning the nature of art is a particular reading of the word *symbol*. He pays considerable attention to defining precisely what he wishes to be understood to mean by the symbolic in art in both the books I have referred to. Putting his distinction as simply as possible, Gadamer repudiates the notion of the symbol in art as 'referential', as pointing to something beyond or outside the work itself. Whilst accepting that much art incorporates symbols used for instance allegorically, this is not what interests Gadamer, or what, in his view, makes the work in question a work of art. It is not symbol as code that he makes central to his understanding (therefore not the notion of 'literacy' beloved of the National Curriculum writers). For Gadamer the work of art operates according to the principle of the *tessera hospitalis*. He has in mind the traditional symbolic practice of breaking a plate or a bowl at the departure of a guest, each of the partners taking one half, the two halves to be joined again in 'recognition' of their mutuality, on the occasion of their reunion. The work of art, Gadamer argues, is never any more than one half of the total experience of art. The experience of art feels like a moment of recognition, or reunion, in which what confronts us in the material world supplies the desired 'other half' necessary to a particular sense of personal integrity or wholeness. This notion of the symbol in art forms a crucial part of Gadamer's argument against 'aestheticism' and the prioritizing of the notions of good taste and connoisseurism. For Gadamer art is a means of apprehending a 'holy order' in the world and is not reserved for a specially educated or sophisticated élite.

Finally, Gadamer appeals to the word *festival* to complete his profile of the experience of art. Here we come closer to the more conventional account of play as 'time-off', recreation and an occasion of indulgence. But that is not the whole story, for festival includes the sacred as well as the profane, is centred upon an experience of wonder and worship, gives itself to ritual and to sacrifice and to prayer as well as feasting. Festival is at once a celebration of that which lies beyond us and which we glimpse and hold to as our personal vision of perfection and the basis of hope and meaning in our lives, whilst at the same time releasing the impulse to celebrate life itself, in an outburst of vitality, indulgence and irresponsibility. Art, Gadamer argues, belongs to the dialectical category of festive activity and will always strike out in the apparently opposite directions we have just been describing. Art is a dialectic in which the sacred and the profane are mutually supportive rather than competitive. Art is the biggest joke and at the same time the most profound truth. Cecil Collins (1994) attempted a depiction of this complex notion in some of his paintings of the Fool. Festival time is time apart – apart from the mundane routines of everyday. (The arts continue to appeal to students where they allow for this dimension – it is their trump card over more stolid subjects in the curriculum.) Clock time loses its grip on holy days. There is a similarly special character to festival sites. The festival is geared to the phenomena of presentation (see 'play' above). Festival emphasizes the notion of a living past informing and accommodating a dynamic present. Festival is an adventure in consciousness.

Such adventures probably have their basis in processes of biological renewal – the drive within the organism to repair its renewable elements and maintain its capacity for vigilance. In humans we have the whole range of what Maslow (1968) called 'Being needs' to attend to. The making imaginative sense of what it means to be a conscious person is what the arts are about. The processes of art comprise principally those delineated by Gadamer. It follows that a real arts education must satisfy criteria generated from those constructs. Arts teachers have always known this. They have not always followed their vocation in these matters. Today we are in danger of losing sight of that vocation altogether. If you are looking for a contemporary account of the role of art in society and in education to complement the account I have just given then I recommend Seamus Heaney's *The Redress of Poetry* (1995) For Heaney the arts provide a way of asserting our humanity against everything in life that threatens it. The arts in schools must never become merely solemn, anymore than they should submit to the pragmatic solution which would make them 'teachable' – as craft or academic studies. The arts in education must be occasions of joy and fury, affirmation and affront. It might take a visit to an exhibition such as the recent one at the Hayward Gallery in London, *Art and Power*, to remind us how vulnerable artists (and arts teachers) can be to pressures both subtle and not so subtle. The consciousness of artists, as Collingwood said, is easily corrupted. If I were looking for a slogan for arts education it would perhaps turn upon the fusion of Adventure with Vigilance. And as for arts teachers, surely their first calling is to be Witnesses – to both these principles. As Collingwood also said, there are no skills to be learnt or taught where expression is concerned. If the beautiful takes our breath away, art allows us to voice our wonder, for instance at 'the glittering and flawless knowledge of perfect ice'.

Our Fifth Alternative Proposal:

The arts in schools must be conceived within a festival framework: committed to the twin principles of hope and redress.

CONCLUSION

In this chapter I have been considering the messages embodied in the revised Orders for Music and Art. I have argued that the documents are threadbare when viewed in terms of intellectual content. I have concluded that they are in most respects useless and repugnant to arts teachers. I have said that they present a seriously inadequate – even a wilfully distorted – account of Art and Music, and that they are thereby likely to disfigure and stunt the teaching of both subjects in a significant degree and for the fore-seeable future. My recent reports on the present situation of the arts in schools give notice of serious consequences flowing from the current situation (Ross and Kamba, 1997). In closing I would like to make one further point. Both sets of Orders claim to be concerned not only that children 'understand' these two subjects but that they also 'enjoy' them. I find no indication in the specifications about how this second objective is to be realized. My present research tells me that there is no chance of children valuing the arts in school unless they also enjoy them, and joy is scarcely the hallmark of the National Curriculum. Two arts subjects notable for their rising popularity with children – Dance and Drama – are officially almost invisible. Theirs is little more than a phantom presence in the revised English and Physical Education Orders, though the schools I have been researching refuse to let them die. Indeed, for sheer enjoyment it would seem there are no other subjects that are their equal. Music teachers have recognized for a long time the uphill task they face, and despite the recent reforms their subject continues to flounder as uninteresting and unenjoyable. Hitherto, Art has done considerably better than any of the arts yet there are now clear and troubling signs that the situation might be changing – and not for the better. In the light – or should that be darkness? – of recent experiences, those of us committed to the continuance of an entitlement curriculum in the creative and expressive arts for all students shall need a clear strategy of subversion if the arts are to survive. The machinery of Educational Reform in the 1980s and 1990s is marked by a destructive cast of mind: iconoclasm on a massive scale has been its impulse, coupled with a regime of coercion and systematic intimidation to create at the very heart of the educational enterprise what a recent commentator described, in reference to the activities of OFSTED as a 'culture of failure'. Walter Benjamin (1992b) characterizes 'the destructive' thus:

> No vision inspires the destructive character. He has few needs, and the least of them is to know what will replace what has been destroyed. First of all, for a moment at least, empty space, the place where the thing stood or the victim lived. Someone is sure to be found who needs this space without its being filled ... The destructive character stands in the front line of the traditionalists. Some pass things down to posterity, by making them untouchable and thus conserving them, others pass on situations, by making them practicable and thus liquidating them. The latter are called the destructive (pp. 157–158).

Our Sixth Alternative Proposal
To teach the arts requires an understanding of the pedagogy of joy, and the courage to cherish the untouchable.

The aim of a restored and renewed arts education is song.

NOTES

1 This paper is a re-worked and extended version of an article originally published in the *Journal of Art and Design Education*, Vol. 14, No. 3 October 1995, National Curriculum Art and Music.
2 see for example, Derry Hannam, 'The Arts and the Adolescent Revisited' in Malcolm Ross (ed.) (1993) *Wasteland Wonderland* Perspective 49, University of Exeter.
3 see for example the work of Keith Swanwick, Michael J. Parsons, Howard Gardner and others – usefully summarized in David J. Hargreaves (ed.) (1989) *Children and the Arts* Milton Keynes: Open University Press.
4 ongoing projects at Exeter University School of Education, directed by Malcolm Ross.

8

The Problems and Persistence of the Spiritual

Lynne Broadbent

The 'spiritual' was identified by HMI in the document *Curriculum 11–16* as one of the eight essential areas of experience to which pupils should be introduced during their period of compulsory schooling. Mention of the spiritual was certainly not new to educational debate, since in 1944 the Education Act had made it incumbent upon every local authority 'to contribute towards the spiritual, moral, mental and physical development of the community' (Education Act 1944), although it has since been a matter of conjecture as to whether the use of the term 'spiritual' at this time was, in fact, any more than a synonym for the term 'religious' (Priestley 1985).

However, unlike the 1944 Education Act, *Curriculum 11–16* was not a legislative document to be swiftly and unquestioningly implemented. It was designed to contribute to discussions about the purposes of the curriculum with an expectation that schools would, subsequently, review existing curricular programmes and consider ways in which the curriculum might be developed and implemented in order to promote pupils' learning through the areas of experience. The document made it clear that the areas of experience did not themselves constitute an actual curricular programme, but rather a checklist for 'curricular analysis and construction' (DES 1977a, p. 6). Furthermore, the eight areas were not to be equated with individual subjects; teachers were encouraged 'to look through the subject or discipline to the areas of experience and knowledge to which it might provide access, and to the skills and attitudes which it may assist to develop' (ibid.).

It was envisaged that planning the curriculum would follow a 'three-dimensional framework' (op. cit., p. 7): the first dimension being the essential areas of experience, the second the subjects or groups of studies through which learning was to be organized, while the third dimension related to the progression planned over the five year period of secondary schooling. However, for such a framework to become a viable basis for curriculum planning within individual schools, it required of teachers an understanding of the breadth and the depth of each area of experience in order that it might be distinctly reflected within the subjects or groups of subjects through which learning was to take place. So, how were teachers introduced to the areas of experience, and specifically, how were they introduced to the spiritual area of experience? How did this introduction match their classroom experience and empower them to meet the perceived need for curriculum development evident in *Curriculum 11–16*? What were the consequences of this for curriculum planning at the time, and what has been its legacy in planning for a common core curriculum both within and after the 1988 Education Reform Act?

DESCRIBING THE SPIRITUAL

Brief descriptions of the eight areas of experience were provided in a supplementary paper to *Curriculum 11–16* (DES 1997a), the spiritual area warranting two, seemingly contrasting, descriptions. The first, which at the time and since has been regarded as the more 'open' description, stated:

> The spiritual area is concerned with the awareness a person has of those elements in existence and experience which may be defined in terms of inner feelings and beliefs: they affect the way people see themselves and throw light for them on the purpose and meaning of life itself. Often these feelings and beliefs lead people to claim to know God and to glimpse the transcendent: sometimes they represent that striving and longing for perfection which characterizes human beings but always they are concerned with matters at the heart and root of existence (DES 1977a, supplement).

This description suggested that the spiritual area was associated with human awareness of inner feelings and beliefs which influence an individual's understanding of self and sense of meaning and purpose in life. It is important to note that while for some this might encompass religious belief, this is not assumed to be necessarily true for all.

The second description appears on first sight to relate more directly to religious believers. It claimed:

> The spiritual area is concerned with everything in human knowledge or experience that is connected with or derives from a sense of God or of Gods. Spiritual is a meaningless adjective for the atheist and of dubious use to the agnostic. Irrespective of personal belief or disbelief, an unaccountable number of people have believed and do believe in the spiritual aspects of human life, and therefore their actions, attitudes and interpretations of events have been influenced accordingly (ibid.).

At its best, this description is opaque; at its worst, it lacks coherence. Quite what is meant by the use of the plural form 'Gods' is unclear, as is the distinction between the atheist and the agnostic. The statement that the term 'spiritual' is meaningless for the atheist is questionable in the light of the seemingly contradictory statement that some people, irrespective of personal belief or disbelief, have believed in the spiritual aspects of human life.

Quite apart from any difficulties inherent within the descriptions themselves, there lies a further and by far more significant difficulty, namely that
there is a distinction between the descriptions offered for the term 'spiritual' and those offered for most of the other areas of experience. Neither
definition is phrased in a language which relates to the development of specific competences, either of a personal or academic nature, nor are they
couched in a language which suggests an overall aim for the personal
development of pupils. This is in sharp contrast to the descriptions of the
mathematical and scientific areas which enumerate practical competences
and to the aesthetic/creative and linguistic areas which contain notions of
personal development. What we have are two rather confusing descriptions
of the spiritual area of experience, not instantly or easily applicable to classroom pedagogy or to curriculum planning.

SEEKING EVIDENCE OF THE SPIRITUAL WITHIN THE CURRICULUM

Supplementary Paper 1 of *Curriculum 11–16* presented selected statements
produced by the HMI Subject Committees who were invited to consider
the contribution of 'their' subject to the thesis of the main paper, which was
to consider a common core curriculum planned according to the three-
dimensional framework and based upon the essential areas of experience.

Of the subjects included, most attempt to identify clear links with the
areas of experience, but only a few make reference to the spiritual: history
adopts a somewhat suspicious and defensive stance, although Classics
defines itself as contributing to the spiritual area through its development
of 'appreciation of the meaning and significance of a fundamental aspect
of human thought and behaviour' (p. 46). Not surprisingly, it is in the
statement on Religious Education where we find the strongest reflection of
the spiritual. The quasi 'objectives' for Religious Education highlight in
tone some of the features of the first description of the spiritual
area:

> In consideration of religion and values, the intention is to help pupils to under-
> stand the nature of religious questions and religious affirmations, and to develop
> a personal and intellectual integrity in dealing with the profoundest aspects of
> their own experience now and in adult life. (op. cit., p. 42)

In a further section entitled 'Reflecting on human existence' we find the
following:

> In some people a feel for certain qualities of the human condition, such as tran-
> sience and mystery, may be arrived at intuitively and exist from an early age.
> More commonly, such insight is the result of later reflection upon experiences
> such as birth, growth, love, friendship and death. This reflection will be assisted
> by the acquisition of certain skills which enable the individual to generalize from
> particular experiences and to handle abstract concepts. Religious education
> seeks to encourage this reflective activity, to foster the formation of personal

convictions and the capacity both to maintain and where necessary to modify them in the light of experience (ibid).

Thus, although there is no explicit reference here to the spiritual area of experience, there are clear indications that if we accept elements of the aforementioned descriptions of the spiritual, then it is strongly reflected within the Religious Education curriculum. However, while there is reference to moral education and to ethical issues, with the possible exception of the linguistic, the statement of Religious Education does not refer to or reflect any other area of experience. Essentially then, it appears that it was difficult for the spiritual to be identified within specific subjects other than Religious Education, or to be cross-referenced with other areas of experience. Housed firmly and almost exclusively within Religious Education, the spiritual area of experience was rendered virtually impotent in terms of curriculum development. This raises the question as to whether the spiritual area of experience was, and is, a redundant commodity or whether its significance to the curriculum and to the education of the whole person has been severely limited by poor definition.

Educational response to *Curriculum 11–16* was, at the time, mixed, with many teachers seeking greater guidance than the document gave over what should be actually taught in the classroom. The *Times Educational Supplement* quoted one headteacher who agreed wholeheartedly that the emphasis of the curriculum needed to be shifted away from learning facts towards concepts and skills, but noted that within the document, this theory 'conflicted with the "teach me" attitude of specialist HMIs who had written other sections devoted to individual subjects' (quoted in TES 23.6. 1978, p. 6).

Another headteacher interviewed by the TES acknowledged the significant influence of the then current writings of philosopher Paul Hirst within the *Curriculum 11–16* document. In his book, *Knowledge and the Curriculum* (1974), Hirst identified seven distinctive 'forms of knowledge', each one 'a unique expression of man's rationality' (p. 25). These forms of knowledge were not 'collections of information, but complex ways of understanding experience which man has achieved' (p. 38). Each form of knowledge had distinguishing features: namely, central concepts, a logical structure through which these concepts linked with experience, distinctive expressions or statements and finally, particular skills for exploring experience. However, Hirst claimed that the forms of knowledge also exhibited common features and that one discipline would make extensive use of the achievements of another. Moreover, he considered that the forms of knowledge were 'firmly rooted in that common world of persons and things that we all share' (op. cit., p. 52).

Writing at the same period, the theologian Hans Kung (1978) referred to the rationalist philosopher, Kant, and to his 'ultimate questions'. These questions were common to human beings and combined 'all the interests of human reason'. Kung cites `What can I know?' which addresses questions of truth, `What ought I to do?' which questions norms and behaviour, and 'What may I hope?' which questions meaning. These questions of truth, norms and meaning were, for Kung, 'those ultimate and yet immediate, perennial questions of human life' (op. cit., p. 75). Kung presents the questions in the following way:

> What can we know? Why is there anything at all? Why not nothing? Where does man come from and where does he go? Why is the world as it is? What is the ultimate reason and meaning of all reality?

> What ought we to do? Why do what we do? Why and to whom are we finally responsible? What deserves forthright contempt and what love? What is the point of loyalty and friendship, but also what is the point of suffering and sin? What really matters for man?

> What may we hope? Why are we here? What is it all about? What is there left for us: death, making everything pointless at the end? What will give us courage for life and what courage for death? (ibid.).

For Kung, these were questions which arose 'in the very midst of man's personal and social life' (ibid.). These are certainly questions that pertain to those 'matters at the heart and root of experience' identified within *Curriculum 11–16*, 'affecting the way people see themselves and throwing light for them on the purpose and meaning of life itself'. There are those who may respond through their belief in God and adopt the beliefs and rituals of religious traditions, while others may respond with a different set of linguistic symbols. Certainly, the questions compel us, whatever our religious persuasion or none, to confront both personal and collective values and they thus provide a bridge between a religious and non-religious view of life. They would also seem to be a bridge between the two descriptions of the spiritual area of experience within *Curriculum 11–16*, and as such may have provided a more useful basis for a description of the spiritual, one which might have better served the prospective contributions of individual subject areas. Indeed, Kung's questions did provide the basis for curriculum guidance within one local education authority – and that guidance did feature the overlapping of the different areas of experience.

In 1980, Hampshire produced a Handbook, *Paths to Understanding* (Hampshire Education Authority, 1980) to accompany the then Agreed Syllabus for Religious Education. The Handbook stated that the Syllabus gave primacy to educational aims and cited three presuppositions underlying the Syllabus:

(1) To ask questions about the meaning and purpose of existence – an activity typical of mature human beings – is educationally more proper than to ignore such questions . . .

(2) Having asked such questions, it is worthwhile to listen to some of the responses men have made

(3) Planned approaches in the curriculum are necessary ... (op. cit., p. 62)

The Handbook went on to say that the curriculum should take account of the many-sidedness of 'man' and referred to a view of 'man' as 'one who seeks, discovers, creates and expresses meaning' (ibid). It quoted Kung and claimed that controversial issues would provide the 'life-blood' of secondary Religious Education, leading pupils towards his questions as they explored religious experiences. Pupils would learn 'how people have interpreted their experiences ... why they felt themselves pressed to such interpretations and answers; and what these implied for them in moral or ritual responses' (ibid).

The Handbook then proceeded to identify the contribution of Religious Education to pupils' spiritual, aesthetic, ethical, linguistic and social and political development. Here, the spiritual is seen as including 'broad concepts' such as the integration of experience, a sense of identity and value, quality of life, and striving for perfection. It is anticipated that through learning and thinking about people who have found a sense of personal identity and purpose through their faith and their allegiance to its corporate expression, pupils will gain awareness of 'experiences of vision, forgiveness and wholeness' (ibid). One result of this learning would be that the 'spiritual area of personality, that relating to beliefs, feelings, aspirations and self-knowledge' would be affected in a way which would prove 'entirely wholesome and enriching' (ibid). Two questions are immediately apparent, firstly whether the descriptions of the spiritual offered here, whilst not definitive, could prove operational in terms of curriculum development, and secondly whether such descriptions could enable the contribution of other curriculum areas to spiritual development to be identified.

The Handbook noted that religions use art, literature, music, architecture and artefacts as means of expressing meaning and that therefore, a study of religion would heighten pupils' awareness of the aesthetic form. Further, it identified strong links between religion and ethics: that by examining the motivations and actions of believers, pupils should develop their ability to discriminate and apply ethical criteria, thus developing knowledge and skills. In relation to linguistic development, in studies of sacred writings and patterns of worship, pupils would encounter different types of language performing different functions. This would again foster the skill of discrimination, here between different literary forms, and develop an appreciation of narrative and poetry. The contribution of Religious Education to social and political development would be based upon the exploration of social institutions within a political framework.

Here then were clearly expressed the contribution of one subject area, Religious Education, not only to spiritual development but to the other areas of experience. Where *Curriculum 11–16* had faltered was in its inability to provide an exemplar which included the spiritual alongside other areas of experience. Had the Hampshire model of curriculum development in Religious Education, with its description of the spiritual firmly located within human values and its explicit 'overlapping' between the areas of experience, been offered as an exemplar, it might well have significantly influenced the response of other subjects to the areas of experience. It is also interesting to note that the Hampshire Handbook stated that if Kung's questions of values were to be addressed in the classroom, then the role of the teacher was of prime importance: that 'if the pupil is to reflect on such matters as birth, love, transience or reconciliation he will need the stimulus which the good teacher can provide' (op. cit., p. 63). The first task of the teacher was to create a point of contact with the pupil's experience through the imaginative use of different approaches. The roles of both teacher and pupil mattered within a context which gave primacy to educational rather than legalistic considerations, and where the learning process took precedence.

LEGISLATING FOR THE SPIRITUAL WITHIN EDUCATION: CURRENT DEVELOPMENTS

The 1988 Education Reform Act legislates for 'a balanced and broadly based curriculum which (a) promotes the spiritual, moral, cultural, mental and physical development of pupils and of society; and (b) prepares such pupils for the opportunities, responsibilities and experiences of adult life (HMSO 1988).

This is the nearest we can find to a philosophical rationale within this highly prescriptive piece of legislation. However, here we have a clear set of values which are perceived as underpinning the curriculum and which reflect many of the concerns of the *Curriculum 11–16* document. The Act seemed to suggest that the purposes of the curriculum lay deeper than the mere fulfilment of the knowledge, skills and understanding embodied within the individual subject areas: that the curriculum should promote the development of the whole person and that 'the spiritual' was one aspect of that development. Furthermore, that the 'spiritual', alongside the moral, cultural, mental and physical development promoted by the school would contribute to the preparation of the pupil for adult life and would thereby have social implications for the wider society. In a speech to the Association of Religious Education Advisers and Inspectors in 1992, David Pascall, the then Chairman of the National Curriculum Council, referred to these Clauses about the curriculum as 'the original vision of the Education Reform Act', a 'vision enshrined in legislation'. The legislators made the promotion of pupils' spiritual development, together with that of their moral, cultural, mental and physical development, a pre-requisite for fulfilling the Act for, following the Education Act of 1992, a school's provision for the spiritual development of its pupils became subject to inspection under the OFSTED Framework for the Inspection of Schools, and it is at this point that the need to define 'the spiritual' became crucial.

Two documents appeared, designed to guide understanding and promote discussion of the spiritual area. The first, *Spiritual and Moral Development – A Discussion Paper*, was published in April 1993 by the National Curriculum Council (NCC) and re-published in September 1995 by its successor, the School Curriculum and Assessment Authority (SCAA). A key feature of the discussion paper was that the potential for spiritual development was open to all pupils irrespective of religious belief or none. It referred to spiritual development as 'applying to something fundamental in the human condition', to do with 'the universal search for individual identity – with our responses to challenging experiences, such as death, suffering, beauty, and encounters with good and evil,' and 'the search for meaning and purpose in life and for values by which to live' (SCAA 1995, p. 3). There are strong echoes here of the descriptions of the spiritual contained within *Curriculum 11–16*. Spiritual development is not 'defined' but rather 'described' through eight interrelated features or aspects, namely 'the development of *personal beliefs* and an appreciation of the relationship between belief and personal identity, *a sense of awe, wonder and mystery*, the experience of *feelings of transcendence* whether of the divine or of the human ability to rise above everyday experiences, *the search for meaning and purpose* and for *self-knowledge*, the capacity to value the individual within *relationships* and the development of a sense of community, and expression of *creativity* through art, music and literature and the use of *feelings and emotions* as a source of growth' (op. cit. pp. 3–4). The discussion paper suggested that most people could relate to these aspects whether they were understood in a purely humanistic or within a religious context.

In February 1994, The Office for Standards in Education (OFSTED) published a discussion paper, entitled *Spiritual, Moral, Social and Cultural Development*, designed to further debate upon what Stewart Sutherland, then Her Majesty's Chief Inspector of Schools, referred to as 'some fundamental questions about the education which we offer to our young people' (OFSTED 1994b, p. 4). The Paper describes the scope of spiritual development in the following way:

> Spiritual development relates to that aspect of inner life through which pupils acquire insights into their personal existence which are of enduring worth. It is characterised by reflection, the attribution of meaning to experience, valuing a non-material dimension to life and intimations of an enduring reality. 'Spiritual' is not synonymous with 'religious': all areas of the curriculum may contribute to pupils' spiritual development.' (op. cit., p. 8)

Spiritual development then is here perceived as essentially personal, relating to the way an individual acquires 'insight', and seems to imply making value judgements about one's existence and experience. This capacity to attribute meaning to experience involves 'reflection' and the 'valuing of a non-material dimension to life' – skills which appear to run counter to a fragmented and materialist popular culture expressed within and outside school life. Both the SCAA and OFSTED discussion papers claim that 'spiritual' is not confined to the development of religious beliefs, is the responsibility of all curriculum areas and of Collective Worship and should be promoted through the ethos of the school. It is also important to note that in both papers 'the spiritual' is no longer described as an area of experience, but linked to the concept of 'development'. The OFSTED discussion paper explores this concept at length and cites it as having dual features, namely, 'how schools develop pupils' and 'how pupils develop' (op. cit, p. 6). This dual process, which will be addressed further, finds some resonance with the notion of planned progression within the *Curriculum 11–16* document.

PREPARING PUPILS FOR ADULT LIFE: THE CONTINUING DEBATE

In January 1996, SCAA convened a conference entitled, 'Education for Adult Life: the spiritual, and moral development of young people'. The aim of the conference was to stimulate debate on matters of shared concern among a range of professionals with responsibility for young people, including parents, governors, employers, religious leaders and academics. Earlier consultations had identified concern over a lack of focus on pupils' spiritual and moral development and its consequences. The conference report, published in July 1996, claimed in its summary of key points that spiritual and moral development were indispensable aspects of education for adult life and linked a concern about spiritual and moral values to the current state of society. Further, while it recognized that many parents and teachers were 'unsure as to how to guide young people', it reiterated the statements in the earlier SCAA and OFSTED papers that spiritual and moral development should be promoted through all subjects within the school curriculum and through the ethos of the school and called for greater attention to be given to relevant teaching and learning strategies to promote spiritual and moral development.

It would appear from the report that there had been a structured and coherent debate on moral development. The discussions addressed the perceived degeneration in moral standards and identified the areas and possible causes of the manifest degeneration, for example, a loss of respect for national leaders, a fragmentation and collapse of historic communities, technological developments and an ethos of materialism and greed. While it was acknowledged that delegates had different expectations of moral development, four clear aims for moral education were offered as a way forward. The aims, each qualified in the ensuing report, included an expectation that young people should become 'knowledgeable about standards of right and wrong' and 'skilled in moral reasoning' (op. cit., p. 9). Here, then was a basis for identifying relevant teaching and learning strategies.

Unfortunately, it appears that the debate on spiritual development did not follow such a structured and coherent path. The report interchanges the terms 'spiritual development' and 'spirituality' without explanation and while the aspects of the spiritual in the earlier SCAA paper (1995) were broadly accepted by the delegates, additional attempts to 'define' the area appear random, confusing and unhelpful in establishing a working definition or description which might serve as a basis for identifying teaching and learning strategies.

However, two key issues appeared to emerge from the debate. The first concerns the relationship between spiritual and moral development. Frequently, within educational discourse, spiritual and moral development are conflated, the spiritual becoming subsumed within the moral and used as a form of quasi-religious coercion to behave morally. Here, however, while spirituality is identified as a possible source of the will to act morally, it is also suggested that behaviour which lacks reference to moral values can inhibit spiritual growth. Thus, earlier descriptions of 'the spiritual' are expanded for it is regarded as having a significant moral dimension and thereby links with another of the areas of experience.

The second issue highlights the need to develop pupils' conceptual framework and skills or aptitudes when considering the spiritual area. Religious and philosophical belief systems are seen as providing young people with a language and conceptual framework through which their own spiritual development might be understood. 'Reflection' and 'learning from experience' are identified as essential factors in spiritual development. These features within the Report strongly reflect elements of the *Curriculum 11–16* document, and indicate both exemplary content (i.e. that related to moral issues) and certain skills required for spiritual development.

Perhaps the most interesting section of the report relates to discussion of the science curriculum. Having agreed that a spiritual and moral dimension could occur in all areas of the curriculum, it was not the remit of the conference to address individual subject areas. Nevertheless, science was debated and a number of points arose. First, contemporary perceptions of science as 'infallible' and the only way to understand experience were noted and were seen as contributing to the demise of spiritual and moral dimensions of the curriculum. Second, it was considered that the pressures of recent curriculum changes had marginalized ethical issues within the science curriculum despite the fact that opportunities for spiritual and moral discussion abounded. Specific examples relating to the status of humankind and the natural world were identified within studies on the environment and genetics and it was considered that students should have a grounding in the philosophy of science. Third, it was recognized that science teachers have a significant role to play in providing an 'objective, balanced and unsentimental approach' to spiritual and moral issues through the application of scientific knowledge and concepts. It seems here that this discussion was reflecting in part the 'three-dimensional framework' at the heart of the *Curriculum 11–16* document: aspects of the spiritual (and moral) areas of experience inherent within the subject were identified and the nature of the science curriculum reappraised in this light. The discussion on Science therefore might be seen as offering a current and clear model for other subjects to reappraise their underlying philosophy, their methodology and their potential contribution to the spiritual and moral development of young people.

It is disappointing that further exemplars of this kind were not addressed, particularly since the findings of a MORI poll cited within the Appendix (op. cit., p. 20) confirm an interest in issues related to 'the status of humankind and human nature' or, in the words of *Curriculum 11–16* 'matters at the heart and root of experience' (DES 1977a, supplement). Of those questioned, 73% of adults and 61% of young people expressed an interest in thinking about what life is for, while 71% and 59% respectively were interested in how the universe began: 65% of adults and 59% of young people were interested in thinking about life after death and more young people than not (47% against 36%) were interested in whether God exists.

The paper, *Education for Adult Life*, might be deemed to take us to the brink of action – it establishes a keen interest in the spiritual, both through the very existence of the conference and through the findings of the MORI poll. It notes the agreement of many delegates that spiritual and moral development is the responsibility of every teacher in every subject, yet a further 'cautionary note' (and there are many within the paper) that some teachers feel uncomfortable and unskilled in these areas seemed to deflect discussion into consideration of three alternative channels for spiritual and moral development, namely personal and social education, economic and political awareness and citizenship education. Further discussion on school and community partnership led to a proposal that a national forum should be established to debate the socially desirable values that schools might promote.

Such a forum, it was felt, could benefit schools and 'give a fresh sense of purpose in national life' (op. cit., p. 18). The forum met and published what became known as its 'Core Values' in a slim SCAA Consultation Document. It defined values and principles for action relating to four areas, namely Society, Relationships, the Self and the Environment. The values themselves were largely uncontentious and were those frequently identified within school 'Mission Statements', yet when five of the 150 member forum asserted that there should be stronger statement on the nature of the family and on marriage, this became the focus of public and political debate. It is difficult to believe that progress in the implementation of strategies to promote spiritual development in schools has not been hijacked by those seeking to adopt the moral high-ground in the political arena.

It is evident then that the spiritual area of experience is still at the heart of educational debate. The question remains however, whether twenty years after the *Curriculum 11–16* document, teachers have gained sufficient understanding of the depth and breadth of the spiritual area of experience to identify its presence within and across individual subjects and to plan for its progression within the curriculum during the period of schooling.

Derek Webster, writing in 1982, found interest in the spiritual 'curious' , since it was a 'vague term often used with other equally imprecise words e.g. development, personality, awareness, maturity and nature' (Webster 1982, p. 85). Quotations from educational documentation have illustrated that while attempts at 'defining' the spiritual usually prove inadequate, they can offer indicators of the breadth of the area: for example, the spiritual finds a reference point within the religious and within the essentially human, to 'matters at the heart and root of existence'; it refers to the intensely personal, to inner thoughts and feelings, yet it also applies to the experience of a sense of community: it is operational within the present yet is is also concerned with ultimate questions.

Can these features be identified within the subjects in the school curriculum? Science, geography, RE and technology are all concerned in varying respects with the relationship of humankind to the external and natural world: they confront us with the need to respond to the issues of value and morality which result from that relationship. History and geography offer opportunities to explore human responses to personal, national and international events both of the past and in the present. The expressive arts speak to and emanate from the imagination, which, Webster claims, 'indicates a distinct order of perception . . . which evokes renewed reality' (op. cit., p. 90). Webster sees the role of the arts in education as 'social and personal in application: that they have emotional and intellectual significance; and that they have both historical and contemporary force' (ibid., p. 91). It appears then, that seen through the lens of the spiritual area of experience, there is a wholeness within these fragmented and often disparate subjects which constitute the school curriculum.

When the SCAA discussion paper identified the eight interrelated aspects of spiritual development, it offered a broad framework through which teachers might develop their understanding of the spiritual area and begin to relate it to classroom pedagogy. The eight aspects focus around three broad areas: first, concepts such as transcendence, religious belief and personal identity; second, experience in the sense of a search for meaning and self-knowledge, and third, relationships, through a sense of community or with the natural world. The SCAA Paper stated that experiencing feelings of transcendence may give rise to a belief in a divine being or may find a reference point in the power of the human spirit to transcend seemingly impossible experiences. Not all feelings of transcendence are located within a specifically religious context and the story of hostage Brian Keenan in *An Evil Cradling* (1992) would be a powerful example of an individual spirit transcending a seemingly impossible experience, as are stories of other individuals confronted with persecution and war, destitution and betrayal. The history and English curriculum have obvious roles here. Recognizing the value of relationships and a search for meaning in life at times of personal suffering are the substance of children's stories such as *Grandpa* and *Badger's Parting Gift*, of *The Diary of Anne Frank*, of many of Shakespeare's plays and of role-play within drama. A sense of awe, wonder and mystery inspired by the natural world engage the science and geography curriculum. These subjects also become engaged in the moral questions related to the use of the environment and the earth's resources. None of these aspects of the spiritual indicates the need to import a new body of knowledge, but rather involve a refocusing of classroom pedagogy in order to draw out the potential within the existing curriculum for promoting spiritual development.

The SCAA Discussion Paper identified a number of learning experiences through which schools might promote pupils' spiritual development (SCAA 1995, p. 8). These included opportunities for pupils to discuss religious and philosophical questions, to be challenged by the beliefs and values of others, to understand why people reach different decisions on spiritual and moral issues and how this affects their daily lives. There should be opportunities to develop relationships with both adults and peers and to experience a sense of community. And there should be opportunities to experience what is aesthetically challenging and to experience silence and reflection. Could these learning experiences possibly become features of curriculum development within an average school?

Michael Young (1995), writing about personal and social development and whole school curriculum policies, claims that a key question lies in 'how schools define their curriculum purposes, and how their specialist subject teaching is developed in relationship to the purposes of the school as a whole . . .' (p. 163). He notes that the demands of subject teaching tend to dominate with individual subjects focusing upon their own subject matter and methodologies and calls for subjects to be *used for* curriculum purposes rather than *used to* define the purposes themselves. This is an issue for subject teaching in both primary and secondary schools. It is also part of the issue raised earlier in respect of the science curriculum. And it is the very same issue which confronted a Hampshire secondary school seeking to develop the spiritual area of the curriculum.

TAKING COGNISANCE OF THE SPIRITUAL : A CASE STUDY

The case study school is a semi-rural Hampshire comprehensive school. In the words of the Deputy Head, it is 'no show-piece school but one which values each and every member of the school community and which has a developed pastoral system'. It is also a school which, early in 1994, was anxious to review its provision for the spiritual and moral development of its pupils. A working group was established, led by the Deputy Head and involving two governors and representatives from the science, maths, PSE, drama and RE departments – eight people in all. Initially the group met on an ad hoc basis but soon decided to convene regularly twice a term.

At its first meeting, the group instigated a review of how spiritual (as well as moral, social and cultural) development was currently promoted through the ethos of the school, through the whole curriculum and through acts of worship. It was acknowledged that a review could have implications for both the school aims (which were also being reviewed), and for the policy on personal development. A review of provision for spiritual development would not therefore be superficial but would affect the whole thinking of the school.

At its second meeting, the group viewed a video on spiritual development, designed for teacher and governor training. It was then decided to devote an INSET day seven months hence to discussion of spiritual development. The INSET would involve the whole staff, and with the comprehensive school as host, they would be joined by the staff of the two feeder primary schools. This initiative represented a significant commitment to the spiritual area of experience on the part of the Senior Management Teams of all three schools.

The INSET day, entitled 'Spiritual Development in Context 5-16' and held in October 1994, was attended by over ninety teachers. The morning sessions were led by two lecturers from higher education. The first session explored the territory of the spiritual with particular reference to the NCC and OFSTED Discussion Papers. Reference to the eight aspects of spiritual development cited in the former allowed for illustrations from across curriculum subjects. A brief practical activity involved the identification of aspects of 'the spiritual' within a children's story and its potential for development across curriculum areas. The exploration of the spiritual through the use of story was extended in the second session through the poetry of Robert Frost and the writing of Brian Keenan, both of which fostered a sense of reflection upon those 'matters at the heart and root of existence'.

Overall, the school reported that the INSET day had significantly heightened awareness of the role of the spiritual within pupils' learning experience and had fuelled continued discussion within individual departments.

More specifically, the maths department had adopted as their particular focus upon the spiritual a sense of awe and wonder in the natural world. The department subsequently engaged pupils in investigative work on patterns in nature. This developed into a project on a 'Maths Garden', an initiative to put maths into the environment. The project was to be in different phases, with the object of transforming a derelict area into a 'quiet' area or garden, for the use of all pupils. Designs conducive to quiet thought were a key consideration for the outer physical landscape was to support the individual's inner reflective landscape: paving stones in circular and semi-circular patterns, brick piers and abstract sculptures. The school's relationship with the wider community expanded as the local Further Education College and past pupils became involved as designers and bricklayers. Developing the skill of reflection, considering questions of meaning and purpose in life, and experiencing a sense of community became part of the process as well as the desired outcome.

The need for this quiet area took on a new meaning when one of the pupils at the school was tragically killed in a road accident. The staff, whose consciousness of basic human issues had been so recently raised, was able to make a swift and committed response. A drama studio temporarily became a quiet space in which friends could fulfil their need to be together and sort through their thoughts.

In the two years following the initial INSET, the Deputy Head reports that while the pace of progress has become slower, the impact upon staff and pupil awareness has been maintained and practice within the school has shifted considerably. The Spiritual and Moral Working Party continues to meet twice termly and has overseen the purchase of material to support spiritual and moral development for the English, maths and modern languages departments. It also recommended that resources which would promote depth of thought should be purchased for collective worship and that these should be linked to the keeping of pupils' 'Diaries of Reflection'. The school's collective worship and personal development policies, and the statement of the school's aims, were consequently rewritten in order to reflect the changes in practice that had been implemented.

The maths garden has been developed and the group involved in this project are now entering a new phase. The school has been selected to work in partnership with a civil engineering charity concerned with sustainable transport systems. This has involved extensive consultation with governors, staff, pupils and members of the local community to consider the development of safe routes to school and the improvement of cycle ways which would be, as far as possible, in keeping with the natural environment. This then draws upon the pupils' respect and sense of moral responsibility for the environment, their awareness of the needs of the local community and their willingness to work collaboratively as members of that community, and their creativity. The new project group has expanded to include the involvement of the geography, science and technology departments.

Following the death of the pupil in a road accident, pupils had raised money for the purchase of trees and a seat to be placed as memorials in the maths garden. A year after the death, a memorial service was held for the school community and for the pupil's family. Pupils were closely involved in both the planning and implementation of the service: the former pupil was remembered through his favourite music and verse, and memories of him were written, spoken during the service and compiled within a book for the relatives to keep. The planning of a community memorial service was, in the words of the Deputy Head, 'very scary – there was always the fear of doing the wrong thing', yet it proved a moving, meaningful and appropriate occasion for all concerned. However, such an occasion could only occur within an existing context of valuing individuals, a strong sense of relationship and community and a willingness to respond 'to challenging experiences of life, such as beauty, suffering and death' (SCAA 1995).

Thus, one school has embarked upon a review of curriculum provision for the spiritual area of experience. In no respect has the process involved a total abandonment of the existing curriculum in terms of content or pedagogy, but rather a reassessment of aims and priorities and a 'refocusing' to ensure that the education of persons lay at the heart of the education process. There is now an awareness in both policy and practice of the need to develop the skill of reflection, to create opportunities in an otherwise crowded curriculum for pupils to engage with questions of meaning and to express these through a variety of linguistic and visual forms. The 'overlaps' between the spiritual, the moral or ethical, the social, the linguistic and the aesthetic areas of experience, absent in the exemplars cited in the *Curriculum 11–16* document, are very much in evidence here.

INSPECTING THE SPIRITUAL: BOON OR BARRIER TO PROGRESS?

Under the OFSTED Framework for the Inspection of Schools, instituted by the 1992 Education Act, the 'spiritual, moral, social and cultural development of pupils' constitutes one of four areas to be inspected (the others being the quality of education, educational standards and efficiency). It is therefore a substantial part of the inspection process and this has provided a spur to schools to ensure that this area of school life finds reflection in both documentation and practice. However, inspection of the spiritual raises debate.

It has already been noted that in both the SCAA and OFSTED discussion papers, 'the spiritual' was no longer described as an area of experience but linked to the concept of development. The OFSTED Paper used the term in two senses, first, how schools develop pupils, that is the process in terms of a school's provision, and second how pupils develop, the outcome of pupils passing through the stages of development provided. The paper also suggested that both areas should be the concern of the inspection process. The difficulties of inspecting pupils' development were identified within the paper itself: it acknowledged that development is not necessarily a continuous process related to pupils' ages, that pupils' development is not necessarily observable during an inspection and that it can be difficult to distinguish between the contribution made by the home, school and the local community. John White (1994) strongly questions the validity of the term 'development' in the context of pupils' spiritual development for it presupposed an innate structure developing into a mature state. Judgements about the presence of spiritual maturity would involve value-judgements about qualities commonly prized. While accepting that parents, teachers and schools can develop qualities in pupils, White claims that 'the whole notion of children developing in these ways just fails to make sense' (p. 371). In the following year, David Trainer, then the HMI with overall responsibility for the inspection of the spiritual states that 'it should be understood by all that there is no question of attempting to "measure" SMSC development' (1995, p. 7). However, he goes on to suggest that 'if this aspect of education is as important as we have argued, then it surely is appropriate that some attempt should be made to assess the quality and success of a school's programme' (ibid). Under the 1995 Guidance on the Inspection of Nursery and Primary Schools, inspectors were required to evaluate what schools actively do to promote pupils' spiritual development, basing their judgements upon the criteria of whether the school 'provides its pupils with knowledge and insight into values and religious beliefs and enables them to reflect on their experiences in a way which develops their spiritual awareness and self-knowledge' (OFSTED 1995a, p. 82). While this in part addresses White's criticism, it would be difficult to envisage making judgements which did not include reference to outcomes in terms of pupils' response.

One further point regarding inspection. David Trainer noted that the Dearing review of the curriculum 'whilst drawing broad attention to the importance of SMSC development, has not seen fit to show how the NC subjects (and RE presumably) might be used for this purpose' (Trainer 1995, p. 3). This in itself could prove an impediment to curriculum development, for until each subject is required to identify its contribution to the spiritual – and to the moral, social and cultural – development of pupils as part of the criteria for subject inspection, then it is unlikely that schools will embark upon a new approach to planning which addresses the 'vision' for the curriculum contained in the 1988 Education Reform Act. And thus, initiatives for a curriculum which has, at its heart, a holistic view of the education process, can all too easily be lost.

IN CONCLUSION

This publication reflects the fact that successive pieces of educational legislation have had at their centre the belief that education in this country is not only about the gaining of knowledge and the acquiring of essential skills . . . but also about personal development in its fullest sense (OFSTED 1994b, p. 1).

In his Foreword to the OFSTED discussion paper, Stewart Sutherland acknowledged that education means more than fulfilling the prescriptions of individual subjects. The paper raised debate about values – both those which are presented to pupils and those which underpin the education process. It recognized the responsibility upon those designing and implementing the curriculum to ensure that 'what is taught and how it is taught are contributing as fully as possible ... to all aspects of pupils' personal development' (p. 2). In both tone and content then this paper is remarkably similar to *Curriculum 11–16*. And it is equally controversial for it forces us to confront the question of what the curriculum is for? Or, in terms of today's pupils, what value has the school added to their personal lives?, What is our vision of education, of the purposes of the curriculum? and what is our vision of the young adult and her/his contribution to society?

In 1977, the way to ensure that the curriculum met the needs of both pupils and society was felt to be by reference to the areas of experience. The spiritual area of experience has maintained its significance in educational debate, only now our understanding of the breadth and depth of the area has developed. We can now formulate descriptions of the spiritual area which are accessible to curriculum planners and which identify the area across subject boundaries. While recognizing that spiritual development might not be linear, we can speak of the school's provision for spiritual development and, as in the OFSTED Handbook, in terms of pupils' capacities. And we can find, as with the Hampshire case study, a school which has taken seriously the contribution of the curriculum to its pupils' spiritual development. All this renders the recent OFSTED discussion paper a provocative document, for it challenges us to harness our professional integrity, enter the debate about, in Stewart Sutherland's words, 'the central questions facing contemporary British education' (OFSTED 1994b, p. 4) and to press towards a curriculum of entitlement which truly addresses the spiritual development of the pupils currently in our schools and of our future generations.

9

Personal, Social and Moral Education in a Democratic Society

A.V. Kelly

Of all the dimensions of experience we are exploring in this book, the personal, social and moral is the one which most obviously cries out for the kind of curricular treatment this general approach advocates. For, within our view of education as development, the personal, social and moral development of the individual is central. And, if, as has been argued earlier, the main thrust of the consequent need to reconceptualize the school curriculum is a shift away from a view of curriculum as a body of knowledge-content to be 'delivered', then the personal, social and moral sphere should offer no problem, since it is difficult, certainly after any kind of serious reflection, to conceive of this area of education in terms of 'knowledge to be acquired or facts stored'.

As is so often the case, however, conceptual clarity has not always prevailed. And there continue to be those people who believe that morality must be seen as a matter of absolutes, and that personal, social and moral education can be viewed as a process of learning what is 'right'. They would thus plan this area of the school curriculum in terms of its content or even its aims and objectives, its behavioural outcomes or performance indicators. To take such a stance is perhaps understandable in those who view the issue from a religious standpoint. It is less acceptable, however, when this position is taken by those officials of SCAA who appear to have hired a time-machine to whisk them into the intellectual past. For in their case, they are either revealing an intellectual inadequacy which is highly disturbing in those who have ultimate responsibility for the education system of the nation, or they are approaching the issue with a political agenda, which is even more unacceptable.

It is, therefore, with an exploration of this issue of moral knowledge and moral absolutes that our discussion of this area of experience will need to begin. For we need to establish that there is no such thing as 'moral knowledge' before we can debunk that approach to moral education which starts from the belief that there is, before we can show why an 'areas of experience' approach is the only viable way of setting about the

161

personal, social and moral education of young people.

Once we have established that position, it will become possible to attempt to unpack what this implies for the organization of the curriculum, and, indeed, of the school system itself.

THE CONCEPT OF 'MORAL KNOWLEDGE'

From the very first, from the point at which human beings began to discuss the education of the young, their moral education has been a central concern. Indeed, before such discussions began, the practice of bringing up the young was firmly centred on teaching them to behave properly. The whole thrust of Plato's discussion of education in *The Republic*, for example, was towards the creation of a form of education which would lead ultimately to perfect morality. And, in the popular mind, there continues to this day an unquestioned conviction that moral upbringing is a significant part of educational provision.

In spite of this age-old concern, however, there has never been anything approaching complete clarity over what this might imply. In part, this has been due to this very concept of 'perfect morality' which Plato assumed and which subsequent generations, especially those which were dominated by religions of all forms, have gladly embraced. For the notion that there is only one version of 'the right' or 'the good' is essential to any religious form of morality. And it is also attractive to politicians for whom the idea of a multiplicity of moral systems complicates life enormously, and for whom the imposition of a single code of values has always appeared to be an attractive means to increased social control. Thus, this notion continues to be prevalent, as religions offer their adherents unquestioned codes of moral behaviour, and politicians and their aides urge us to return to 'the basics', to absolute values, although they appear to have no better understanding of what these are than we do ourselves.

Two developments in recent times, however, have shown this view to be no longer tenable, if indeed it ever was. First, totalitarianism, in the many forms in which we have experienced it over the last century or so, has demonstrated the social, political, cultural and ethnic dangers of assuming that there is one truth and that those who possess it have every right to impose it on those whose inadequacies cause them to fail to recognize or appreciate it, or whose cultural, ethnic or religious backgrounds lead them to different beliefs and practices.

To advocate such an approach to education in this sphere, therefore, is to be engaged in an activity which is essentially political in its thrust, and, further, political in a seriously sinister sense. For the attempted imposition of any one set of values is an act of totalitarianism, a denial of the fundamental democratic values of freedom – of opinion, of thought, of speech – and a rejection of that moral and cultural pluralism which characterizes most modern-day societies and which in any genuinely democratic society must be protected and indeed celebrated (Kelly 1995).

Second, developments in our understanding of human knowledge during the twentieth century have made it clear that in no sphere, not even in the 'hard', 'factual' sphere of scientific and technological knowledge, as other chapters in this book amply demonstrate, can human beings generate knowledge about which they are entitled to be confident, and even less dogmatic. Knowledge in all spheres, including the mathematical, as Paul Ernest argues in Chapter 3, must be recognized as contextual, and thus as provisional, tentative, uncertain and requiring constant challenge and questioning (Kelly 1986, 1995). This is the central tenet of that movement which has come to be known as postmodernism, and, whatever view one takes of that multi-faceted intellectual phenomenon, it is difficult to deny the force of that underpinning principle.

And this reinforces our earlier claim that to take any other view of knowledge is to put democracy itself at risk, since it is to deny that free interplay of opinion which must be its very essence (Kelly 1995). For 'more often than not, democracy is now defined as the political system which most effectively protects the freedom of individuals to make their own autonomous choices and implement their own private preferences' (Levitas 1986).

To take a view of moral principles as being fixed or static, then, is to deny that plurality of values and cultures which characterizes most societies in the late twentieth century, since 'in any modern state the people is bound to be . . . *diverse*' (Wollheim 1962, p. 72). It is to deny to the individual all right to his/her own opinion on a range of issues. It is to deny democracy itself. And, perhaps most importantly, it is to deny people the right to be human beings. For, despite that legacy of the ancient world which leads us to believe that 'man' is a rational animal, it is far more plausible to see that what distinguishes human beings from the rest of the animal kingdom is their capacity for principled behaviour.

To be fully human is to be capable of making moral judgments, of making decisions which take account of the concerns and interests of others, of acting according to one's principles rather than merely according to want or desire. Human behaviour is principled rather than merely goal-directed behaviour. And to behave in a manner which is not characterized in this way, to act out of blind adherence to imposed or instilled rules or precepts, to 'do as one is told', or to be motivated by nothing more elevated than a fear of punishment or a desire for reward is to be less than human; it is to be less than moral; for it is to display the kinds of behaviour which are more typical of lower forms of animal life.

To accept any concept of moral *knowledge*, of moral *absolutes*, any notion that morality is a matter of *knowing* what is right rather than of making one's own moral judgments, is to encourage a relapse into this latter form of behaviour. It is thus to deny human beings their essential privilege of freedom of choice, of being human. And it is to put at risk the continuation of genuinely democratic forms of social living, since the essence of these must be some notion of unity in diversity rather than unity through an imposed homogeneity.

WHAT IS PERSONAL, SOCIAL AND MORAL EDUCATION?

The implications of this for the planning of personal, social and moral education are quite profound. In particular they require that we cease to plan it in terms of knowledge to be transmitted, rules to be learned or patterns of behaviour to be instilled. They demand a process or developmental approach to curriculum planning, since to plan by the prespecification of curriculum content or, worse, of behavioural objectives is not only unsatisfactory, it is positively dangerous and counter-productive, since it puts at risk the development of the individual as an autonomous person. Moral behaviour can only be seen as a process; otherwise it ceases to be moral behaviour and becomes mere automaton-like obedience (or disobedience) to the instructions, and thus the control, of others.

To educate someone morally, socially or personally, then, is to assist him/her in the process of developing this capacity for making moral judgments. Anything less than this, or different from this, is mere moral instruction and thus a form of indoctrination.

In this of course moral education is no different from any other form of genuine *education*. For to be educated in any field, as this book is designed to demonstrate, is to be assisted to develop appropriate understandings, to acquire powers of critical awareness; to learn to challenge and question everything which is presented to one as knowledge, and to reach one's own conclusions on all matters. True education in its entirety is a process of personal development. Anything short of this – and there is plenty of it about – is mere training, instruction or even, as we have just seen, indoctrination. Use of the term 'education' must be seen as implying that conditions such as those just listed are being satisfied, and thus as offering us this useful and important conceptual distinction between this and other kinds of teaching activity.

There are several aspects of this form of education in the moral, social and personal sphere which we need to identify.

First, we must note that it is the very antithesis of authoritarianism. It is a matter of learning to be self-directed rather than 'doing as one is told'. For moral behaviour implies moral responsibility, as the daily work of any lawcourt in a democratic society illustrates, and that in turn means that one's behaviour must be freely chosen. The notion of free will is central to any discussion of morality or of personal autonomy, and there is an important distinction to be made, as Aristotle pointed out a long time ago, between actions performed *willingly* and those performed *not unwillingly*. Truly moral behaviour is freely chosen and thus carries full responsibility. Actions performed out of obedience, out of inculcated habit, or out of respect for, or fear of, an authority, may be performed 'not unwillingly' but they are not freely chosen, so that they cannot warrant full responsibility. In short, they are not fully moral. To educate someone personally or morally, then, does not mean telling them how to think and behave; it means assisting them in the process of learning to think consciously about their behaviour and to make their own decisions. And to educate them socially is to enable them to do this with full regard for the social context of their lives.

Second, to be morally educated is to have come to a recognition that moral behaviour is a matter of acting in accordance with one's principles rather than out of expediency. It is a matter of doing something because one believes it to be right rather than because one sees it to be useful, profitable or offering some kind of 'pay-off', indeed sometimes when it is none of these things. We will note later how difficult it is to develop this kind of understanding in children in the context of a society which has come to be characterized by competition and a self-seeking expediency, and within a curriculum which is similarly characterized. Difficult as it might be, however, it is central to personal, social and moral education. For there can be no concept of morality which is not tied to the notion that moral behaviour is principled behaviour, and thus no concept of moral education which does not embrace the need to assist young people towards such principled behaviour.

Moral education, then, must start with an awareness of the need to promote the development of the ability to generate one's own freely chosen moral principles and to recognize the need to make one's judgments and to structure one's behaviour according to those principles.

The development of such principles, however, is not a matter of plucking them out of the air. They can only be of value if they are the result of careful reasoning. Hence it is necessary to lead young people towards the kinds of understanding which are necessary for the development of moral principles.

It is also necessary to encourage them to recognize that, although the choice of those principles is not a matter of acquiring some kind of 'moral knowledge', many kinds of knowledge are relevant to the implementation of them or the making of judgments in relation to them.

This was a major thrust of what was perhaps the most influential of the Schools Council's curriculum projects, the Humanities Curriculum Project (HCP) (Schools Council 1970). For that project was designed to encourage young people to address issues of current social importance, issues such as relations between the sexes, living in cities and war and peace. In line with what was said above about the importance of freedom of opinion, the project team decided from the outset that it would be improper to plan work of this kind with clearly predetermined objectives concerning its intended outcomes, but that, rather, the essence of the project should be the procedural principles to which teachers and pupils would be expected to adhere.

What is of interest to us here is that one of those principles was that pupils should be encouraged to recognize the importance of *informed* opinion, that, while all shades of view were to be tolerated and protected, uninformed, 'top-of-the-head' opinions were not acceptable. Thus it was hoped that pupils would not only learn that they have a right to their own view but also that they have a responsibility to ensure that any view they reach is based on the fullest possible awareness of all 'facts' relevant to the holding of that view.

This is the way in which knowledge enters into moral learning, not as 'moral knowledge' or knowledge of right and wrong, but as knowledge of all kinds and from all sources which may be relevant to the making of moral judgments and, indeed, to acting on them. And there can be no doubt that a recognition of the need for such knowledge and the role that it plays in decision making must be another central component of moral education.

A further kind of knowledge we need is a knowledge of how our actions are likely to impinge on others. And, as an important dimension of that, we need to understand the feelings of others and to recognize that these matter, to appreciate that our behaviour can seldom be completely 'self-regarding', that it always affects others and that how it affects others must be an important consideration in any judgments we make.

This takes us into a whole new area of personal, social and moral education. For so far we have discussed it as if it were a purely cognitive matter and moral behaviour merely a matter of reasoned calculation. A moment's thought, however, will reveal how important to both is the affective or emotional dimension. We need to be able to understand and, indeed, to have control of our emotions if we are to be able to reach balanced moral judgments and, perhaps more importantly, to act on those judgments. For, as St Paul once said, 'the good I would I do not, and the evil that I would not that I do'. From the very first, the intervention of the emotions, of pleasure, of Plato's 'beast with many heads', of Christianity's 'original sin', between judgment and action has been recognized as the major barrier to moral behaviour. Reaching informed judgments is one thing; translating them into action often quite another.

Moral 'knowledge', then, is procedural rather than propositional. And personal, social and moral education is the complex process of promoting a range of capabilities, all of which contribute to an ability to develop our own moral principles, to reach informed judgments in the light of those principles on moral issues of every kind, from those big global issues we are constantly being made aware of to the personal day-to-day problems we must resolve in our own lives, and, where appropriate, to translate those judgments into action, whether such action is totally comfortable for us as individuals or not.

THE PRACTICE OF PERSONAL, SOCIAL AND MORAL EDUCATION

The contribution of school subjects

It will be apparent, even from this brief outline of what it means to educate someone personally, socially and morally, that every school subject has its contribution to make to the process. Indeed, in so far as any school subject has claims to be genuinely educational, it must, as has been argued above, demonstrate its contribution to this aspect of human development. It should also be apparent, however, that that contribution will seldom take the form of offering bodies of subject knowledge or the attainment of objectives, but must be recognized as contributing to a *process*. It will also be clear, therefore, that it requires a reconceptualization of most school subjects, so that, in so far as they have a contribution to make to personal, social or moral education (and of course in so far as they are seeking to make that contribution) they must be conceived and planned in such a manner as to make that possible.

We can recognize the contribution which might be made to personal, social and moral development by English, by drama, by history, by social studies, by physical education and so on, but we cannot leave it to chance whether that contribution materializes or not; we cannot offer these subjects in the form of curriculum content and hope that their moral impact will occur automatically, as if by osmosis, or as some kind of by-product. If our concern with personal, social and moral development is serious and genuine, we must plan in such a way as to capitalize on what these subjects have to offer. We must acknowledge the importance of their contribution to that holistic form of experience we are suggesting a genuine form of education ought to be. And that means that we must focus on what they have to offer to human development rather than merely on their contribution to the acquisition of knowledge. We must think about their intrinsic, personal, developmental potential rather than merely their instrumental, utilitarian or vocational value.

The National Curriculum for England and Wales has failed to recognize, or has deliberately rejected, the notion that education must in part be concerned to contribute to the personal development of young people, and has concentrated on the teaching of that knowledge which its architects regard as useful. Other chapters reveal the inadequacies of this approach in all areas of the curriculum, the degree to which it falls short of being *education* in any significant sense that one can give to that term. What we must note here is its consequent inability to cater for the needs of personal, social or moral development. For its structure and its underlying rationale, its model of curriculum, are such as to require that we offer subjects to pupils as bodies of knowledge to be assimilated rather than as vehicles for their own growth and development, and, specific to the present context, it denies us the opportunity of capitalizing on the contribution those subjects might make to personal, social and moral growth and development.

Moral education as a separate curriculum area

It is for this reason that separate arrangements have had to be recommended for what is now called the personal and social education of children and young people (the dropping of the term 'moral' perhaps has its own significance), arrangements outside of, and supplementary to, the National Curriculum. For, while this aspect of education has been designated by the National Curriculum Council as a function of the 'whole curriculum' (NCC 1990c), and while this description suggests that it should therefore be addressed in all areas of the curriculum, in reality it means that, because it cannot be so addressed within their content-based structure, it has to be picked up by other means. Fundamentally, it has been recognized as a casualty of the National Curriculum and as consequently requiring some form of first aid.

The idea of moral education as a separate area of the curriculum, or at least as requiring its own concentrated treatment, is not of course new. It is after all the essence of the Humanities Curriculum Project to which we referred earlier. Hitherto, however, such separate activity has been seen as necessary to supplement and focus what was going on elsewhere. Every subject, and indeed every teacher, has been recognized as having a contribution to make, as having a responsibility for, moral education. As the Newsom Report (CACE 1963, para.160) said, 'teachers can only escape from their influence over the moral and spiritual development of their pupils by closing their schools'.

Now, however, the terms of the National Curriculum, and the legal demands which teachers have to meet, require little more of them than that they 'deliver' their specialist subjects in accordance with the attainment targets set and prepare their pupils for the regular tests they must face. Furthermore, the use of those test results to form 'league tables' by which they and their schools will be externally judged creates a climate in which the performance of pupils in tests must naturally loom very much larger than than their development – personal, social, moral or otherwise.

Hence provision for moral education, or personal and social education, must now be made as compensatory for, rather than as supplementary to, the basic curriculum. For that basic curriculum is now no longer supportive in itself of personal, social or moral development.

The influence of the educational environment

The problem goes deeper than this, however. For the scenario we have just uncovered is also one in which that basic curriculum can be seen not only as not supportive of personal, social and moral development, but also as positively damaging and counter-productive to it.

Teachers have been aware for a long time of the difficulties, perhaps the impossibility, of promoting a proper form of moral education in a climate which is not itself supportive of that process and does not reflect a similar set of moral values to those being propagated, when the ethos of the home, the school or, indeed of society itself is not conducive to what the educational process is focused on. And more than two decades ago this conviction was given the considerable support of another Schools Council project, Lifeline (McPhail et al. 1972). A major feature of the philosophy underlying that project was the belief that 'the basic form of motivation lies in treating others with consideration' (Downey and Kelly 1978, p. 184), and this led to the view that at the practical level 'moral education cannot be taught as a separate entity, since living the considerate life is a matter concerning the whole life of the school' (ibid.).

That project team, therefore, took the view that any serious attempt at moral education must be backed by the organization and structure of the school, that that organization and that structure must themselves demonstrate an adherence to the principles upon which the approach to moral education itself is founded, that schools and teachers must 'practise what they preach'.

It was the same kind of thinking which prompted many people to question the ethics underlying practices such as selection and streaming and their impact on the moral and social development of the pupils exposed to them – at whatever level – the strongest argument against them, apart from the evidence of their manifest inaccuracies, being their divisive social effects (Ferri 1971; Hargreaves 1972; Kelly 1975, 1978).

Those practices, however, are being reasserted, reinforced and re-established by the National Curriculum, its associated policies and the consequent pressures on schools and teachers. And, further, it is now not merely the organizational context of education which is militating in this way against a proper form of personal, social or moral education; it is the curriculum itself. For the curriculum which has now been imposed by government on schools, teachers and children is overtly competitive and divisive and offers an open invitation to pupils (and, indeed, to teachers too) to be self-seeking rather than collaborative or considerate in their interactions with each other.

As Lynne Broadbent reminds us in Chapter 8, Ofsted (1994) has itself stressed the importance of the ethos of the school for the personal, social, moral and spiritual development of its pupils. What it has failed to recognize, however, or is unwilling to acknowledge, is that the ethos of any school is largely a function of its curriculum, and that the curriculum which Ofsted itself is concerned to impose and maintain creates an ethos which it is difficult to reconcile with the kinds of moral values Ofsted itself seems to wish to promote.

Not only, then, does the existence of this compulsory curriculum make it difficult for schools and teachers to find space for anything which might be called personal or social or moral education; in its very essence it can be seen to be working against the potential effectiveness of any such activities they might succeed in making space for. It is difficult, if not impossible, to persuade young people of the importance of mutual tolerance, support, consideration, collaboration in a context where for most of the working week the emphasis is on intolerance, competition and self-centredness, and especially when it is the latter kinds of value which have been encouraged to flourish in society at large.

Problems of law and order

In the sphere of personal, social and moral education, it is already beginning to appear that one result of adopting that form of curriculum and imposing it on our schools is a significant increase in law and order problems among young people, even young children. To establish a form of education whose fundamental values are those of competition, and thus of success and failure, is to establish a set of standards according to which large numbers of children and young people must fail. And to extend the application of these standards to the youngest pupils in our schools is to ensure that that sense of failure for many of them comes very early in their school careers. We thus now have the phenomenon of alienation and general disaffection from school, which was once associated only, or mainly, with the secondary sector of schooling, appearing conspicuously in infant schools (Barrett 1989).

Nor should this surprise us. For, if we attempt to force upon all children a diet which is inappropriate, unpalatable and, indeed, in many cases, indigestible, we must expect them to reject it. And with that rejection will go all of the values, personal, social and moral, which a proper form of education in a democracy should be seeking to promote. Those who can digest what is offered will be imbibing a set of values which, as we have seen, are difficult to reconcile with genuinely democratic living. And those who find the fare indigestible will not only reject those values – they will, having been offered no alternative, reject the very concept of social or moral principles. Thus, neither group will have a form of personal, social or moral education which one can justify; and the latter group will grow up with no sense of social or moral responsibility at all.

Disaffection from school begins with personal failure and rejection, and it leads very quickly to a reciprocal rejection of all that school stands for. And, since, not unreasonably, schools are seen as representative of what society stands for, this process also encompasses an alienation from society itself, deriving from a sense of rejection by society. It is unreasonable to expect those who hold no stake in society to accept an obligation to, or a responsibility for, society. If rights imply duties, then, conversely, duties imply rights, so that we cannot expect those whose rights are not respected by society to accept any of the reciprocal duties towards it. And to offer such people courses in citizenship is a mere charade, since the concept of citizenship entails that very sense of belonging and participation which these people do not have. Such courses can only ever be an attempt at inculcating obedience by covertly coercive methods.

Currently society has a growing body of people who, for reasons of rejection of one form or another, do not have – and, worse, have no reason to have – any sense of belonging, responsibility or loyalty to the society in which they exist but of which they do not see themselves as significant members.

Membership of this growing underclass is being swelled by youngsters who, from the earliest age, have experienced little beyond rejection and failure in the schooling system which, in their most formative years, is their main, even only, direct contact with society. Hence, unless some action is taken to mitigate this process, problems of alienation, disaffection and thus of law and order will continue to escalate.

Prevention is the only effective solution to this growing problem. For there is no cure, once the disease has taken hold. It is the causes which must be addressed not the symptoms. Those symptoms are the marks of an unhealthy society and must be recognized as such, rather than being dismissed as the responsibility merely of an aberrant section of society. The increasing volume of law and order problems, therefore, cannot be effectively tackled by punitive measures. These problems will not be solved by building bigger prisons, by converting former holiday camps into detention centres, by lowering the age of criminal responsibility, or even by bringing corporal punishment back into our schools. They can only be mitigated if we address their causes, and those causes are to be found to a large extent located in the school curriculum.

It would seem that the present – ill-thought out, haphazard and 'bolt-on' – approach to personal, social and moral education is not only failing to achieve what is needed in a democratic society, it is also, in harness with curriculum policies as a whole, leading to an escalation of social problems, especially in the field of law and order, but perhaps also more widely in the overall social and moral health of society. If we are to arrest this process, then an alternative approach is urgently needed.

TOWARDS AN ALTERNATIVE FORM OF PERSONAL, SOCIAL AND MORAL EDUCATION

If we are to identify and generate a genuine alternative approach to education in this field, we must now return briefly to the debate over the status and validity of moral standards and principles with which we began this chapter.

It was argued at the outset that, for several reasons – most notably the pluralist nature of the modern society and the resultant uncertainty concerning all forms of human knowledge – an absolutist position is now untenable. To suggest, however, that the only alternative to such a position is a relativist 'free-for-all' is to fall into the twin traps of over-simplicity and naive polarization which unfortunately characterize too much current thinking, perhaps especially in the realm of so-called educational theory. There is a middle ground; and it is crucial – for society as well as for education – that we gain the clearest possible picture of what this is.

In considering the forms of curricular provision which are appropriate to personal, social and moral education, we must begin by remembering that the main concern is, or should be, the initiation of the young into a democratic society. The concern is with socialization; but in a democratic context this is not, or should not be, the kind of socialization which has rightly been criticized as a form of indoctrination, a process of seeking to ensure political obedience and compliance. Rather it is socialization into a liberal society, in which freedom and equality are the key features rather than authoritarianism and privilege. Democracy is a moral as well as – even more than – a political system (Kelly 1995). And as such, it offers a perfectly justifiable set of moral values and principles, which not only can, but must, form the basis of personal, social and moral education in such a society.

I have argued elsewhere (Kelly 1995) that the key features of any genuinely democratic moral system are freedom, bringing with it as a corollary respect for the freedom of others, equality, again in conjunction with a willingness to grant this to others, a respect for these and all other human rights deriving from them, and an acknowledgement of the demands of popular sovereignty, an acceptance of responsibility for the governance of society. (This latter point takes us of course into the associated realm of political education which will be the subject of the next chapter.)

It is not difficult to deduce from this basic position the moral 'virtues' which we are perfectly entitled to seek to inculcate in the young as we attempt to prepare them to take their places in a democratic society. We must, as was suggested earlier, encourage them to think for themselves on all issues and assist them in doing so. We must also, however, make it clear to them that a corollary of this is a respect for and tolerance of the right of others to their opinions, thoughts and preferences. We must promote in them a sense of social justice, which will include an acceptance of social and cultural equality and a recognition of democratic human rights. We must teach them the importance of honesty and openness. And we must seek to persuade them of the importance of accepting their share of responsibility for the management of society, along with an awareness that the quality of life in society, of their own lives as well as those of others, depends on them, and that responsibility for it cannot, or at least should not, be shuffled off onto others, especially when those others are likely to exploit such apathy.

What is of value in a democratic society, what makes for quality of life in such a society, is not merely the individual freedom which such a society should offer, but moreso the diversity – cultural, ethnic, moral, political and religious – which it promotes and renders possible. What is unacceptable, therefore, is all forms of intolerance – cultural, racial, religious, political -, not only because such intolerance creates tensions which diminish the quality of life for everyone, but also because such intolerance denies us the cultural richness which the social diversity itself makes possible.

To offer the young an appropriate form of personal, social and moral education, then, is to initiate them into democratic values of this kind. And the justification for this is not to be found in the law of God nor in any absolutist or rationalist philosophical system, and certainly not in the authoritarian pronouncements of our 'superiors'. It is to be found in the concept of democracy itself, and what the very notion of democratic living implies for standards and principles of social behaviour.

In adopting this approach to the personal, social and moral education of young people, then, we are not abrogating our responsibility for positive teaching. Equally, however, we are not meeting that responsibility by offering spurious absolutes of a kind they may well come to reject. We are merely drawing attention to the logic of the democratic system. For that system requires of all who wish to be a part of it, and to share its benefits, that they accept as a basic moral tenet respect for, and tolerance of, the views, habits, practices, customs, religious beliefs and, in general, the codes of behaviour of their fellow citizens – always on the assumption that these in themselves are such as to conform to the democratic moral template.

And we are at the same time seeking to make clear to young people that democratic freedom entails responsibility, that rights entail duties, and, above all, that how they use their freedom, meet their responsibilities, enjoy their rights, fulfil their duties, is a matter of judgment and the resolution of conflicting demands, not blind obedience to catch-all 'moral absolutes'. Assisting young people to make such judgments and resolve such conflicts must be the central task of this dimension of education and, indeed, of education in its totality in a genuinely democratic context.

It is only in this direction, then, that a tenable – and workable – model of personal, social and moral education will be found. If we are to find it, and if we are to make any headway in the ever more crucial fight against those law and order problems which are proliferating in modern society, we need to become a good deal clearer than most people currently are about what it is we are trying to do, and are justified in trying to do.

In this respect, the most sensible and viable approach to personal, social and moral education in schools which has emerged (or, at the time of writing, appears to be emerging) from official sources is the expected recommendation of the National Forum for Values in Education and the

Community, that all pupils should be required to engage in compulsory community service. Questions are rightly being asked about the practicability of implementing such a proposal, although it would seem that, if it has proved practicable to involve large numbers of pupils in work experience, it should not be difficult to extend this to, or co-ordinate it with, experience in aspects of community work.

A more serious drawback is that contrary ethos we noted earlier which has been introduced into schools and the school curriculum through the National Curriculum and its associated policies. In proposing compulsory community service, the group acknowledged that the values currently being promoted in society are success, wealth, winning and 'not getting caught', and suggested that schools should seek to offset this by concentrating on values such as those of compassion, fairness, freedom, justice, respect and responsibility. We have noted earlier the difficulties of promoting such values in the teeth of a prevailing ethos in society which is contrary to them. We have also noted how much more difficult this is when that prevailing contrary ethos has permeated the schools and the school curriculum. We must note now, therefore, that a fundamental change in curricular policies as a whole will be necessary if any approach to personal, social and moral education, even one which includes a compulsory community service element, is to succeed. It is, however, a step in the right direction, and might take us closer to what we are recommending here, namely the establishment of a genuinely democratic set of social and moral values.

An important feature of this kind of development is the fact that it provides opportunities for society outside the school to reinforce what the schools are attempting to achieve in this dimension of education, and thus indicates to young people that concern for their personal, social and moral development is not confined to the school, to their teachers and parents, but is of importance to society as a whole. In this connection one must commend initiatives, such as that which is taking hold in various regions of the Isle of Wight, of electing Youth Councils with powers not only to voice opinions but also to influence decisions on a variety of local issues.

Effective forms of personal, social and moral development must in some form be located in the wider community and must be reinforced by activities supported, and indeed initiated, by agencies outside the schools.

BARRIERS TO PROGRESS

In suggesting this democratic approach to personal, social and moral education, we are of course moving into the closely associated realm of political education, which is to be the subject of the next chapter. Before, we make way for that, however, we must briefly consider some of the barriers which exist to block the path of any effective movement towards this kind of democratic moral system, and some of the positive dangers of accepting the inferior alternatives which are currently being peddled. For, if we are to make progress in this direction, we must begin by resisting and rejecting attempts to approach the planning of this area of the curriculum from other perspectives.

The first barrier is that contradictory ethos endemic to the present National Curriculum whose negative effects on personal, social and moral education we have just noted yet again.

A second barrier is that adherence to the notion of moral knowledge and moral absolutes which we discussed at the beginning of this chapter. There is one version of this approach which we must be especially wary of. For, in addition to the dangers inherent in the 'moral absolutes' of NCC, SCAA and now QCA, there are potential disasters also, for example, in seeking to resolve this problem by reasserting the moral values of the Judaeo-Christian tradition, as we have been urged to do by leading members of the established church, such as the Archbishop of Canterbury (Carey 1996).

For it is precisely the failure of that tradition which has created for us the problems we must now address. If we seek to inculcate values which have no more substantial backing than tradition, even a religious tradition, we must not expect this policy to be effective in a social context in which tradition is recognized as – by definition – outmoded, as modernist rather than as postmodernist, as inevitably to be transcended by intellectually newer forms of thought.

And, if we seek to base those values on a particular set of religious beliefs, on nothing more substantial than the fear of God, then we will be falling into two further traps. For, first, we will be offering moral principles of a kind which we suggested earlier is questionable in the context of a democratic society of free persons. And, second, such principles will also prove practically ineffective in a society in which the underpinning religious beliefs are rejected, not only by those who adhere to different forms of religious faith but also by that growing body of people who adhere to no religious faith whatsoever.

To associate morality with religion in this way must bring the danger, which is a major factor in those law and order problems we are increasingly concerned about, that to have rejected religion will seem to many people, as it clearly does at present, as entailing the rejection of all moral principles also, and a consequent loss of all sense of moral obligation. And so the baby will go down the drain with the bath-water.

Isn't there a danger that this will give children the message that being moral is necessarily connected with being religious? And if they are not religious believers, they may well think that morality can be dispensed with too. Morality and religion are separate and it is crucially important to keep moral and religious education separate, too, for excellent practical and theoretical reasons. (White 1994, p. 8)

It is precisely this association of religion with morality which has led to our present situation. To reassert moral and spiritual values, through, for example, compulsory Christian assemblies in schools and the compulsory teaching of Christian values, is to make the same error again. It is certainly not a route towards correcting it. For, where this does not meet with total indifference and rejection, it will be seen as an attempt to establish precisely that alienating form of religious apartheid the fruits of which we are currently reaping in Northern Ireland – and in many places elsewhere in the world. In fact, in the context of modern commercialism, it begins to look like a device to drum up business for an ailing enterprise. And that is no basis for curriculum planning in an area of such importance to society as well as to the individual.

Those with a vested interest in religions of one form or another may regret the fact, but we are living in a secular society, and such a society requires a secular form of morality. To try to impose something different on it is not only to be doomed to failure, it is also to be inviting further disaster. And it is to be selling society short. For a society with any claims to being a cohesive unit is entitled to a clear statement of those values which give it cohesion, which hold it together as a unit, which comprise its moral cement. And, in the case of any genuinely democratic society, that cement is the moral values of democracy itself. To offer it spurious forms of morality which it is claimed derive from religious beliefs most of its members do not embrace is to attempt to hoodwink it, and this is unacceptable in democratic terms. It is even to be questioned whether religious values are themselves democratic or consistent with democratic principles. Certainly, if we are right to regard tolerance as a major moral principle of democracy, it is difficult to see much evidence of adherence to this in most forms of religion.

A democratic society is held together by democratic values. And it is this we must recognize and fully explore if we are to tackle effectively the moral issues which we face, and especially if we are to provide young people with a set of moral principles which they can recognize the point of and which they are, as a result, far more likely to embrace.

Absolutism, then, in its traditional sense offers no solution to the problems of personal, social and moral education. On the other hand, it is simplistic to recognize no alternative to this other than an anarchic relativism. Democratic theory can provide all of the absolutes we need for a perfectly coherent form of social morality and a perfectly acceptable set of moral principles. What it cannot, and should not do, is to dictate in detail how these principles are to be applied or implemented. That is a matter for the moral judgment of the individual.

For not the least merit of the democratic moral system is that it can offer moral principles of a kind and in a manner which will not compromise individual freedom or autonomy. It is of the essence of democracy that it should seek to promote, and, indeed, to maximize, individual autonomy. Other forms of morality do not, and cannot, offer such a facility. If, then, we see morality as the practice of principled behaviour within a social context, we must recognize democracy as the only form of social and political organization which is consonant with such a definition – both theoretically and practically.

We must also recognize the implications of this for the curriculum as a whole. For it reinforces the central theme of this book, that personal development through a wide range of experiences is, or should be, the central concern of any genuinely educative curriculum, as well as underlining a point which was made at the beginning of this chapter, that personal, social and moral education is pivotal to this process.

In proposing an alternative direction for personal, social and moral education, then, one which stresses the need to develop a secular morality within a democratic context, we are proposing a new direction for education as a whole. And, in doing so, we must also advocate that any national curriculum in its totality must be founded on, and must reflect, the same democratic, moral and, indeed, educational principles.

10

Political, Social and Economic Education for Democratic Citizenship

Gwyn Edwards

In the *Curriculum 11–16* working papers Her Majesty's Inspectorate (DES 1977a, p. 6) identified the 'social and political' as one of the essential 'areas of experience' in which pupils should be offered properly thought out and progressive experience during the period of compulsory schooling. Indeed, the 'political and social' area of experience received considerable attention, both directly and indirectly, in the working papers. Section 2 'Schools and society' explored the relationship between pupils' educational needs and the diverse expectations of society and Section 3, 'Schools and preparation for work', underlined the obligation of schools to equip pupils for adult life, especially in relation to the world of work. Together, these sections portrayed a world characterized by political and economic tension, multiple expectations, rapidly changing value systems, the emergence of unanticipated social needs, increased leisure, and exponential technological development. Consequently, it was argued, 'the greater will be the need for a basic political and economic education for all' (op. cit., pp. 11–12). Speculating on the needs of pupils in a world of change and uncertainty, HMI concluded:

> They will need to understand different viewpoints, appreciate conflicting motives, resist tendentious influences, and appraise critically. They will need to make choices and understand the implications of choices made. They will therefore require not only basic knowledge of how society is run and how resources are distributed but also an introduction to citizenship involving not so much a study of institutions but of issues, not of constitutional forms but of political motivation and of the criteria for making political choices (op. cit., p. 12).

Similar themes permeated the two supplementary papers 'Economic understanding' and 'Political competence'. The former recognized that 'schools are already dealing with members of an economy and a polity' (op. cit., p. 53) in that some pupils are citizens by virtue of their right to vote and that 'virtually all pupils in secondary schools are consumers and most of them enjoy some kind of an an income' (ibid.). On this basis, it was acknowledged that 'if it is intended seriously that England should be a democracy,

... all citizens should be aware of the main economic and political issues so that they may consider them in an informed and intelligent way' (ibid.).

Significantly, much emphasis was given in the working papers to the interrelatedness of political, social and economic structures and processes. For example, the supplementary paper 'Economic understanding' highlighted the fact that 'economics is very intimately bound up with social, political and ethical questions' (op. cit., p. 54) and contended that 'if it is a purpose of a curriculum to add to young people's social and political competence, then economic knowledge is a necessary condition of educational value' (ibid.). It is somewhat surprising, therefore, that the 'economic' was not identified as an area of experience in its own right. From what was written, however, it is reasonable to conclude that economic understanding was viewed by HMI as a necessary and integral dimension of the social and political area of experience.

Read retrospectively, in the light of subsequent events, *Curriculum 11–16* appears optimistic, visionary and radical. However, it was not without tensions and contradictions, three of which are particularly significant to this chapter. First, HMI delineated 'two distinct and yet interdependent roles' (p. 9) that education has in relation to society, 'each acting upon the other' (ibid.). One is concerned 'with equipping young people to take their place as citizens and workers in adult life, and to begin to form attitudes to the prevailing patterns of standards and behaviour' (ibid.). The other has responsibility for educating the autonomous citizen, 'a person able to think and act for herself or himself, to resist exploitation, to innovate and to be vigilant in the defence of liberty.' It was acknowledged that 'these two functions do not always fit together' (ibid.) but the implications of this were not addressed. Second, HMI recognized the 'plurality of interest and groups in society as a possible strength' (ibid.) but clearly had no truck with those groups 'who see society as it is presently constituted as oppressive and objectionable' (ibid.). What they had in mind was 'the "virtuous citizen", probably living as part of a family, in a largely urban, technology-based industrial society, with minority cultures, working in general towards a social harmony which can accommodate change and differences' (ibid.). Third, attention was drawn to the serious constraints 'imposed by an outdated school organization or ethos, taken over from the attitudes and assumptions of previous decades and circumstances' (op. cit., p. 13) – including didactic teaching styles, content laden syllabuses, competitive examinations and hierarchical management structures – yet no necessity was seen for any significant restructuring of the curriculum. On the contrary, it was argued that most of the knowledge necessary for social and political objectives can be transmitted through established subjects or a combination of them and, therefore, does 'not require the introduction of new subjects into the curriculum' (ibid.).

The curricular structure that best facilitates social, political and economic education has always been a contentious matter. As Beck (1978, p. 70) notes, the received view 'is that, in so far as these areas are an appropriate part of the school curriculum at all, they are most suitably studied through established school subjects, particularly history, geography and religious education'. But, although widely endorsed, this view is not universally accepted. Crick and Porter (1978, p. 27) claim that 'political literacy teaching is most successful where it is done through courses which have been constructed with exclusive political literacy objectives'. In a similar vein, The Politics Association (Brennan 1981, p. 142) 'expresses some reservations about the approach to political education through traditional subjects as a general strategy'. History, it observes, 'may be a necessary condition for political understanding, but it is not, of itself, a sufficient condition' (op. cit., p. 263). It goes on to argue that 'social, economic, and political concepts are inter-related and that there are considerable advantages in the development of teaching strategies which will enable each of these fields of study to inform and enliven the other' (ibid.). This view is not without support. Porter (1983, p. 20) suggests that 'social education, by virtue of the fact that it deals in part with the relationship between individuals and society, must have a political dimension'. For Blyth (1994, p. 14) 'an economic perspective cannot appear in any curriculum unless moral and social issues are considered too'. And in relation to geography, Dear (1996, p. 181) argues 'that economic, political and socio-cultural spheres provide a *multi-foundational* basis for the discipline'.

THE HUMANITIES CURRICULUM

No area of the school curriculum has a monopoly on promoting social, political and economic understanding but few would dispute that it is a central concern of that area broadly categorized as the humanities. It follows, therefore that the nature and efficacy of the provision for social, political and economic education will depend to a large extent on how the humanities curriculum is conceptualized and structured. Complications immediately arise, however, from the lack of any consensus on what actually constitutes the humanities. According to Eisner (1984, p. 115), 'the variety of conceptions of the humanities are as diverse as the disciplines and fields of study that are said to constitute them.' Marx (1975, p. 6) points out that 'no one has ever devised a clear set of distinctions for assigning some academic pursuits to the humanities and others to the social sciences'. Roberts (1984, p. 155), likewise, draws attention to 'endless confusion about the differences . . . between humanities and the social sciences.' Jarrett (1973, p. 47) observes that 'in England [and Wales] humanities often embraces, and is even slanted towards, the social sciences', a tendency which concerns White (1973, p. 58) in that 'the sociologizing of the humanities curriculum undervalues the contemplative side of our nature'.

It comes as no surprise, therefore, to find substantial differences in how the humanities curriculum is conceived in schools and, by implication, in how political, social and economic education is organized within it. Historically, a conception of humanities as a collection of discrete subjects has established itself firmly in the school curriculum with geography, history and religious education emerging as the dominant, if not exclusive, subjects. However, although deeply entrenched, this conception has been challenged at various times to varying degrees. For example, early in the century Mackinder (1913, p. 7) had advocated the teaching of geography and history as a combined subject on the grounds that subjects 'exist only in books and not in the real world'. And in the inter-war period the Association of Education for World Citizenship had campaigned for the inclusion of additional subjects in the curriculum – notably political science and economics.

In the 1950s a combination of post-war social and economic reconstruction and educational reorganization arising from the 1944 Education Act created a climate conducive to a fundamental reappraisal of the humanities curriculum. Of particular concern at the time was the need to educate young people for their responsibilities as citizens in a democratic society, and to equip them with the necessary skills and understandings to cope with life in the complex, pluralistic and ever-changing world they would inherit. Moreover, the establishment of secondary education for all, together with the raising of the school leaving age, posed the additional challenge of devising a curriculum that would maintain the motivation and attention of a large cohort of non-academic pupils. In response to these multiple demands, arguments were presented for broadly-based social studies courses that would be more in tune with the interests and experiences of the pupils and more directly related to the needs and realities of a modern industrialized society. The aims of such courses, it was envisaged, would be:

> To combine the material of history, geography and civics together with relevant material from other subject fields, into a single integrated background course, through which the child can come to appreciate the interrelatedness of all the elements of his environment and to feel himself to be closely associated with the past and present struggles and achievements of mankind, and to have a personal contribution to make towards future progress (Hemming 1949, p. 25).

Early attempts to broaden and/or integrate the humanities curriculum, however, had limited impact and history and geography, supported by powerful subject associations, were able to maintain their dominant position. Moreover, the subject-based status quo was officially endorsed in a series of government reports, white papers and pamphlets which collectively did much to shape post-war educational policy and practice. The Spens Report (Board of Education 1938, p. 159), for example, advised that 'proposals for unifying subjects should be entertained with some caution' and the Norwood Report (Board of Education 1943, p. 57) rejected claims for the introduction of additional social subjects into the curriculum on the grounds that 'nothing but harm can result ... from attempts to interest pupils prematurely in matters which imply the experience of an adult'. In a similar vein, the Ministry of Education (1949) pamphlet *Citizens Growing Up* acknowledged that 'one essential purpose of education is to nurture the development of the future citizen' (p. 20) but assumed that this could be accomplished through traditional subjects 'logically and naturally with no distortion' (p. 22). More pointedly, it asserted that to the teachers of history and geography 'belongs the task of introducing the pupil to the political, economic and social life in which he is about to share' (p. 24).

Despite the formidable odds, the mid-1960s heralded the beginning of a more determined and sustained effort to reconceptualize the humanities curriculum. Often this resulted in little more than a reorganization of the subject matter of established subjects. More radical approaches, however, challenged the legitimacy of the traditional subject-based humanities curriculum, and highlighted the sterility of the learning experiences it often engendered. Academic subjects were seen as arbitrary social constructions, rather than logical necessities, and their content was considered to be remote from the interests, experiences and needs of the majority of pupils. Such assumptions underpinned many of the humanities projects developed in the 1970s under the auspices of the Schools Council. The Keele Integrated Studies Project, for example, examined the possibilities of integration in the humanities area of the curriculum and sought ways of relating knowledge to the experiences, feelings and beliefs of students. Similarly, the Humanities Curriculum Project constructed a humanities curriculum around a number of controversial issues considered to be closely related to the lived experiences and practical concerns of the adolescent pupil. This project made an explicit commitment to a set of pedagogical principles that encouraged the pupils to exercise their judgement and express their feelings about the significance of topics and materials they encountered.

In addition, the 1970s and 1980s witnessed attempts to accommodate in the humanities curriculum a kaleidoscope of newly emerging areas of study, perspectives or themes, including Peace Studies; Urban Studies; World Studies; Women's Studies; Media Studies; Global Education; Development Education; and Multicultural Education. Supporters of the New Right viewed these initiatives as evidence of a pervasive left-wing bias in the curriculum that was undermining traditional social and educational values. For Scruton, (1986, p. 107) Peace Studies had 'a dubious intellectual status [and] no practical application, being ... mere opinion-making of a propagandist kind'. Similarly, Ellis-Jones (1986, p. 161) claimed that Women's Studies was 'propagandist, intolerant and unscholarly'. And Hill (1986, p. 116) saw Urban Studies as 'largely a bid to get all the major preoccupations of modern Marxism on to the timetable'. Even so, regardless of their political intent, or educational merit, these initiatives constituted, at the time, a further significant challenge to the traditional subject-based humanities curriculum.

W(H)ITHER THE 'POLITICAL' AND THE 'ECONOMIC' IN THE HUMANITIES CURRICULUM?

We noted earlier that in *Curriculum 11–16* HMI identified 'economic understanding' and 'political competence' as two fundamental aims of education in a democratic society. And we noted also that HMI recognized a potential conflict between these aims. It is somewhat surprising therefore that within the 'shifting mosaic' of the humanities curriculum, as described above, the 'political' and 'economic' dimensions have, until recently, received relatively little attention Moreover, since their emergence, they have experienced mixed and contrasting fortunes with significant consequences for the kind of humanities curriculum being advocated in this chapter.

The Political

Prior to 1970 very little provision was made for political education during the compulsory years of schooling. What did exist was confined almost exclusively to a minority of pupils in the latter stages of secondary education. This consisted of GCE A and O level courses in British Constitution or British Government and Politics for 16–18 year olds and a medley of non-examination civics and citizenship courses for lower achieving 14–16 year olds. With few exceptions, these courses 'concentrated on the formal structure and institutions of central government' (Harber 1984, p. 116), were 'descriptive and legalistic in character' (Brennan 1981, p. 45), lacked 'real cognitive penetration' (ibid.) and were 'marked by an implicit deference for the status quo' (Homan 1995, p. 5).

In contrast, the 1970s heralded a period of growing optimism for political education. From a state of 'pervasive stagnation' in the 1960s, Heater (1977) detected a 'burgeoning of interest'. Similarly, Whitty (1979, p. 112) noted that 'after a decade of quiet gestation, the political education movement has now become a force to be reckoned with'. By the end of the decade 79% of middle and secondary schools in England and Wales claimed to be providing some form of political education (Stradling and Noctor 1983) 'albeit, in many cases, a modest provision through subjects such as history and general studies' (Porter 1983, p. 21).

The cause of political education was considerably strengthened by the founding of the Politics Association in 1969. In 1974, the Association, in partnership with the Hansard Society, obtained a three-year grant from the Nuffield Foundation to fund a Programme for Political Education in secondary schools and colleges of further education. The main aim of the programme was to enhance political literacy by which was meant 'the knowledge, skills and attitudes needed to make a man or woman informed about politics; able to participate in public life and groups of all kind, both occupational and voluntary; and to recognize and tolerate diversities of political and social values' (Crick and Porter, 1978, p. 1). Politics was seen as inevitably concerned with conflicts of interests and ideals. Hence, it was claimed:

> A politically literate person will ... know what the main political disputes are about; what beliefs the main contestants have of them; how they are likely to affect him [sic]; and he will have a predisposition to try to do something about it in a manner at once effective and respectful of the sincerity of others (op. cit., p. 33).

The Programme advocated a shift in emphasis from the transmission of political knowledge to the development of political skills and values, and a shift in emphasis from the study of political institutions to an engagement with political issues. Moreover, it sought to broaden the conception of politics beyond the affairs of state and political parties to embrace the activities of every day life. The politically literate person, it was envisaged, would have the ability to recognize the political dimension of any human situation.

The Programme was structured around 12 basic concepts drawn from 'terms used in every day life' but which would be 'employed more precisely and systematically than is usual' (op. cit., p. 14). The 12 concepts related to government (power; force; authority; order), relationships (law; justice; representation; pressure) and people (natural rights; individuality; freedom; welfare). Additionally, the programme identified a set of procedural values without which it was claimed 'there cannot be any reasonable study or practice of politics' (op. cit., p. 64). These were freedom, toleration, fairness, respect for truth and respect for reasoning.

Interestingly, Pat and John White (1976) critiqued the Programme on a number of counts, two of which have particular relevance to this chapter. First, they saw limitations in what they perceived as a purist view of political education in that it took no account of significant economic concepts. They acknowledged that 'political issues are not necessarily economic ones', but argued that, 'in practice, many of the most important political decisions depend on economic considerations' (p. 265). Second, they felt that the Programme failed to address 'the precise relationship between the individual's interests and those of the community as a whole' (p. 259). As they saw it, there was an emphasis on individualistic aims – 'on the individual and what political involvements might be expected to yield for him' (ibid.) – as against moral or community-based aims.

Despite the notable gains that political education made during the 1970s there were voices of caution. Whitty (1979), for example, found good grounds for expressing some concern about the political education movement, especially its popularity amongst politicians. Their support, he argued, was associated with a 'belief that it could assist in preserving the status quo and in bolstering respect for it' (p. 113). Indeed, he found little evidence within public pronouncements that political education was 'intended to provide a central context for meaningful and critical education' (p. 112). Beck (1978, p. 72), too, advised 'caution and scepticism' on the ground that:

an officially sponsored programme of political 'education' might turn out to be little more than an attempt to adjust the aspirations of young people to 'realistic' levels and to instil 'appropriate' and 'responsible' (i.e. uncritical) attitudes to 'the world of work'. In short there is a danger that political education will mean political *socialization*.

As it turned out, these voices of caution were of little consequence for in the 1980s political education underwent a spectacular reverse of fortunes. The cross-party consensus of the 1970s collapsed in the face of a sustained attack on political education by supporters of the New Right. In response to pressure, New Right Sections 44 and 45 of the Education (No 2) Act 1986 forbade 'the promotion of partisan political views in the teaching of any subject in the school' and required that such steps as are reasonably practicable be taken 'to secure that where political issues are brought to the attention of pupils . . . they are offered a balanced presentation of opposing views'. Any remaining hopes for political education were effectively swept away in the 1988 Education Act which gave the Secretary of State for Education unprecedented powers, including absolute control over the school curriculum. Having assumed such control, he was not now going to allow a curriculum that would encourage any serious questioning of the legitimacy and authority of the political status quo. The only glimmer of hope was provided by the the inclusion of Education for Citizenship as one of five cross-curricular themes the National Curriculum Council considered to be 'essential parts of the whole curriculum' (NCC 1990b, p. 4).

Economic Education

Like political education, there has, historically, been little explicit provision for economic education in the school curriculum except in the form of examination courses for sixth form pupils. A survey in 1976 found that only 14% of schools offered economic courses below sixth form level. Moreover, the pupils that benefited from these courses were predominantly high achieving boys, their numbers estimated to be little more than 2% of the age group (Ryba 1986). However, there was in the 1970s and 1980s a growing interest in economic education in some guise or other.

The reasons for this are not too difficult to locate. The world oil crisis in 1973 terminated an era of sustained economic growth in the Western industrialized nations and precipitated a period of major economic and industrial restructuring (Kerr 1994). This restructuring, in turn, brought about sweeping changes in the nature of work and a marked reduction in the size of the work-force. Consequently, the 1970s heralded a period of rising unemployment, especially amongst the young. Moreover, a view was emerging that many school leavers lacked the necessary understandings, skills and dispositions to take advantage of what employment opportunities were available. It came as no surprise, therefore, that the Government White Paper which followed Callaghan's Ruskin Speech in 1976 echoed 'the feeling that the educational system was out of touch with fundamental needs for Britain to survive economically in a highly competitive world through the efficiency of its industry and commerce' (DES 1977b, p. 2). Young people, it was argued, were 'not sufficiently aware of the importance of industry to our society,' and they were 'not taught much about it' (ibid.). They left school 'with little or no understanding of the workings, or importance, of the wealth-producing sector of our economy' (p. 34). Henceforth, it was envisaged that education would 'contribute as much as possible to improving industrial performance and thereby increasing the national wealth' (p. 6). Thus, education was seen as the source of, a scapegoat for and the solution to Britain's economic decline.

Such sentiments were reiterated in all subsequent official government statements on the curriculum. *The School Curriculum* (DES 1981, p. 18) asserted that 'pupils need to be given a better understanding of the economic base of our society and the importance to Britain of the wealth creating process' and *The Organization and Content of the School Curriculum* (DES 1984b, p. 8) affirmed that 'every pupil should study, ... under whatever guise, ... the principles of a free society and some basic economic awareness.' The White Paper *Better Schools* (DES 1985, p. 16) conjectured:

> The economic stresses of our time and the pressures of international competition make it more necessary than ever before that Britain's work-force should possess the skills and attitudes, and display the understanding, the enterprise and adaptability that the pervasive impact of technological advance will increasingly demand.

In response, it advocated a curriculum that brought education and training 'into closer relation in a variety of ways' and had 'preparation for employment as one of its principal functions' (op. cit., p. 16). Moreover, it 'regarded as important that both pupils and teachers should have greater awareness of the wealth-creating function of industry and commerce' (ibid.). Consistent with these imperatives, the Council for the Accreditation of Teacher Education (CATE) in its criteria for the approval of initial teacher training courses stipulated that the educational and professional studies element of such courses should 'enable students to appreciate their task as teachers within the broad framework of ... the values and the economic and other foundations of the free and civilized society in which their pupils are growing up, and the need to prepare pupils for adulthood, citizenship and the world of work' (DES 1989, p. 10).

In line with government policy, a myriad initiatives and projects have been launched that endeavour to promote economic and industrial understanding in the curriculum in order, primarily, to meet perceived economic needs of the country. Prominent among these are the Economics Education 14–16 Project, the Schools Curriculum Industry Project (SCIP), the Technical and Vocational Education Initiative (TVEI), the Mini-Enterprise in Schools Project (MESP) and the Educating for Economic Awareness Project.

The cumulative impact of these initiatives and projects is not easy to gauge. In a survey on economic understanding in the school curriculum carried out in 1985, albeit using a small sample, HMI (DES 1987 p. 7) noted that 'Despite the increasing recognition by ... schools ... that economic understanding should be an important part of the curricular experience of all pupils, there was less progress towards an appreciation of what economic understanding might actually consist'. The survey indicated that 'economic understanding was better where [pupils] had received explicit teaching in the field' (p. 17) which led HMI to the conclusion that 'cross-curricular approaches might have to be supported by specific timetabled provision to be effective' (ibid.). And in a HMI report on mini-enterprises (DES 1990c) 'what was considered to be least well handled in primary schools was the development of economic and industrial understanding' (p. 5). Moreover, in secondary schools it was found that 'a proportion of students were getting a distorted view of the real trading world' (p. 8) and 'a false impression was being created in the minds of many ... as to the characteristics of the real market-place' (p. 11).

In light of what had gone on before, it is somewhat surprising that no explicit provision was made for economic education in the National Curriculum, especially as one of the statutory requirements of the 1988 Education Act is a curriculum that 'prepares pupils for the opportunities, responsibilities and experiences of adult life'. Instead, it was left to the National Curriculum Council to make good the deficit by including Economic and Industrial Understanding as one of its cross-curricular themes (NCC 1990a).

THE NATIONAL CURRICULUM AND ITS LEGACY

By the mid-1980s social, political and economic education had established a firm foothold in the humanities curriculum, either as discrete subjects or as key elements of an integrated framework. Much of what had been achieved, however, was rendered obsolete in 1988 with the imposition of a subject-based National Curriculum. Henceforth, geography, history and religious education were to be the legally sanctioned standard bearers of the humanities curriculum.

Prospects for a broad, integrated humanities curriculum, and for social, political and economic education within it, were bleak from the start. The History and Geography Working Groups differed significantly in how they saw the two subjects relating to each other, and in how they perceived their own subject contributing to the promotion of social, political and economic understanding. The final report of the Geography Working Group (DES 1990a) reflected and reinforced the aspirations of many geographers to align their subject substantially with science, rather than the humanities. The report reaffirmed the place and status of the physical and scientific elements of geographical studies on the grounds that they are integral to a balanced and complete understanding of the subject' (p. 7). Conversely, it played down geography's links with the humanities by asserting that the skills of the subject are 'frequently different from the skills of research and inter-pretation developed through history and are more closely related to mathematical and scientific skills' (p. 74). Consequently, it was argued, 'great care must be exercised in developing formal links between his-tory and geography, especially in the context of combined courses' (ibid).

In contrast, the final report of the History Working Group asserted that 'history and geography make closely-related contributions to learning' (DES 1990b, p. 182). More specifically, it claimed that:

> they benefit from each other's methods of enquiry, involving investigation of human issues and values, the interpretation of partial or distorted evidence, an attempt to see issues from other people's points of view and the making of rea-soned judgements. [Furthermore], some of the skills of geography . . . are useful to pupils in their study of history, the two subjects share themes such as trans-port, industry, agriculture, settlement, and population, to which each brings its own perspective [and] all patterns and issues of concern to geographers have their roots in past conditions and arrangements' (ibid).

In Section 7 of its final report, the Geography Working Party acknowledged that geography has an important role to play in promoting political, social and economic understanding but provided no explicit structure or guid-ance for its realization in practice. In contrast, the History Working Group incorporated political, economic, and social understanding into the History National Curriculum itself. In their final report (DES 1990a) the pro-grammes of study were structured around four dimensions of the study of history, namely Political; Economic, technological and scientific; Social and religious; and Cultural and aesthetic. The Working Party regarded this PESC formula as one of the most significant contributions towards achiev-ing balance in the history curriculum.

It is now clearly evident that a concerted effort was made by an ad hoc alliance of neo-conservative politicians (and their advisers) and self-appointed educational 'experts' to influence the deliberations, and subse-quent recommendations, of both the History and Geography Working Parties, although the degree to which they succeeded is debatable. What is beyond dispute, however, is the degree to which the outcomes were manip-ulated by direct government intervention. Mrs Thatcher herself saw it as 'absolutely right' for history teaching to concentrate on names, dates and events. Pupils, she asserted, should know 'the great landmarks of British history' (quoted in *The Independent*, 5.4.90). Echoing her concern, John McGregor (Secretary of State for Education, 1989–1990) requested the History Working Party to place more emphasis on facts and knowledge. In turn, his successor Kenneth Clarke (Secretary of State for Education, 1990–1992) removed political issues from the geography draft orders. Nor did he see a role in geography for 'people's attitudes and opinions' (quoted in *TES*, 18.1.91). Moreover, Clarke made his opposition to integrated humanities and topic work abundantly clear. In such contexts, he argued, pupils 'simply do not learn enough about individual subjects' (quoted in *TES*, 17.5.91). Thus, he saw the National Curriculum as a means of rescuing history and geography 'from near extinction as valid subjects in some schools' (quoted in *The Guardian* 26.3.91).

As the inadequacies of a subject-based National Curriculum became increasingly apparent, the National Curriculum Council endeavoured to redeem the situation by bolting on a framework of 'cross-curricular elements', comprising 'dimensions skills and themes' (NCC 1990a), designed to 'tie together the broad education of the individual subjects and augment what comes from the basic curriculum' (p. 2). Five cross-curricular themes, assumed to be 'essential parts of the whole curriculum' (p. 4), were identified – namely, Economic and Industrial Understanding; Careers Education and Guidance; Health Education; Education for Citizenship; and Environmental Education. This, however, only compounded the problem by imposing additional burdens on an already overloaded curriculum. Therefore, it came as little surprise when, in April 1993, John Patten, the Secretary of State for Education, invited Sir Ron Dearing, Chairman of the School Curriculum and Assessment Authority, to review the National Curriculum, albeit within the somewhat narrow remit of slimming down the curriculum, improving the central administration, simplifying the testing arrangements and reviewing the ten-level scale for recognizing children's attainment. Following an interim report in July, the final report, *The National Curriculum and its Assessment*, was published in December 1993. It could be argued that the general approval it received from the educational community was misplaced in that the underlying assumptions of the National Curriculum were never questioned – for it was not in the remit to do so – and its deeply flawed structure remained intact.

In a speech to the British Academy in July 1988 Kenneth Baker (Secretary of State for Education, 1986–1989) paid particular tribute to the contribution of the humanities to civilized life:

> In this country, as nowhere else, the tradition of humanities teaching has continued vitality and relevance. I am quite clear that every civilized society, to remain civilized, needs to develop in its citizens the aptitudes and intuitions which flow from an engagement with the humanities. The humanities are an inter-related effort to give intellectual expression to the significance of what it is to be human.

It is ironic, therefore, that the National Curriculum which he instigated has in practice resulted in a narrow, fragmented, emasculated humanities curriculum that does justice neither to the constituent subjects themselves, nor to the pursuit of the broader civilizing aims that a humanities curriculum should seek to foster. Social, political and economic education, if it exists at all, now flounders at the margins of the curriculum where it clings hopefully to the cross-curricular themes and/or personal and social education programmes as a potential, if tenuous, lifeline. But, as research has shown, the cross-curricular themes have been marginalized to such an extent that their recovery is unlikely without a substantial revision of the National Curriculum subject orders (Whitty et al., 1994). Consequently, opportunities for pupils to develop a critical understanding of the society in which they live, and of their agency within it, have been severely curtailed. It will be argued in the next section that such opportunities are essential prerequisites for preparing young people for active participation in a democratic society, and for the furtherance of the democratic ideal itself.

EDUCATION, DEMOCRACY AND CITIZENSHIP

Few would seriously dispute that a free, publicly-funded system of education is an essential requirement for any society that claims to be democratic. Beyond basic provision, however, there is very little agreement on what education in a democratic society should actually entail. In practice, much would depend on the meaning attributed to the term democracy. For there is no fixed, unitary conception of democracy. It is an essentially contested concept that over the course of history has undergone a number of substantial revisions. It could be argued that our present understanding of democracy is derived, predominantly, from the economic and political reality of Western capitalist societies. Here, within the framework of a capitalist economic ethic, 'contemporary' liberal democracy emerged and is now firmly established. In the words of Barber (1992, p. 242), 'Democracy was ... reborn in the modern world with capitalism as its midwife'. This tradition of democracy, Macpherson (1973, p. 5) argues, 'had been built in a market economy, whose ethos was competitive maximization of utilities'. As such, it embodies a view of human beings as 'asocial, egotistic individuals whose fundamental motivation in acting is the satisfaction of their own interest' (Gould 1988, p. 4) and, thereby, privileges individual freedom as the fundamental democratic imperative. The need for collective political participation is, therefore, considered to be minimal, its limited function being primarily to remove the obstacles and guarantee the rights for individuals to pursue their self-interest. Moreover, this conception of democracy has been reinforced by growing scepticism of the possibility or desirability of direct participation by citizens in the affairs of large, modern nation states. Thus, in its present form, democracy has become little more than competition between ruling elites for the votes of the people – and the consequent right to govern – at periodic, free elections. It is, according to Schumpeter (1943, p. 242), 'a certain type of institutional arrangement for arriving at political-legislative and administrative decisions' in which the political ignorance and apathy of citizens is viewed as acceptable, or even necessary (Pateman 1970).

In response to the perceived limitations of 'contemporary' Western liberal democracy, there is now a growing argument for a return to the 'classical' form in which human beings are envisaged as purposeful, self-determining agents, for whom participation in the practical problems of public affairs in pursuit of the common good is seen as a means of advancing their intellectual, emotional and moral development. For Macpherson (1973, p. 8), it is consistent with a view 'that the end or purpose of man [sic] is to use and develop his uniquely human attributes or capacities' which, he suggests, could be taken to include 'the capacity for rational understanding, for moral judgement and action, for aesthetic creation and contemplation, for the emotional activities of friendship and love, and, sometimes, for religious experience' (p. 4). Viewed thus, education and democracy are mutually supportive processes.

There is growing support also for the view that the upheavals and transformations the world is currently experiencing require nothing less than a fundamental rethinking of democracy (Mouffe 1992; Gould 1998; Held 1996). Some of the rethinking focuses specifically on the need for democratic politics to acknowledge and confront the inequalities that are inevitably created by a capitalist market economy. It is argued that the economic policies and practices of modern Western societies constitute a formidable, if not insuperable, obstacle to the realization of the democratic ideal. As Dahl (1985, p. 68) points out, 'If citizens are unequal in economic resources, so are they likely to be unequal in political resources; and political equality will be impossible to achieve.'

Inevitability, this tension – some would argue incompatibility – between democracy and free market capitalism manifests itself in education and with far-reaching implications. Brosio (1991, p. 36), for example, sees the school's role as occupying 'a contested site where two, historically powerful and contradictory, imperatives clash.' In his view:

> The capitalist economic imperative requests that schools produce competent, willing workers; whereas, the democratic egalitarian perspective requests that public education develop critical, well-rounded, citizen-workers who are committed to complex roles beyond work – and who may use their critical skills to analyse capitalist work relations, and command of the economy (pp. 35–36).

Thus, he contends, 'authentic democracy – and education for democratic empowerment – must necessarily struggle against the hegemony of capitalism' (op. cit., p. 31). MacIntyre (1987, p. 16) goes even further in claiming that 'the two major purposes which teachers are required to serve are, under the conditions of Western modernity, mutually incompatible'. Only under certain types of social and cultural conditions, he argues, can both purposes be satisfied 'within one and the same educational system' (ibid).

On the other hand, Novak (1982, p. 14) for example, argues that 'political democracy is compatible in practice *only* (my emphasis) with a market economy'. Moreover, he claims that the imperatives of capitalism are consistent with the basic tenets of Judaeo-Christian theology and, thereby, he endeavours to establish its moral superiority over other forms of economic organization. Such arguments have been mobilized by neoliberals to justify the free-market ideology that has dominated government thinking throughout the 1980s and 1990s, especially during the Thatcher years. Even so, the resulting economic and social policies have not gone unchallenged. And, significantly, some of the most pointed criticism has come from religious organizations. The Report of the Archbishop of Canterbury's Commission on Urban Priority Areas (1985, pp. 16–17), for example, argues that the Church 'has a duty to question the morality of economic philosophies' and calls for 'a more open debate ... about economic policies and about the type of society present economic policies are shaping'. It goes on to argue that the creation of wealth must always be accompanied by just distribution. In a similar vein, leading Methodists call for a reversal of the government's 'market-oriented, competitive, individualistic philosophy' (cited in *The Guardian* 22.4.93) and, conversely, a return to co-operative, egalitarian and community-oriented policies.

These criticisms highlight once again the fundamental tension between free-market capitalism and participatory democracy. It has been argued that the Conservative government's interest in citizenship education was a response to the criticisms of its neoliberal policies and an attempt to reconcile the tension embodied therein (Mouffe 1988). Nowhere is this more evident than in the views expressed by Douglas Hurd (Foreign Secretary, 1989–1997). He argues (1988, p. 14):

> A social policy founded on ideals of responsible and active citizenship is compatible with free market economic policies ... Those qualities of enterprise and initiative which are essential for the generation of material wealth are also needed to build a family, a neighbourhood, or a nation which is able to draw on the respect, loyalty and affection of its members.

An alternative, or additional, interpretation of the Conservative government's interest in citizenship education is that it represented a quick-fix solution to what it perceived to be a growing moral malaise in society. The white paper *Choice and Diversity* (DES 1992, p. 7), for example, states that 'the ethos of any school should include a clear vision of the values within it, and those of the community outside'. Few would take issue with this statement. Appropriate values, however, are thought to include 'respect for people and property; honesty and consideration for others; trust, fairness and politeness' (DES 1992a, p. 7).

This somewhat narrow, instrumental view of citizenship education is reflected also in the National Curriculum Council cross-curricular guidance documents *Education for Citizenship* (DES 1992c) and *Education for Economic and Industrial Understanding* (DES 1992b). The former, Homan (1995, p. 6) argues, is 'distinguished by its cautiousness', being little more than 'retreat into the safe haven that was occupied by civics'. Its emphasis on 'order and stability', 'shared values', 'family life' and 'voluntary service' suggests an attempt is being made to align future citizens more solidly behind the status quo. Beneath the surface rhetoric of the document lurks a neo-conservative image of the active citizen, caricatured by Ignatieff (1991, p. 26) as 'the good-hearted, property-owning patriot, who serves as an unpaid JP if asked, does jury service, gives a day a week to meals on wheels, checks that the old-age pensioner next door is tucked in on cold days, and so on'. Further interrogation of the document reveals a number of strategic blindspots and concealments. For example, schools are seen as being responsible for inculcating in their pupils 'respect for the rule of law' (NCC 1990b, Foreword) but not for inviting them to question or challenge laws that might be considered unjust, repressive or outdated. Pupils are required to understand and appreciate 'the importance to society of wealth creation' (op. cit., p. 8) but must remain ignorant of debates pertaining to its just distribution. And pupils are expected to show 'a constructive interest in community affairs' (op. cit., p. 4) but nowhere is it suggested that this could extend to political activism or non-violent civil disobedience.

Thus, it could be argued that the cross-curricular themes constitute an inadequate basis for promoting citizenship education in a democracy. As Gutmann (1993, p. 3) points out, 'Education should prepare citizens for consciously *re-producing* (not replicating) their society' and, therefore, 'must institute practices of democratic deliberation and decision-making . . . for children to the extent necessary for cultivating their capacities for democratic deliberation' (op. cit., p. 5). For Engle and Ochoa (1986, p. 514), 'rather than demanding a passive acceptance of authority, democracies must produce citizens who have a reasoned commitment to democracy and the capacity for criticism, questioning, decision making and active participation in public affairs'. Giroux (1980, p. 357) makes a similar claim:

> If citizenship education is to be emancipatory it must begin with the assumption that its major aim is not to fit students into existing society; instead, its primary purpose must be to stimulate their passions, imaginations and intellects so that they will be moved to challenge the *social, political and economic* forces that weigh so heavily upon their lives (my emphasis).

There is substantial support, therefore, for the view that a model of citizenship education which prepares adequately for active, meaningful and informed participation in public life cannot be accommodated within the present National Curriculum structure. The Citizenship Foundation (1994), for example, in written evidence submitted to the the Paul Hamlyn National Commission on Education in 1992, called for 'a fundamental review of the place of the humanities and social sciences within the curriculum' on the grounds that it is 'entirely unsatisfactory that significant elements of citizenship education should be relegated to second class status and left to the mercy of an individual school's curriculum policy' (op. cit., p.62). The National Commission on Education itself considers 'the teaching of citizenship of great importance' and recommends its inclusion – together with English, mathematics, natural science, technology and a modern foreign language – in a compulsory core that would take up 50% of curriculum in Key Stage 1 (ages 5–7) and 70% in Key Stages 2 and 3 (ages 7–14).

Of equal concern is the extent to which education in general is being systematically recast as little more than an instrumental means to economic productivity and efficiency. It is now almost taken to be axiomatic by the major political parties that the purpose of schooling is primarily, if not exclusively, to serve the needs of a competitive market-economy. In the foreword to a DfEE (1996) consultative document, *Equipping Young People for Working Life*, Gillian Shephard (Secretary of State for Education and Employment, 1994–1997) affirmed the previous government's intention 'to bring our [educational] system in line with the needs of a modern, competitive economy' (p. 1). Thus, she she went on to say, 'we must do all we can to help . . . young people to acquire the skills, knowledge and understanding they will need to be part of a highly adaptive workforce' (ibid.). Despite a recent change of government, there appears to be no significant change in how the fundamental purposes of education are being perceived. On the contrary, the obsession with comparing the achievements of our educational system, in instrumental economic terms, with those of 'our main industrial competitors' seems to have intensified under New Labour.

THE WAY FORWARD: EDUCATION FOR DEMOCRATIC CITIZENSHIP

I have implied throughout this chapter that the National Curriculum is predicated on a seriously flawed logic that renders it ill-equipped to meet the educational challenges of the twenty-first century. In this final section I wish to argue that an education for democratic citizenship necessitates a radical reordering of the epistemological and pedagogical imperatives of the curriculum in general and the humanities curriculum in particular. Nothing less will do. The suggestions that follow are not intended to be absolute or inclusive; rather they are indicative of the kinds of changes that need to be implemented in the school curriculum if education for democratic citizenship is to have any real meaning or substance.

The only defensible curriculum in a society which claims to be democratic is one that is founded on the principles of democracy itself. Democracy is rooted in a belief that people have the desire to work together in pursuit of the common good, and that given the opportunity they are capable of acquiring the intellectual and moral virtues this demands. Schools, therefore, should be sites where present and future generations learn and practise the art of democratic living. The curriculum should not be fixed and centrally imposed. Rather, it should be negotiated between schools and their communities and between teachers and their pupils, albeit within a commonly agreed framework arrived at through open and informed debate. This requires a belief that even in a pluralistic society people share some core values and purposes which, through dialogue, can be identified and pursued. To believe otherwise is to forgo the possibility of democratic living. Indeed, a principal purpose of education should be concerned with helping young people acquire a set of guiding principles that will enable them to live their lives meaningfully, constructively and cooperatively in the midst of the uncertainty and unpredictability they will increasingly encounter.

Democracy, Peters (1979, p. 474) argues, is a way of life 'in which as much as possible is decided by discussion rather than by authoritative fiat'. To decide matters by reasoned discussion, he maintains, 'requires truth-telling, respect for persons, and the impartial consideration of interests, as under-lying moral principles' (ibid.). Barber (1984) too, puts talk at the heart of democracy. He identifies nine functions of democratic talk which 'converge towards a single, crucial end – the development of a citizenry capable of genuinely public thinking and political judgment and thus able to envision a common future in terms of genuinely common goods' (p. 197). With talk, he argues, 'we can invent alternative futures, create mutual purposes, and construct competing views of community . . . talk is not *about* the world, it is talk that makes and remakes the world' (p. 177). Therefore, he claims, 'a democracy that does not institutionalize talk will soon be without autonomous citizens' (p. 190). Moreover, discussion is a reciprocal process that involves listening as well as speaking. As Gould (1988, p. 88) points out, 'the deliberative process of democratic decision-making requires that each participant not only permit the others to express their view and offer their judgments but take the others' views seriously into account in arriv-ing at his or her own judgment'. It follows that education for democratic citizenship requires that pupils are given the opportunity to acquire and develop the art of discussion, and to cultivate those virtues that are intrin-sic to it. Such a view is not new. The Humanities Curriculum Project was developed on the principle that in dealing with controversial human issues in the classroom 'the basic teaching strategy should be one of discussion rather than instruction'. The social studies project Man: A Course of Study likewise gave sanction and support to open-ended discussion in which pupils 'learn to listen to others as well as express their own ideas', and 'where definitive answers to many questions are not found' (Hanley et al. 1970, p. 5).

Opportunities for pupils to develop social, political and economic under-standing – in terms of knowledge, skills and values – should be explicitly and systematically planned for within a broad, integrated and flexible humanities curriculum. The content of such a curriculum should be derived from the 'basic principles, axiomatic questions [and] pervasive themes' (Bruner 1977, p. ix) pertaining to the social, political and economic dimensions of human experience, rather than from a narrow and arbitrary selection of academic subjects. In such a curriculum, the depth and quality of learning should have precedence over the breadth of content coverage. As Engle and Ochoa (1986) point out, 'a curriculum purporting to prepare citizens in a democracy . . .. must provide a more probing treatment of problems, ideas, values and materials, covering fewer topics than usual, and going deeper into each'. Gardner, too, maintains (1995) that schools attempt to cover too much with superficial understandings (or non-understandings) being the inevitable result. For him 'it makes far more sense to spend a significant amount of time on key concepts, generative ideas, and essential questions and allow students to become thoroughly familiar with these notions and their implications' (p. 208). This view accords with Bruner's (1966) notion of the spiral curriculum in which basic ideas are continually revisited in order to deepen the understanding of them that comes from learning to use them in progressively more complex forms.

Social, political and economic activities are inextricably intertwined and reciprocally related, and, moreover, are becoming increasingly global in scope and impact. Students, therefore, need opportunities to develop what Pike and Selby (1988, p. 34) term 'systems consciousness'. This involves both 'the ability to think in a systems mode' and 'an understanding of the systematic nature of the world.' In the words of Davies (1990, p. 22), they should be 'encouraged to see phenomena and events as bound up in complex, interactive and multi-layered webs in which relationship is everything'.

Students should also be given opportunities to acquire what Keats calls Negative Capability by which he means the capability 'of being in uncertainties, mysteries and doubts without any irritable reaching after fact and reason' (quoted in Trilling 1955, p. 32). This requires a humanities curriculum that avoids premature closure on controversial issues by giving sanction and support to open-ended enquiry. Education for democratic citizenship should enable learners to gain an appreciation of the provisionality and contestability of knowledge, and encourage them to rely on independent reasoning, rather than the authority of experts, as the source of truth. As Elliott (1991, p. 142) puts it, 'an educationally worthwhile process involves a reflexive attitude towards the nature of knowledge, on the part of both the teacher and students'.

The kind of humanities curriculum I am proposing here has major implications for the preservice and inservice education of teachers. It would require teachers who could work competently, confidently and creatively at the interface of a number of academic disciplines and cross easily into different cultural spheres. Teachers would need to become what Giroux (1992) calls 'border intellectuals' with a capacity to 'both problematize and take leave of the cultural, theoretical and ideological borders that enclose them' (op. cit., p. 142). This would entail an abandonment of 'the safe zone of identity' afforded by traditional subject structures in order to open up alternative visions and possibilities. Such a move is in sharp contrast to the present endeavours of the Teacher Training Agency and the Office for Standards in Education to confine teachers securely at the heartlands of the officially sanctioned National Curriculum subjects.

CONCLUSION

Peters (1975) claims that education consists of 'the discovery of what it means to be human and should, above all things, sensitize us to the predicaments in which we are placed as human beings'. In a similar vein, Maxwell (1984) in his preface calls for a new kind of rational inquiry 'devoted to the enhance-ment of wisdom' which gives intellectual priority to the personal and social problems we encounter in our lives as we strive to realize that which is desir-able and of value'. In his view, this involves 'the dual tasks of articulating our problems of living, and proposing and criticizing possible solutions, namely possible human actions' (p. 3). As the twenty-first century approaches it is becoming obvious that the predicaments and problems we face are increasingly global in both scope and impact. Nor do they fit neatly into traditional academic categories. On the contrary, disciplinary bound-aries are being blurred to the point where the notion of a distinct discipline is becoming problematic (Matless 1992). What we are witnessing, Geertz (1983, p. 20) claims, 'is not just another redrawing of the cultural map – the moving of a few disputed borders, the marking of some more picturesque mountain lakes – but an alteration in the principles of mapping'.

The 1988 Education Act legislates for 'a balanced and broadly based cur-riculum which (a) promotes the spiritual, moral, cultural, mental and phys-ical development of pupils at the school and of society; and (b) prepares such pupils for the opportunities, responsibilities and experiences of adult life' (HMSO 1988). As a general statement of intent, few would take issue with these broad aims, but it is simplistic to assume that they are most effectively realized through the study of an arbitrary collection of largely academic subjects. What the 1988 Education Act failed to provide was a coherent rationale whereby its broad aims could be translated into a National Curriculum that could be adapted to meet the needs of schools operating in a variety of contexts and circumstances. In the absence of a coherent rationale, we have inherited a fragmented, over-prescriptive, con-tent-laden, assessment-driven National Curriculum that fails to meet the interests and needs of many of the pupils it purports to serve. Indeed, it comes as no surprise to find that a recent national survey has revealed a lack of relevance, stimulus and accessibility in relation to subject content as one of the major causes of pupil disaffection with schools in England (Kinder 1997).

Whether we like it or not, education is caught up in the turbulence of exponential change the outcomes of which are increasingly unpredictable. What is required now is a National Curriculum framework that seeks to rediscover the intrinsic purposes and principles of education and that gives schools the freedom and incentive to respond flexibly, creatively and responsibly to the needs of their pupils in an uncertain and rapidly changing world. Above all else, we need to educate young people in ways that will enable them to engage actively, critically and effectively in the affairs of their society in order for them to have a voice in the shaping of their destiny. Few would seriously dispute that the humanities curriculum has a crucial role to play in this endeavour. In the words of Ravitch and Finn:

> Well taught and well learned, the humanities are the strongest democratizing force that formal education can muster. . . . They liberate the mind, they inform the citizens, they hone the intellect, they supply criteria by which assertions and claims can be judged and they train the analytical skills that give such judgments power. . . . Knowledge of the humanities . . . engages one in serious considerations of what it means to be wise, ethical and moral. (1984, pp. 241–243).

Emergent Principles for an Alternative National Curriculum

A number of basic principles have underpinned, and emerged from, all the contributions to the debate which this book has set out to fuel. Some of them are listed here, in summary, as the beginnings of a guide to whatever reforms come to be undertaken in relation to official policies for educational provision.

FUNDAMENTAL PRINCIPLES

1. The following principles are predicated on an assumption that any national curriculum to be formulated is intended to be appropriate for a **democratic** society.
2. While education is essentially a political matter, nothing but damage can ensue from treating it as a **party**-political matter.
3. The school curriculum is an essential element in the safeguarding of democracy, so that it cannot properly be framed or controlled by the representatives of any one political ideology, especially those who support a non-democratic ideology.
4. For the same reason, curriculum planning cannot be left to self-seeking educrat careerists.
5. Education is the responsibility of society as a whole, and, as such, should be under the direction of intelligent and committed lay-persons working closely, and in genuine collaboration, with informed, expert and caring professionals. The establishment of a democratically formed Teaching Council is long overdue.
6. In a democratic society schools exist to provide an education for life, so that education must be planned as human development and not merely in terms of the acquisition of knowledge – as developmental rather than incremental, as a process rather than as a product.
7. The essentials of such an education for life are personal enrichment, political empowerment and personal/social/moral adjustment and responsibility.
8. The assumption has to be made (although it must be carefully monitored) that this is also the most effective route to economic success – for society as a whole as well as for each individual.

199

9. A democratic national curriculum must be planned holistically, not as a collection of discrete syllabuses.
10. All subject/knowledge-**content** is politically loaded, so that, even if the selection of curriculum content must always be ideologically driven, the manner of its **presentation** must be such as to invite challenge, questioning, critique, debate rather than mere assimilation and regurgitation.
11. A democratic education will seek to encourage pupils and teachers to be creative and expressive rather than passive.
12. Democratic education must be recognized as essentially a collaborative rather than a competitive activity.
13. The curriculum must be framed, therefore, not primarily in terms of its **content** but as a set of **guidelines** delineating the **democratic** entitlement of every young citizen.
14. The assessment of individual attainment within such a curriculum must be qualitative rather than quantitative; it must concentrate not on the assimilation of selected knowledge-content but on the development of processes and powers of critical reasoning and evaluation.
15. A curriculum so framed cannot be operated by remote control or through a system of external testing and the application of sanctions. Its implementation must involve greater professional freedom and scope for the exercise of professional judgment by teachers.
16. The training of teachers (both initial and in-service) must again become the **education** of teachers, and must regain its former focus on the development of an understanding of young people, a recognition of the importance of caring for them and the acquisition of appropriate powers of professional judgment.

References

Alexander, R., Rose, J. & Woodhead, C. (1992) *Curriculum Organization and the Classroom: A discussion document*, DES, London

Almond, L. (1984) Aspirations in Physical Education, pp. 9–11 in Mawer and Sleap (eds.) (1984)

Andrews, G. (ed.) (1991) *Citizenship*, Lawrence and Wishart, London

Apple, M. (1979) *Ideology and the Curriculum*, Routledge, London

Archer, L.B. (1980) The mind's eye, *The Designer*, January 1980, p. 9

Armstrong, N. (1984) Why implement a health related fitness programme?, *British Journal of Physical Education*, Vol. 15, No. 6, pp. 173–175

Arnold, M. (1909) The Function of Criticism, pp. 1–25 in *Essays Literary and Critical*, Dent, London

Arnold, M. (1932) *Culture and Anarchy*, Cambridge University Press, London

Ascher, M. (1991) *Ethnomathematics: A Multicultural View of Mathematical Ideas*, Brooks/Cole, Belmont, CA

Asprey, W. and Kitcher, P. (eds.) (1988) *History and Philosophy of Modern Mathematics*, University of Minnesota Press, Minneapolis

Baker, K. (1988) *Key Role: Humanities in Society*, lecture given at the British Academy, 7 July, 1988

Bakhtin, M. (1929) The problem of speech genres, pp. 91–7 in Morson (ed.) (1986)

Barber, B.R. (1984) *Strong Democracy: Participatory Politics for a New Age*, University of California Press, Berkeley

Barber, B.R. (1992) *An Aristocracy for Everyone: The Politics of Education and the Future of America*, University of California Press, Berkeley

Barrett, G. (1989) *Disaffection From School? The Early Years*, Falmer, London

Barthes, R. (1972) *Mythologies* (A. Lavers, tr.) Cape, London

Bartolini-Bussi, M.G. (1991) Social interaction and mathematical knowledge, *Proceedings of PME-15*, pp. 1–16, Assisi, Italy

Beck, J. (1978) Social and political education: a question of priorities, *Cambridge Journal of Education*, Vol. 8, No. 3, pp. 66–77

Bell, A.W., Kuchemann, D. and Costello, J. (1983) *A Review of Research in Mathematical Education: Part A, Teaching and Learning*, NFER-Nelson, Windsor

Benjamin, W. (1992a) *Illuminations*, Fontana, London

Benjamin, W. (1992b) *One-Way Street and Other Writings*, translated by Edmund Jephcott and Kingsley Shorter, Verso, London

Berkeley, G. (1710) *The Principles of Human Knowledge*, Fontana Library (1962), Collins, Glasgow

Bernstein, B. (1967) Open schools, open society?, *New Society* 14.9.67

Beveridge, M. (ed.) (1982) *Children Thinking Through Language*, Arnold, London

Black, P. (1995) Looking for a new relationship – science and popular culture, paper presented at the 1995 annual conference of the Association for Science Education INSET Services

Black, P. (1996) Curriculum Change: Dream or Nightmare, *Education in Science*, No. 168. pp. 8–9

Black, P. & Harrison, G. (1985) In Place of Confusion Nuffield Chelsea Curriculum Trust, London

Blake, N. (1996) Between postmodernism and anti-modernism, *British Journal of Educational Studies*, Vol. 44, No. 1, pp. 42–65

Blenkin, G.M. and Kelly, A.V. (1981, 1987) *The Primary Curriculum*, Harper and Row (Second edition, 1987, Paul Chapman), London

Blenkin, G.M. and Kelly, A.V. (eds.) (1988, 1996) *Early Childhood Education: A Developmental Curriculum*, Paul Chapman, London

Bloom, B.S. (ed.) (1956) *Taxonomy of Educational Objectives I, Cognitive Domain*, McKay, New York

Blyth, W.A.L. (1994) Beyond economic and industrial understanding: An economic perspective in the primary curriculum, *British Journal of Education and Work*, Vol. 7, No. 1, pp. 11–7

Bourdieu, P. and Passeron, J. (1977) *Reproduction in Education, Culture and Society*, Sage, London

Brennan, T. (1981) *Political Education and Democracy*, Cambridge University Press, Cambridge

Brooke, P. and Humm, P. (eds.) *Dialogue and Difference: English into the Nineties*, Routledge, London

Brooker, P. (1987) Why Brecht, or Is the English after cultural studies?, pp. 20–31 in Green in association with Hoggart (eds.) (1987)

Brosio, R.A. (1991) The continuing conflict between capitalism and democracy: ramifications for Schooling-Education, *Educational Philosophy and Theory*, Vol. 23, No. 2, pp. 30–45

Brown, S., Fauvel, J. and Finnegan, R. (eds.) (1981) *Conceptions of Inquiry*, Methuen, London, in association with Open University Press

Bruner, J.S. (1960, 1977) *The Process of Education*, Harvard University Press, Cambridge, Massachusetts

Bruner, J.S. (1966) *Towards a Theory of Instruction*, Norton, New York

Buber, M. (1965) *The Knowledge of Man*, Allen and Unwin, London

Buber, M. (1966) *Between Man and Man*, Collins, London

Callinicos, A. (1989) *Against Postmodernism*, Polity Press, Cambridge

Cohen, l. & Mannion, L. (1994) *Research Methods in Education*, Routledge, London

Cantona, E. (1995) *My Story* (quoted in *The Daily Telegraph* 25/6/1994)

Carey, G. (1996) Morality is more than a matter of opinion, *The Daily Telegraph*, 5/7/96, p. 26

Carr, D. (1979) Aims of Physical Education, *Physical Education Review*, Vol. 2, No. 2, pp. 91–100

Carr, W. (1991) Education for democracy? A philosophical analysis of the National Curriculum, *Journal of Philosophy of Education*, Vol. 25, No. 2, pp. 183–91

Citizenship Foundation (1994) The importance of citizenship in *Insights into Education and Training*, papers selected by Paul Hamlyn Foundation/National Commission on Education. Heinemann, London.

Cole, M., Hill, D. and Rikowski, G. (1997) Between postmodernism and nowhere: the predicament of the postmodernist, *British Journal of Educational Studies*, Vol. 45, No. 2, pp. 187–200

Collingwood, R.G. (1938) *The Principles of Art*, Clarendon, Oxford

Collins, C. (1994) *The Visions of the Fool and Other Writings*, Golgonooza, Ipswich

Crick, B. and Porter, A. (eds.) (1978) *Political Education and Political Literacy*, Longman, London

Crump, S. (1995) Towards action and power: post-enlightenment pragmatism, *Discourse: Studies in the Cultural Politics of Education*, Vol. 16, No. 2, pp. 203–217

Dahl, R. (1985) *A Preface to Economic Democracy*, Polity Press, Cambridge

Davies, I. (1990) History teachers: the secret agents of political education, *Social Science Teacher*, Vol. 20, No. 1, pp. 21–4

D'Ambrosio, U. (1985) Ethnomathematics and its place in the history of pedagogy of mathematics, *For the Learning of Mathematics*, Vol. 5, No. 1

Dear, M. (1996) Practising postmodern geography, *Scottish Geographical Magazine*, Vol. 111, No. 3, pp. 179–181

Deuchar, S. (1996) Time to reinvent the spiel, letter to the *Times Educational Supplement* 19.4.96

Dewey, J. (1916) *Democracy and Education*, Macmillan, New York

Dollimore, J. and Sinfield, A. (eds.) (1985) *Political Shakespeare*, Manchester University Press, Manchester

Doll, W.E. (1989) Foundations for a post-modern curriculum, *Journal of Curriculum Studies*, Vol. 21, pp. 243–253

Donald, J. (1989) Beyond Our Ken: English, Englishness and the National Curriculum, pp. 13–30 in Brooke and Humm (eds.) (1989)

Dowling, P. (1988) The Contextualizing of Mathematics: Towards a Theoretical Map, in Harris, M. (ed.) (1991) *Schools, Mathematics and Work*, Falmer, London

Dowling, P. and Noss, R. (eds.) (1991) *Mathematics Versus the National Curriculum*, Falmer, London

Downey, M.E. and Kelly, A.V. (1978) *Moral Education*, Harper and Row, London

Doyle, B. (1989) *English and Englishness*, Routledge, London

Driver, R. (1983) *The Pupil as Scientist?*, Open University Press, Milton Keynes

Duff, B.E. (1990) "Event" in Dewey's philosophy, *Educational Theory*, Vol. 40, No. 4, pp. 463–470

Durand, J. (1995) Who owns science?, *Independent*, 20.6.95

Eisner, E.W. (1982) *Cognition and Curriculum: A Basis for Deciding What to Teach*, Longman, New York and London

Eisner, E.W. (1984) Can the humanities be taught in American public schools, pp. 112–129 in Lander (ed.) (1984)

Eisner, E.W. (1996) *Cognition and Curriculum Reconsidered*, Paul Chapman, London

Elliott, J. (1991) *Action Research for Educational Change*, Open University Press, Milton Keynes

Ellis-Jones, A. (1986) Women's Studies: No fit subject for schools or Higher Education, pp. 161–8 in O'Keefe (ed.) (1986)

Engle, S.H. and Ochoa, A. (1986) A curriculum for democratic citizenship, *Social Education*, Vol. 50, No. 7, pp. 514–525

Ernest, P. (ed.) (1989) *Mathematics Teaching: The State of the Art*, Falmer, London

Ernest, P. (1991) *The Philosophy of Mathematics Education*, Falmer, London

Ernest, P. (1997) *Social Constructivism as a Philosophy of Mathematics*, State University of New York Press, Albany, New York.

Ernest, P. (1994a) The Dialogical Nature of Mathematics in P. Ernest (ed.) (1994b) *Mathematics, Education and Philosophy*, Falmer, London.

Fauvel, J. (1991) Using history in mathematics education, *For the Learning of Mathematics*, Vol. 11, No. 2, pp. 3–6 & 16

Fauvel, J. and Gray, J. (eds.) (1987) *The History of Mathematics: A Reader*, Macmillan, Basingstoke

Ferri, E. (1971) *Streaming: Two Years Later*, NFER, Slough

Feyerabend, P. (1978) *Against Method: Outline of an anarchist theory of knowledge*, Verso, London

Foucault, M. (1981) *The History of Sexuality: Vol. 1*, Penguin, Harmondsworth

Freire, P. (1972) *Pedagogy of the Oppressed*, Penguin, Harmondsworth

Freire, P. (1974) *Education for Critical Consciousness*, Sheed and Ward, London

Freire, P. (1976) *Education: The Practice of Freedom*, Writers and Readers Cooperative, London

Gadamer, H-G. (1975) *Truth and Method*, Sheed and Ward, London

Gadamer, H-G. (1986) *The Relevance of the Beautiful and Other Essays*, Cambridge University Press, Cambridge

Gardner, H. (1984) *Frames of Mind. The Theory of Multiple Intelligences*, Heinemann, London

Gardner, H. (1995) Reflections on multiple intelligences: myths and messages, *Phi Delta Kappa*, Vol. 77, No. 3, pp. 200–9

Gardner, P. (1994) Representations of the Relationship Between Science and Technology in the Curriculum, *Studies in Science Education*, Vol. 24. No. 1, pp. 1–13

Geertz, C. (1983) *Local Knowledge*, Basic Books, London

General Synod of the Church of England (1995) *Faith in the City: A Call for Action by Church and Nation*, Church House Publishing, London

Gerdes, P. (1988) Of possible uses of traditional Angolan sand drawings in the mathematics classroom, *Educational Studies in Mathematics*, Vol. 19, No. 1, pp. 3–22

Gewirtz, S., Ball, S. and Bowe, R. (1996) *Markets, Choice and Equity in Education*, Open University Press, Basingstoke

Giddens, A. (1995) Keynote address to the annual conference of the Standing Conference on Studies in Education, Royal Society of Arts, London

Giroux, H. (1980) Critical theory and rationality in citizenship education, *Curriculum Inquiry*, Vol. 10, No. 4, pp. 329–366

Giroux, H. (1990) *Curriculum Discourse as Postmodernist Critical Practice*, Deakin University Press, Geelong, Victoria

Giroux, H. (1992) *Border Crossings: Cultural Workers and the Politics of Education*, Routledge, New York

Giroux, H. and McLaren, P. (1992) Writing from the margins: geographies of identity, pedagogy and power, *Journal of Education*, Vol. 174, No. 1, pp. 7–30

Giroux, H. and Simon, R. (1988) Critical pedagogy and the politics of popular culture, *Cultural Studies*, Vol. 2, No. 3, pp. 294–320

Glasersfeld, E. von (1995) *Radical Constructivism: a way of knowing and learning*, Falmer, London

Goldin, G.A. (1987) Cognitive representational systems for mathematical problem solving, pp. 125–145 in Janvier (ed.) (1987)

Goodfellow, M. (1990) The world of work, *Times Educational Supplement* 9.2.90

Goodson, I. and Medway, P. (eds.) (1990) *Bringing English to Order: The History and Politics of a School Subject*, Falmer, London

Gordon, P. and Lawton, D. (1978) *Curriculum Change in the Nineteenth and Twentieth Centuries*, Hodder and Stoughton, London

Gould, C.C. (1988) *Rethinking Democracy*, Cambridge University Press, Cambridge

Green, B. (ed.) (1993) *The Insistence of the Letter: Literacy Studies and Curriculum Theorizing*, Falmer, London

Green, B. (1995) Post-curriculum possibilities: English teaching, cultural politics and the post-modern turn, *Journal of Curriculum Studies*, Vol. 27, No. 4, pp. 391–409

Green, M. in association with Hoggart, R. (eds.) (1987) *English and Cultural Studies: Broadening the Context*, Murray, London, for the English Association

Gutman, A. (1993) Democracy and democratic education, *Studies in Philosophy and Education*, Vol. 12, No. 1, pp. 1–9

Halpin, D., Fitz, J. and Power, S. (1993) *The Early Impact and Long-Term Implications of the Grant-Maintained Schools Policy*, Trentham, Staffordshire

Hamilton, D. (1993) Texts, literacy and schooling, pp. 46–57 in Green (ed.) (1993)

Hampshire Education Authority (1980) *Paths to Understanding*, Hampshire

Hanley, J.P. et al. (1970) *Curiosity, Competence, Community* (evaluation of Man: A Course of Study), Education Development Centre Inc., Cambridge, Massachusetts

Hannam, D. (1993) The arts and the adolescent revisited, pp. 97–114 in Ross (ed.) (1993)

Harber, C. (1984) Politics and political education in 1984, *Educational Review*, Vol. 36, No. 2, pp. 113–120

Hargreaves, A. (1994) *Changing Teachers, Changing Times: Teachers' Work and Culture in a Post-modern Age*, Cassell, London

Hargreaves, D. (1972) *Interpersonal Relations in Education*, Routledge and Kegan Paul, London

Hargreaves, D. (ed.) (1989) *Children and the Arts*, Open University Press, Buckingham

Harlen, W. (1980) Matching, pp. 53–70 in Richards (ed.) (1980)

Harlen, W. (1992) *The Teaching of Science*, David Fulton, London

Harré, R. (1983) *Personal Being*, Blackwell, Oxford

Harvey, D. (1990) *The Condition of Postmodernity*, Blackwell, Oxford

Haydon, G. (ed.) (1987) *Education and Values: the Richard Peters Lectures*, University of London Institute of Education, London

Heaney, S. (1995) *The Redress of Poetry*, Oxford University Press, Oxford

Heater, D. (1977) A burgeoning of interest: political education in Britain, *International Journal of Political Education*, Vol. 1, No. 4

Hebdidge, D. (1986) Postmodernism and 'The Other Side', *Journal of Communication Enquiry*, Vol. 10, No. 2, pp. 78–98

Held, D. (1996) *Model of Democracy* (second edition), Polity, London

Hemming, J. (1949) *The Teaching of Social Studies in Secondary Schools*, Longmans, Green and Co., London

Hiebert, J. (ed.) (1986) *Conceptual and Procedural Knowledge; The Case of Mathematics*, Erlbaum, Hillsdale, NJ

Hill, D. (1986) Urban studies: closing minds?, in O'Keefe (ed.) (1986)

Hirst, P.H. (1974) *Knowledge and the Curriculum*, Routledge and Kegan Paul, London

Homan, R. (1995) Participation and Control, *Westminster Studies in Education*, Vol. 18, No. 1, pp. 5–13

Hooper, R. (ed.) (1971) *The Curriculum: Context, Design and Development*, Oliver and Boyd in association with the Open University Press, Edinburgh

Hoyle, E. (1969) How does the curriculum change? 1. A proposal for enquiries, *Journal of Curriculum Studies*, Vol. 1, No. 2, pp. 132–141, also pp. 375–398 in Hooper (ed.) (1971)

Hoyrup, J. (1980) Influences of institutionalized mathematics teaching on the development and organisation of mathematical thought in the pre-modern period, pp. 43–5 in Fauvel and Gray (eds.) (1987)

Hurd, D. (1988) Citizenship in the Tory democracy, *New Statesman*, Vol. 115, No. 2979, p. 14

Hyland, J.L. (1995) *Democratic Theory*, Manchester University Press, Manchester

Ignatieff, M. (1991) Citizenship and moral narcissism, pp. 26–36 in Andrews (ed.) (1991)

Inglis, F. (1993) *Cultural Studies*, Blackwell, Oxford

Inman, S. and Buck, M. (1995) *Adding Value: Schools' Responsibility for Pupils' Personal Development*, Trentham, Stoke-on-Trent

Inner London Education Authority (ILEA) Afro-Caribbean Language and Literacy Project in Further and Higher Education (1990) *Language and Power*, Harcourt Brace Jovanovich, London

Ive, M. (1997) Cited from talk given at the Design and Technology Association (DATA) Conference, Birmingham, June, 1997

Jakobson, R. (1981) Two aspects of language and two types of aphasic disturbance, pp. 239–259 in *Selected Writings II*, Mouton, The Hague

Janvier, C. (ed.) (1987) *Problems of Representation in the Teaching and Learning of Mathematics*, Erlsbaum, Hillsdale, NJ

Jarrett, J.R. (1973) *The Humanities and Humanistic Education*, Addison-Wesley, Reading, Massachusetts

Jarvis, T. (1991) *Children and Primary Science*, Cassell Educational, London

Jeffery, J. (1988) *Technology across the curriculum: a discussion paper*, Unpublished paper, University of Exeter School of Education

Johnston, J. (1995) The gap between public perceptions of science and the realities of science. Paper presented at the NAARST Conference, San Francisco

Jones, K. (ed.) (1992) *English and the National Curriculum: Cox's Revolution*, Kogan Page, London, in association with the London Institute of Education

Jones, M. (1984) Primary school Physical Education: a view from within, pp. 44–5 in Mawer and Sleap (eds.) (1984)

Joseph, G. (1991) *The Crest of the Peacock: Non-European Roots of Mathematics*, Tauris, London and New York

Keenan, B. (1992) *An Evil Cradling*, Hutchinson, London

Kelly, A.V. (ed.) (1975) *Case Studies in Mixed Ability Teaching*, Harper and Row, London

Kelly, A.V. (1978) *Mixed-Ability Grouping*, Harper and Row, London

Kelly, A.V. (1986) *Knowledge and Curriculum Planning*, Paul Chapman, London

Kelly, A.V. (1989) *The Curriculum: Theory and Practice* (Third edition), Paul Chapman, London. Previews edns. 1997, 1982.

Kelly, A.V. (1990) *The National Curriculum: A Critical Review* (Updated edition 1994), Paul Chapman, London

Kelly, A.V. (1995) *Education and Democracy: Principles and Practices*, Paul Chapman, London

Kerr, D. (ed.) (1994) *Developing Economic and Industrial Understanding in the Curriculum*, London, David Fulton

Kinder, K. (1997) Causes of disaffection: the views of pupils and education professionals, *EERA Bulletin*, Vol. 3, No. 1, pp 3–11

Kirk, D. (1988) *Physical Education and Curriculum Study*, Croom Helm, London

Kitcher, P. and Aspray, W. (1988) An Opinionated Introduction, in W. Aspray and P. Kitcher, (eds.) *History and Philosophy of Modern Mathematics*, University of Minneapolis Press, Minneapolis

Kosslyn, S.M. (1979) Imaging and cognitive development: a teleological approach, in Seigler (ed.) (1979), p. 295

Kuhn, T. S. (1970) The Structure of Scientific Revolutions, University of Chicago Press, Chicago

Kung, H. (1978) *On Being a Christian*, Collins, London

Labov, W. (1970) *The Logic of Non-Standard English*, National Council of Teachers of English, Champaign, Illinois

Lacan, J. (1977) *Ecrits*, Tavistock, London

Lacan, J. (1979) *The Four Fundamental Concepts of Psycho-Analysis*, Penguin, Harmondsworth

Lakatos, I. (1976) *Proofs and Refutations: the Logic of Mathematical Discovery* (edited by J. Worrall and E. Zahar) Cambridge University Press, Cambridge

Lakoff, G. and Johnson, M. (1980) *The Metaphors We Live By*, University of Chicago Press, Chicago

Lander, B. (ed.) (1984) *The Humanities in Precollegiate Education*, University of Chicago Press, Chicago

Lankshear, C. (1993) Curriculum as literacy: reading and writing in 'New Times', 154–174 in Green (ed.) (1993)

Laslett, P. and Runciman, W.G. (eds.) (1962) *Philosophy, Politics and Society* (Second Series), Blackwell, Oxford (reprinted in 1964 and 1967)

Lather, P. (1991) *Getting Smart: Feminist Research and Pedagogy Within the Postmodern*, Routledge, New York

Lave, J. (1988) *Cognition in Practice*, Cambridge University Press

Lawton, D. (1975) *Class, Culture and the Curriculum*, London, Routledge

Lawton, D. (1981) The curriculum and curriculum change in education in the '80s, pp. 115–130 in Simon and Taylor (eds.) (1981)

Lawton, D. (1988) Ideologies of education, pp. 10–20 in Lawton and Chitty (eds.) (1988)

Lawton, D. (1989) *Education, Culture and the National Curriculum*, Hodder and Stoughton, London, Sydney, Auckland and Toronto

Lawton, D. and Chitty, C. (eds.) (1988) *The National Curriculum*, Bedford Papers 33, Institute of Education, London

Levin, D.M. (ed.) (1987) *Pathologies of the Modern Self: Postmodern Studies in Narcissism, Schizophrenia and Depression*, New York University Press, New York

Levitas, R. (1986) *The Ideology of the New Right*, Polity Press, Cambridge

Layton, D. (1990) *Inarticulate Science?*, Occasional papers No. 17, University of Liverpool

Layton, D. (1993) Technology's Challenge to Science Education

Lowe, R (1862) *British Parliamentary Debates. Third Series 1862*, Vol. CLXV, Col.238, quoted in Selleck (1968), p. 15

Lyotard, J-F. (1984) *The Postmodern Condition: A Report on Knowledge*, University of Minnesota Press, Minneapolis, Minn.

MacIntyre, A. (1987) The idea of an educated public, pp. 15–36 in Haydon (ed.) (1987)

Mackinder, H. (1913) Teaching geography and history as a combined subject, *The Geography Teacher*, No. 7, pp. 4–9

Macpherson, C.B. (1973) *Democratic Theory: Essays in Retrieval*, Clarendon Press, Oxford

Mandela, N. (1995) *Long Walk to Freedom*, Abacus, London

Marx, K. (1872) The fetishism of commodities, pp. 435–443 in McLellan (ed.) (1987)

Marx, L. (1975) Technology and the study of man, pp. 435–443 in Niblett (ed.) (1975)

Maslow, A.H. (1968) *Towards a Psychology of Being*, Van Nostrand Reinhold Company, New York

Matless, D. (1992) An occasion for geography: landscape, representation and Foucault's corpus, *Environment and Planning D: Society and Space*, Vol. 10, No. 1, pp. 41–56

Mawer, M. and Sleap, M. (eds.) (1984) *Physical Education Within Primary Education*, The Physical Education Association of Great Britain and Northern Ireland

Maxwell, S. (1984) *From Knowledge to Wisdom*, Blackwell, Oxford

Masterman, L. (1992) *Teaching the Media*, Routledge, London

McCormack, R. & Murphy, P. (1994) Learning the Processes in Technology, paper presented to the British Educational Research Association Annual Conference, Oxford University

McIntosh, P.C. (1968) *Physical Education in England since 1800*, Bell, London

McLaren, P. (1988) Culture or canon? Critical pedagogy and the politics of literacy, *Harvard Educational Review*, Vol. 58, No. 2, pp. 211–234

McLellan, D. (ed.) (1987) *Karl Marx: Selected Writings*, Oxford University Press, Oxford

McLure, J.S. (1986) *Educational Documents: England and Wales 1816 to the Present Day*, Methuen, London

McMurty, J. (1991) Education and the market model, *Journal of Philosophy of Education*, Vol. 25, No. 2, pp. 209–217

McPhail, P., Ungoed-Thomas, J.R. and Chapman, H. (1972) *Moral Education in the Secondary School*, Longmans, London

Medway, P. (1990) Into the sixties: English and English society at a time of change, pp. 1–46 in Goodson and Medway (eds.) (1990)

Mellin-Olsen, S. (1981) Instrumentalism as an educational concept, *Educational Studies in Mathematics*, Vol. 12, No. 3, pp. 351–367

Merleau-Ponty, M. (1973) *The Prose of the World*, Northwest University Press, Evanston

Millar, R. (1996) Designing a curriculum for public understanding in science, Education in Science, No. 166, pp. 8–9

Morson, G.S. (ed.) (1986) *Bahktin: Essays and Dialogues on His Work*, University of Chicago Press, Chicago and London

Mouffe, C. (ed.) (1992) *Dimensions of Radical Democracy*, Verso, London

National Foundation for Educational Research (1995) *The Arts in their View*, NFER, Slough

Niblett, W.R. (ed.) (1975) *The Sciences, the Humanities and the Technological Threat*, London University Press. London

Novak, M. (1982) *The Spirit of Democratic Capitalism*, Touchstone, New York

Nunes, T., Schliemann, A.D. and Carraher, D.W. (1994) *Street Mathematics and School Mathematics*, Cambridge University Press

Oakeshott, M. (1933) *Experience and its Modes*, Cambridge University Press, Cambridge

Oakeshott, M. (1959) *The Voice of Poetry in the Conversation of Mankind*, Bowes and Bowes, Cambridge

O'Keefe, D. (ed.) (1986) *The Wayward Curriculum*, The Social Affairs Unit, London

Parry, J. (1989) The Physical Education curriculum from 5–16, pp. 235–251 in Rayner and Wiegand (eds.) (1989)

Pascall, D. (1992) *Standards in Education*, an address given to the Association of Religious Education Advisers and Inspectors, July

Pateman, C. (1970) *Participation and Democratic Theory*, Cambridge University Press, Cambridge

Peters, R.S. (1966) *Ethics and Education*, Allen and Unwin, London

Peters, R.S. (1973) *The Philosophy of Education*, Oxford University Press

Peters, R.S. (1975) Subjectivity and standards, pp. 139–156 in Niblett (ed.) (1975)

Peters, R.S. (1979) Democratic values and educational aims, *Teachers College Record*, Vol. 80, No. 3, pp. 463–482

Phenix, P.H. (1964) *Realms of Meaning*, McGraw-Hill, New York

Phillips, D. (1994) The importance of citizenship, pp. 59–63 in *Insights into Education and Training*, Papers selected by Paul Hamlyn Foundation National Commission on Education

Piaget, J. (1926) *The Language and Thought of the Child*, Routledge, London

Pike, G. and Selby, D. *Global Teacher, Global Learning*, Hodder and Stoughton, London

Playfair, L. (1870) On Primary and Technical Education, quoted in Selleck (ed.) (1968) p. 15

Polanyi, M. (1958) *Personal Knowledge*, Routledge and Kegan Paul, London

Polanyi, M. (1964) *Science, Faith and Society*, University of Chicago Press, Chicago

Popper, K.R. (1968) *The Logic of Scientific Discovery*, Hutchinson, London

Popper, K.R. (1979) *Objective Knowledge* (revised edition), Oxford University Press, Oxford

Porter, A. (1983) *Teaching Political Literacy: Implications for Teacher Training and Curriculum Planning*, University of London Institute of Education, London

Priestley, J.G. (1985) Towards finding the hidden curriculum: a consideration of the spiritual dimension of experience in curriculum planning, *British Journal of Religious Education*, Vol. 7, No. 3, pp. 112–9

Quicke, J. (1996) Self, modernity and a direction for curriculum reform, *British Journal of Educational Studies*, Vol. 44, No. 4, pp. 364–376

Quine, W.V.O. (1960) *Word and Object*, MIT Press, Cambridge, MA.

Raleigh, M. (1981) *The Languages Book*, ILEA English Centre, London

Ravitch, D. and Finn, C. *Against Mediocrity*, Holmes and Meier, New York

Rayner, M. and Wiegand, P. (eds.) (1989) *Curriculum Progress 5–16: school subjects and the national curriculum debate*, Falmer, London

Read, H. (1931) *The Meaning of Art*, Faber and Faber Ltd, London

Reid, W.A. (1993) Literacy, orality and the functions of curriculum, pp. 13–26 in Green (ed.) (1993)

Restivo, S. (1992) *Mathematics in Science and History*, Kluwer, Dordrecht

Richards, C. (ed.) (1980) *Primary Education: Issues for the Eighties*, Adam and Charles Black, London

Richardson, M. (1948) *Art and the Child*, University of London Press, London

Roberts, F. (1984) Precollegiate humanities, leadership curriculum issues, pp. 154–170 in Lander (ed.) (1984)

Rogers, R. (1995) *Guaranteeing an Entitlement to the Arts in Schools*, Royal Society of Arts, London

Rorty, R. (1979) *Philosophy and the Mirror of Nature*, Princeton University Press, New Jersey

Rosenthal, S. (1993) Democracy and education: a Deweyan approach, *Educational Theory*, Vol. 43, No. 4, pp. 377–89

Ross, M. (1991) The Hidden Order of the Arts Curriculum, *British Journal of Aesthetics*, Vol. 31, No. 2, pp. 111–121

Ross, M. (ed.) (1993) *Wasteland Wonderland*, Perspectives 49, University of Exeter

Ross, M. (1995) National Curriculum art and music, *Journal of Art and Design Education* Vol. 14, No. 3, pp. 271–6

Ross, M. and Kamba, M. (1997) *State of the Arts in Five English Secondary Schools*, University of Exeter School of Education, Exeter

Ross, M., Radnor, H., Mitchell, S. and Bierton, C. (1993) *Assessing Achievement in the Arts*, Open University Press, Buckingham

Rotman, B. (1993) *Ad Infinitum The Ghost in Turing's Machine: Taking God Out of Mathematics and Putting the Body Back In*, Stanford University Press, Stanford, California

Ruskin, J. (1898) *Unto This Last*, George Allen, Orpington and London

Russell, T et al. (1991) *Primary SPACE Reports*, Liverpool University Press, Liverpool

Ryba, R. (1986) Integrating economic learning into the social science curriculum: the contribution of economics, *Social Science Teacher*, Vol. 16, No. 1, pp. 11–17

Sampson, E.E. (1989) The deconstruction of self, pp. 1–19 in Shotter and Gergen (eds.) (1989)

Saxton, J. and Miller, S. (1996) Design and designing: What's in a word?, *Journal of design and Technology Education* Vol. 1, No. 2, pp. 110–118

Schon, D. (1983) *The Reflective Practitioner. How Professionals Think in Action*, Temple Smith, London

Schools Council (1969) *Humanities for the Young School Leaver: an Approach through Religious Education*, Evans Methuen Educational, London

Schools Council (1970) *The Humanities Project: An Introduction*, Heinemann, London

Schumpeter, J.A. (1943) *Capitalism, Socialism and Democracy*, Allen and Unwin, London

Scruton, R. (1986) Peace studies: no true subject, pp. 107–115 in O'Keefe (ed.) (1986)

Secondary Heads Association (1995) *Whither the Arts?: The State of the Expressive Arts in the Secondary School*, S.H.A., Leicester

Seigler, R.S. (ed.) (1979) *Children's Thinking: What Develops?*, Erlbaum, Hillside, NJ

Selleck, R.J.W. (ed.) *The New Education 1870–1914*, Pitman, London

Sells, L. (1976) The mathematics filter and the education of women and minorities, paper presented at the annual conference of the American Association for the Advancement of Science, Boston

Simon, B. (1974) *The New Nations and the Educational Structure*, 1780–1870, Lawrence and Wishart, London

Simon, B. and Taylor, W. (eds.) (1981) *Education in the Eighties*, Batsford, London

Skemp, R.R. (1976) Relational understanding and instrumental understanding, *Mathematics Teaching*, No. 77, pp. 20–6

Smithers, A. and Robinson, P. (1992) *Technology in the National Curriculum: Getting it Right*, Engineering Council

Staffordshire County Council Education Committee (1985) *Dance Curriculum Guidelines 5–18 Years*

Stander, D. (1989) The use of the history of mathematics in teaching, in Ernest (ed.) (1989), pp. 241–6

Steen, L.A. (1988) The Science of Patterns, *Science*, Vol. 240, No. 4852, pp. 611–616

Stenhouse, L. (1967) *Culture and Education*, Nelson, London

Stenhouse, L. (1975) *An Introduction to Curriculum Research and Development*, Heinemann, London

Stenhouse, L. (1980) Reflections, in Stenhouse (ed.) (1980), pp. 244–262

Stenhouse. L. (ed.) (1980) *Curriculum Research and Development in Action*, Heinemann, London

Stradling, R. and Noctor, M. (1983) *The Provision of Political Education in Schools: a National Survey*, University of London Curriculum Review Unit, London

Stubbs, M. (1976) *Language, Schools and Classrooms*, Methuen, London

Trainer, D. (1995) The inspection of spiritual and moral development, SPES, *A Magazine for the Study of Spiritual, Moral, Social and Cultural Values in Education*, Issue No. 2, pp. 3–4, RIMSCUE Centre, University of Plymouth

Trilling, L. (1955) *The Opposing Self*, Secker and Warburg, London

Trudgill, P. (1983) *On Dialect: Social and Geographical Perspectives*, Blackwell, Oxford

Tymoczko, T. (1986) *New Directions in the Philosophy of Education*, Birkhauser, Boston

Ulmer, G. (1981) The Post-Age, *Diacritics II*, pp. 39–56

UNESCO (1982) *Declaration on Media Education*, Grunwald, Federal Republic of Germany

Usher, R.S. (1989) Locating experience in language: towards a poststructuralist theory of experience, *Adult Education Quarterly*, Vol. 40, No. 1, pp. 23–32

Vygotsky, L.S. (1962) *Thought and Language*, MIT Press, Cambridge, Mass.

Vygotsky, L.S. (1978) *Mind in Society*, Harvard University Press, Cambridge, Mass.

Wadsworth, P. et al. (1993) *Nuffield Primary Science* (schemes), Collins Educational, London

Walkerdine, V. (1982) A psychosemiotic approach to abstract thought, pp. 129–155 in Beveridge (ed.) (1982)

Walkerdine, V. (1988) *The Mastery of Reason*, Routledge, London

Walkerdine, V. (1989) Femininity as Performance, Oxford Review of Education, Vol. 15, No. 3, pp. 267–279

Walkerdine, V. (1989b) *Counting Girls Out*, Virago, London. Reprinted 1998 by Falmer Press, London

Warnock, M. (1977) *Schools of Thought*, Faber and Faber, London

Watts, M. (1991) Questions of Policy: Some Lost Opportunities in the Making of Primary Science, Peacock A. (eds.) *Science in Primary Schools, the Multicultural Dimension*, MacMillan Education, London

Webster, D.H. (1982) Spiritual growth in Religious Education, pp. 85–95 in *Religious Education and the Imagination: Aspects of Education 28*, University of Hull Institute of Education

Wetton, P. (1988) *Physical Education in the Nursery and Infant School*, Croom Helm, London and Sydney

Whitaker, K. (1984) Physical Education within Primary Education: Introduction, pp. 5–6 in Mawer and Sleap (eds.) (1984)

White, J. (1973) *Towards a Compulsory Curriculum*, Routledge and Kegan Paul, London

White, J.(1988) An unconstitutional national curriculum, pp. 113–122 in Lawton and Chitty (eds.) (1988)

White, J. (1994) Instead of OFSTED: a critical discussion of OFSTED on 'Spiritual, Moral, Social and Cultural Development', *Cambridge Journal of Education*, Vol. 24, No. 3, pp. 369–377

White, P. (1994) Citizenship and 'spiritual and moral development' *Citizenship*, Vol. 3, No. 2, pp. 7–8

White, P. and White, J. (1976) A programme for political education: a critique, *Teaching Politics*, Vol. 5, No. 3, pp. 257–271

Whitehead, A.N. (1932) *The Aims of Education and Other Essays*, William and Norgate, London (reprinted 1945)

Whitty, G. (1979) Political education: some reservations, *The Social Science Teacher*, Vol. 8, No. 3, pp. 112–116

Whitty, G., Rowe, G. and Aggleton, P. (1994) Discourse in Cross-curricular Contexts: limits to empowerment, International Studies in Sociology of Education, Vol. 4, No. 1

Williams, R. (1961) *The Long Revolution*, Chatto and Windus, London

Willinsky, J. (1993) Lessons from the literacy before schooling, pp. 58–74 in Green (ed.) (1993)

Winnicott, D.W. (1971) *Playing and Reality*, Tavistock, London

Wittgenstein, l. (1956) *Remarks on the Foundation of Mathematics*, Blackwell, Oxford

Wollheim, R. (1962) A paradox in the theory of democracy, pp. 71–87 in Laslett and Runciman (eds.) (1962)

Wolpert, L. (1992) *The Unnatural Nature of Science*, Faber, London

Young, M. (1995) The future basis for 14–18 entitlement, pp. 161–179 in Inman and Buck (eds.) (1995)

Zaslavsky, C. (1973) *Africa Counts*, Lawrence Hills, New York

Zinman, J.M. (1968) *Public Knowledge*, Cambridge University Press, Cambridge

Zizek, S. (1989) *The Sublime Object of Ideology*, Verso, London

Government reports and other official publications referred to in the text

Assessment of Performance Unit (1983) *Aesthetic Development*, HMSO, London

Assessment of Performance Unit (1987) *Design and Technological Activity: A Framework for Assessment*, HMSO, London

Assessment of Performance Unit (1989) *National Assessment: The APU Science Approach*, HMSO, London

Board of Education (1921) *The Teaching of English in England: Being the Report of the Departmental Committee Appointed by the President of the Board of Education to Inquire into the Position of English in the Education System of England* (The Newbolt Report), HMSO, London

Board of Education (1931) *Primary Education* (The Hadow Report), HMSO. London

Board of Education (1933) *Syllabus of Physical Training for Schools*, HMSO, London

Board of Education (1938) *Report of the Consultative Committee on Secondary Education with Special Reference to Grammar and Technical High Schools* (The Spens Report)

Board of Education (1943) *Curriculum and Examinations in the Secondary School: Report of the Committee of the Secondary Schools Examination Council* (The Norwood Report)

Central Advisory Council for Education (1959) *15 to 18* (The Crowther Report), HMSO, London

Central Advisory Council for Education (1963) *Half Our Future* (The Newsom Report), HMSO, London

Central Advisory Council for Education (1967) *Children and Their Primary Schools* (The Plowden Report), HMSO, London

Department for Education (1992) *Choice and Diversity* (White Paper), HMSO, London

Department for Education (1995) *English in the National Curriculum*, HMSO, London

Department for Education and Employment (1996) *Equipping Young People for Working Life*, DfEE, London

Department of Education and Science (1975) *A Language for Life* (The Bullock Report), HMSO, London

Department of Education and Science (1976) *The Curriculum 11 to 16*, HMSO, London

Department of Education and Science (1977a) *Curriculum 11–16*, HMSO, London

Department of Education and Science (1977b) *Education in Schools: A Consultative Document*, HMSO, London

Department of Education and Science (1979a) *Aspects of Secondary Education in England: A Survey by HM Inspectors of Schools*, HMSO, London

Department of Education and Science (1979b) *Curriculum 11–16. Supplementary Working Papers: Physical Education*, HMSO, London

Department of Education and Science (1981) *The School Curriculum*, HMSO, London

Department of Education and Science (1982) *Mathematics Counts* (The Cockcroft Report), HMSO, London

Department of Education and Science (1984a) *Curriculum 11–16: Towards a Statement of Entitlement*, HMSO, London

Department of Education and Science (1984b) *The Organization and Content of the 5–16 Curriculum*, HMSO, London

Department of Education and Science (1985a) *The Curriculum from 5 to 16: Curriculum Matters 2*, HMSO, London

Department of Education and Science (1985b) *Mathematics from 5 to 16* (Curriculum Matters 3), HMSO, London

Department of Education and Science (1985c) *Science 5–16: A Statement of Policy*, HMSO, London

Department of Education and Science (1985d) *Better Schools*, HMSO, London

Department of Education and Science (1987) *Economic Understanding and the School Curriculum*, HMSO, London

Department of Education and Science (1988a) *National Curriculum Task Group on Assessment and Testing: A Report*, DES, London

Department of Education and Science (1988b) *National Curriculum: Design and Technology Working Group Interim Report*, HMSO, London

Department of Education and Science (1989) *Initial Teacher Training: Approval of Courses* (Circular 24/89), HMSO, London

Department of Education and Science (1990a) *Geography Final Report*, HMSO, London

Department of Education and Science (1990b) *History Final Report*, HMSO, London

Department of Education and Science (1990c) *Mini-enterprises in Schools: Some Aspects of Current Practice*, HMSO, London

Department of Education and Science (1992) Choice and Diversity: A New Framework for Schools, HMSO, London

Department for Education (1995) *Science in the National Curriculum*, HMSO, London

Her Majesty's Inspectorate (1979) *Aspects of Secondary Education, Supplementary Information on Mathematics*, HMSO, London

Her Majesty's Inspectorate (1985) *Mathematics from 5–16*, HMSO, London

Her Majesty's Inspectorate (1992) *Report on the First Year of National Curriculum Technology*, HMSO, London

Institute for Public Policy Research (IPPR) (1993) *Education: A Different Version* IPPR, London

Manpower Services Commission (MSC) (undated) *Economic Awareness Across the Curriculum*, MSC, London

Ministry of Education (1949) *Citizens Growing Up*, HMSO, London

National Curriculum Council (1987) National Curriculum Science Working Group Interim Report, NCC, York

National Curriculum Council (1989a) *Science in the National Curriculum*, London HMSO

National Curriculum Council (1989b) *Science Non-Statutory Guidance*, London, HMSO

National Curriculum Council (1989c) *The Whole Curriculum* (NCC Circular No. 6), NCC, York

National Curriculum Council (1990a) *The Whole Curriculum: Curriculum Guidance 3*, NCC, York
National Curriculum Council (1990b) *Education for Economic and Industrial Understanding: Curriculum Guidance 4*, NCC, York
National Curriculum Council (1990c) *Education for Citizenship: Curriculum Guidance 8*, NCC, York
National Curriculum Council (1991) *Science in the National Curriculum*, London HMSO
National Curriculum Council (1992) *Spiritual and Moral Development: a Discussion Paper*, NCC, York
Office for Standards in Education (1994a) *Science and Mathematics in Schools – A Review*, HMSO, London
Office for Standards in Education (1994b) *Spiritual, Moral, Social and Cultural Development*, HMSO, London
Office for Standards in Education (1995a) *Guidance on the Inspection of Nursery and Primary Schools*, HMSO, London
Office for Standards in Education (1995b) *Guidance on the Inspection of Secondary Schools*, HMSO, London
School Examinations and Assessment Council (1991) *The Assessment of Performance in Design and Technology* SEAC, London
Schools Council (1975) *Educating Through Design and Craft* (Schools Council Design and Craft Education Project), Edward Arnold, London
Schools Curriculum Assessment Authority (1994) *Science in the National Curriculum: Draft Proposals*, SCAA, London
Schools Curriculum Assessment Authority (1995) *Spiritual and Moral Development*, SCAA Discussion Papers No. 3, SCAA, London
Schools Curriculum Assessment Authority (1996) *Education for Adult Life: the Spiritual and Moral Development of Young People*, SCAA Discussion Papers No. 6, SCAA, London
Schools Curriculum Assessment Authority/Department for Education and Employment (1996) *Science Key Stage 2 Test A, Levels 3–5*, SCAA, London
School Curriculum Development Committee (undated) *Educating for Economic Awareness: A Basic Entitlement in the School Curriculum* (Curriculum Issue No. 4), SCDC, London

Author Index

212

Subject Index